T0301440

Crisis and the Failure of Economic Theory

NEW DIRECTIONS IN POST-KEYNESIAN ECONOMICS

Series Editors: Louis-Philippe Rochon, *Laurentian University, Sudbury, Canada* and Sergio Rossi, *University of Fribourg, Switzerland*

Post-Keynesian economics is a school of thought inspired by the work of John Maynard Keynes, but also by Michal Kalecki, Joan Robinson, Nicholas Kaldor and other Cambridge economists, for whom money and effective demand are essential to explain economic activity. The aim of this series is to present original research work (single or co-authored volumes as well as edited books) that advances Post-Keynesian economics at both theoretical and policy-oriented levels.

Areas of research include, but are not limited to, monetary and financial economics, macro and microeconomics, international economics, development economics, economic policy, political economy, analyses of income distribution and financial crises, and the history of economic thought.

Titles in the series include:

Post Keynesian Theory and Policy
A Realistic Analysis of the Market Oriented Capitalist Economy
Paul Davidson

Inequality, Growth and 'Hot' Money
Pablo G. Bortz

The Financialization Response to Economic Disequilibria
European and Latin American Experiences
Edited by Noemi Levy and Etelberto Ortiz

Crisis and the Failure of Economic Theory
The Responsibility of Economists for the Great Recession
Giancarlo Bertocco

Crisis and the Failure of Economic Theory

The Responsibility of Economists for the Great Recession

Giancarlo Bertocco

University of Insubria, Italy

NEW DIRECTIONS IN POST-KEYNESIAN ECONOMICS

 Edward Elgar
PUBLISHING

Cheltenham, UK • Northampton, MA, USA

Published by
Edward Elgar Publishing Limited
The Lypiatts
15 Lansdown Road
Cheltenham
Glos GL50 2JA
UK

Edward Elgar Publishing, Inc.
William Pratt House
9 Dewey Court
Northampton
Massachusetts 01060
USA

A catalogue record for this book
is available from the British Library

Library of Congress Control Number: 2016957234

This book is available electronically in the **Elgar**online
Economics subject collection
DOI 10.4337/9781785365355

ISBN 978 1 78536 534 8 (cased)
ISBN 978 1 78536 535 5 (eBook)

Typeset by Columns Design XML Ltd, Reading

Printed on FSC approved paper

Printed and bound in Great Britain by Marston Book Services Ltd, Oxfordshire

Contents

List of figures and tables   vii
Acknowledgements   ix

Introduction   1

PART I   THE CRISIS AND THE MAINSTREAM THEORY

1   A brief description of the crisis   13
2   Mainstream economists and the crisis   20
3   The limits of the mainstream theory   40

PART II   AN ALTERNATIVE THEORETICAL APPROACH

4   Keynes and the monetary theory of production   57
5   Finance and risk   69
6   Saving decisions, wealth and speculation   92
7   Money and crisis   109

PART III   THE ENDOGENOUS NATURE OF THE CRISIS AND
            THE POLICIES FOR A GOOD LIFE

8   The endogenous nature of the subprime crisis   139
9   Overcoming the crisis: which policies?   169
Conclusions   198

Bibliography   203
Index   229

Figures and tables

FIGURES

2.1 Federal funds rate (real and counterfactual percentages)   22
2.2 The boom and the collapse of the real estate sector compared with
    the counterfactual hypothesis   23

TABLE

7.1 Real-exchange economy (C–M–C') and monetary economy
    (M–C–M')   129

Acknowledgements

The roots of this book lie in the years I spent in the Department of Economics at the University of Pavia. I have a debt of gratitude to the people I met and with whom I worked in those years: Alberto Sdralevich, Giorgio Lunghini, Nicolò De Vecchi, Carluccio Bianchi, Franco Campanella, Anna Carabelli, Gioacchino Garofoli, Carlo Giannini, Guido Montani, Pietro Muliere, Renzo Rampa, Luisa Rosti and Gianni Vaggi.

At the Department of Economics of the University of Insubria I found the ideal place to continue my research work. I wish to thank the Dean, Alberto Coen Porisini, the director of the department, Matteo Rocca, and my colleagues for allowing me to spend a sabbatical year during which I could lay the foundations of this work. I also wish to thank the exceptionally helpful and attentive staff of the department secretariat and of the library. I am also grateful to Giorgio Rampa for hosting me in his department during the sabbatical year.

I have a major debt to Andrea Kalajzić for his efforts and contribution to making the first version of this book readable, and to Hervé Baron, Riccardo Bellofiore, Francesco Bertocco, Lelio De Michelis, Giorgio Grasso, Lorenzo Pecchi and Lino Sau for their helpful comments on an earlier version of the book. I wish to thank Francesco Brioschi, the publisher of my first work on the crisis.

Finally, I want to thank Angela, my precious and wonderful life companion, who has not read a single line of this book, but knows each and every detail of it.

To Alessandro, Enzo, Francesco, Maria and the little Camilla

Introduction

> You cannot see a crisis coming if you have theories and models that assume
> that the crisis is impossible. (Adair Turner 2016, p. 246)

I decided to write this book because the economists' attitude towards the
current crisis struck me as somewhat passive. With this, I do not mean
that economists failed to deal with the crisis – indeed, thousands of
studies have been published on this topic. What I am actually suggesting
is that the economics profession is learning nothing from this crisis. I
believe there are two fundamental lessons that we, as economists, should
learn from the current crisis. First, we should recognize the limitations of
the mainstream economic theory developed over the last 40 years.
According to this theory, in a market economy in which the price system
is free to work without major obstacles, a disastrous crisis, such as the
recent one, cannot occur. The attitude of the majority of the economics
profession before the eruption of the crisis can be described by the
opening words of Robert Lucas's presidential address to the annual
meeting of the American Economic Association in 2003:

> Macroeconomics was born as a distinct field in the 1940s, as a part of the
> intellectual response to the Great Depression. The term then referred to the
> body of knowledge and expertise that we hoped would prevent the recurrence
> of that economic disaster. My thesis in this lecture is that macroeconomics in
> this original sense has succeeded: its central problem of depression prevention
> has been solved, for all practical purposes. (Lucas 2003, p. 1)

The adoption of a theoretical model which maintained that market
economies are structurally stable implied, of course, that the economists
were not able to predict the onset of a catastrophic crisis. This is why
public opinion fiercely criticized the economics profession. Nevertheless,
the economists' responsibilities go beyond their inability to foresee the
crisis since, by elaborating a theoretical model which ruled out the
occurrence of this event, the economics profession enabled the paralysis
of the financial system and the subsequent deep recession. In fact, this
theory led the vast majority of economists to neglect the signs of
instability that emerged during the Great Moderation and provided the
theoretical endorsement for the behaviours and choices that created the

conditions for the outbreak of the crisis (see, for example, Madrik 2014; Wolf 2014).

The first lesson to be learnt from this crisis is that economic theories are not abstract constructions, extraneous to the real world, but they produce significant consequences for the welfare of a society. After the outbreak of the crisis, even some of the economists who were more closely linked to the mainstream theory acknowledged the limits of the orthodox theory. Alan Greenspan, who chaired the Federal Reserve from June 1987 to January 2006, is one of the most important examples. Before the crisis, Greenspan had always shown a deep trust in the markets' self-regulating abilities. Nevertheless, during a hearing before the House Committee on Oversight and Government Reform of the United States Congress, Greenspan admitted that the financial crisis had led him to question the validity of the mainstream theoretical model:

> I made a mistake in presuming that the self-interests of organizations, specifically banks and others, were such that they were best capable of protecting their own shareholders and their equity in the firms. ... The problem here is something which looked to be a very solid edifice, and, indeed, a critical pillar to market competition and free markets, did break down. And I think that, as I said, shocked me. I still do not fully understand why it happened and, obviously, to the extent that I figure out what happened and why, I will change my views. ... I found a flaw in the model that I perceived as the critical functioning structure that defines how the world works, so to speak. ... That's precisely the reason I was shocked. Because I had been going for forty years, or more, with very considerable evidence that it was working exceptionally well. (Quoted in Cassidy 2009, pp. 5–6)

Greenspan's words highlight the second lesson that economists should learn from the crisis, namely the necessity of developing a new theoretical approach that can provide a sound explanation of the phenomenon of economic crises and of the role of finance in modern market economies.

1. THE CRISIS AND THE NEED FOR A NEW THEORETICAL MODEL

Looking at the last hundred years, one can identify at least two historical moments in which the economics profession was driven by significant and unexpected phenomena to abandon the then generally accepted theory and to replace it with a different paradigm. The first dates back to the 1930s, when the Great Depression undermined confidence in the neoclassical theory, according to which economic crises were nothing more than accidental phenomena, bound to die out spontaneously thanks to the normal functioning of the markets. In 1936, the publication of John Maynard Keynes's *General Theory of Employment, Interest and Money* brought to the fore a revolutionary theoretical approach whereby economic crises were structural phenomena. Keynes stated that, if left to themselves, market economies typically produce significant fluctuations of output and employment. During the 1950s and1960s, the neoclassical theory was replaced by a new orthodoxy, consisting in a specific interpretation of Keynes's thought that became known as the Neoclassical Synthesis.

The second turning point occurred in the 1970s, when the Western economies were hit by a new global crisis characterized by a combination of low growth and high inflation, known as 'stagflation'. This new phenomenon led economists to question the assumption that Keynesian policies can ensure high output growth rates coupled with low, or at least stable, inflation rates. In those years, Milton Friedman developed a strong criticism of the then dominant theoretical approach, emphasizing how Keynesian policies were substantially ineffective in situations in which workers were not affected by the 'monetary illusion'.

Friedman's criticism did not generate a theoretical revolution, but rather a counterrevolution that drove the economics profession to re-accept the conclusions of the pre-Keynesian neoclassical theory. The return to the old theory was based on an apparently sound argument: if the levels of output and employment were not influenced by Keynesian policies, then they evidently depended only on the working of unfettered markets. Accordingly, the only effective policy consisted in eliminating every barrier that prevented markets from functioning efficiently. The new version of the neoclassical theory became known first as 'monetarism' and then as 'new classical macroeconomics'. This modern reformulation of neoclassical principles formed the theoretical foundation of the neoliberal ideology that led industrialized countries, beginning with the administrations of Ronald Reagan in the United States and Margaret Thatcher in the UK, to adopt a series of policies aimed at liberalizing capital movements, deregulating markets and privatizing public enterprises.

Because of recent events, economists are now in a situation similar to that experienced during the 1930s and the 1970s. The question economists now face is whether this crisis has uncovered substantial limits of the currently dominant theory. The answers to this basic question are splitting the economics profession. 'Conservative economists' believe that recent events should not question the foundations of the theoretical model developed in the last few decades,[1] while 'critical economists' maintain that this crisis has emphasized fundamental flaws in the mainstream theory and that it is time for a significant change in the dominant paradigm. With different arguments and varying intensity, the latter thesis is supported by Nobel laureates such as Akerlof, Krugman, Phelps, Shiller, Solow and Stiglitz, and by other prominent economists.[2]

Nevertheless, almost ten years after the outbreak of the crisis, most of the economics profession continues to accept the mainstream theoretical model. There is a deep contradiction between a theory that denies even the possibility of a disastrous crisis and the factual reality. This contradiction becomes apparent if one looks at the explanations of the crisis elaborated by mainstream economists. In fact, it is not easy to identify the origins of the crisis by using a theoretical model which states that market economies cannot be subject to significant turbulences. In the first part of this book, I will show that, in order to explain the causes of the financial crisis and the subsequent Great Recession, mainstream economists are forced to use concepts and relationships that are inconsistent with the dominant theory. The deep contradiction between the analysis of the origins of the crisis made by conservative economists and the orthodox theory, highlights the inability of most of the economics profession to explain the functioning of modern economic systems and the need to develop an alternative theoretical model.[3]

2. THE LIMITS OF THE MAINSTREAM THEORY

To overcome the contradiction between theory and reality, mainstream economists consider the current crisis as an accidental event, a phenomenon that is external to the normal functioning of the economic system. This argument is developed by interpreting the crisis in two ways: 1) as the result of an unpredictable shock, a 'black swan' (see Taleb 2007); and 2) as a consequence of the mistakes made by the Federal Reserve and the US banking system. Depending on the degree of responsibility assigned to these two culprits, three different explanations of the crisis can be identified.

The first explanation blames the US monetary authorities for adopting an overly expansive policy after the collapse of the stock market in 2000 and the terrorist attacks on the Twin Towers on 11 September 2001. According to this explanation, the Federal Reserve favoured the development of the real estate bubble that burst in the summer of 2007. The second explanation assigns the main responsibility for the crisis to the

US banking system. The most rigorous version of this interpretation was elaborated by Raghuram Rajan (2006, 2010), who claims that, under the pressure of a system of distorted incentives, the US banking system created an excessive amount of risk that, in the end, triggered the crisis. Finally, the third explanation is provided by Ben Bernanke, the successor to Alan Greenspan as Chairman of the Federal Reserve from 2006 to 2013. Bernanke (2005, 2007b, 2010a) states that the huge amount of liquidity that fuelled the housing bubble was not the by-product of the Fed's expansive monetary policy, but it was rather generated by an excessive accumulation of savings in the oil-producing countries and in the emerging Asian countries, particularly China.

All these explanations regard the crisis as an exogenous phenomenon that is unrelated to the normal dynamics of a market economy (see Galbraith 2014). The position of mainstream economists can be compared to the attitude of those that, after a plane crash, immediately rule out the possibility that it may have been caused by a structural problem, and that, consequently, attribute the responsibility to the pilot. Nevertheless, this parallelism is unconvincing, as the 'drivers' blamed for the eruption of the crisis were considered to be the best in the world. In fact, until the outbreak of the crisis, Alan Greenspan was acclaimed as the best Chairman since the institution of the Federal Reserve. In addition, the US financial system was unanimously recognized as the most advanced in the world, a benchmark for the financial sector of every other country.[4] Thus, it is difficult to understand how the best pilots, who were flying the most sophisticated aircraft in the world, could have caused a catastrophe.

Furthermore, the explanations based on the idea that the current crisis is the result of mistakes made by specific economic actors must be questioned because they are inconsistent with the mainstream theory. In the economic system described by mainstream economists, neither the monetary authorities nor the banking system is supposed to make mistakes resulting in a catastrophic crisis. The monetary authorities have no reason to adopt policies that contrast with the goal to achieve stability in the general price level, while the banking system is not expected to suddenly lose its ability to channel resources collected from savers towards the most productive investments.

The interpretations of the crisis elaborated by mainstream economists are based on concepts and relationships that are completely at odds with the fundamental propositions of the orthodox economic theory. In other words, they refer to an economic reality that is very different from the world described by the mainstream theory. The interpretation that blames the Federal Reserve is in contrast with the neoclassical theory of money, which coincides with the quantity theory of money. According to this theory, the monetary authorities control the amount of money but not the supply of credit, which instead depends on saving decisions. Nevertheless, when mainstream economists explain the origins of the crisis, they assume the existence of a relationship between the expansionary monetary policy implemented by the Federal Reserve, the increase in the supply of credit by the banks and the housing bubble that developed in the United States.

The explanation that identifies the roots of the crisis in the behaviour of the US banking system is also in sharp contrast with the traditional theory of finance. In Rajan's (2006, p. 52) view, the US banking system generated a real 'iceberg of risk'. However, in the orthodox theory of finance, the banks are mere intermediaries that transfer resources from savers to businesses. Banks thus do not create any risk; on the contrary, they are supposed to reduce the risks associated with the transfer of saved resources, since, compared with savers, they develop a special expertise in evaluating the borrowers' characteristics.

Finally, even Bernanke's interpretation of the origins of the crisis is not consistent with the mainstream theory. Bernanke argues that the accumulation of a huge amount of savings in the emerging Asian countries accounts for the development of both the dot.com bubble that burst in 2000 and the housing bubble that exploded in the summer of 2007. But, again, the existence of a relationship between an increased propensity to save in the emerging countries and the development of speculative bubbles in the United States is inconsistent with the standard theory of finance. According to this theory, an expansion of the flow of savings is highly positive, as it causes an increase in the flow of investments. Furthermore, the identification of a link between saving decisions and the development of a bubble presupposes the introduction of the concepts of 'speculation' and of 'speculative bubbles' in the orthodox theoretical model. However, as the first part of this book will explain, these concepts are completely neglected in the traditional macroeconomic theory.

Hence, all the interpretations of the origins of the crisis elaborated by mainstream economists are in sharp contrast with the fundamental pillars of the orthodox theory of finance. In the neoclassical world, the monetary authorities do not control the supply of credit, which instead depends on the economic agents' saving decisions, and the banks do not create risks, as they act as intermediaries allocating saved resources to the most profitable uses. In such an economy, a crisis cannot occur, since the monetary authorities are responsible for fixing the rate of growth of the money stock in accordance with the targeted inflation rate. Moreover, the assumption that the whole banking system suddenly loses its ability to transfer saved resources to the most competitive enterprises is quite unrealistic.

Paradoxically, the Great Recession can only be explained by considering an economic system featuring the characteristics highlighted by the conservative economists' interpretations of the crisis, even though such a system greatly differs from the world described by the neoclassical theory of finance, as: 1) the supply of credit does not depend on saving decisions, but on the decisions taken by the monetary authorities and the banking system; 2) the banks can create risks; and 3) the phenomenon of speculation is highly relevant. Therefore, the conclusion drawn in the first part of this book is that the current crisis should lead the economics profession to develop an alternative theoretical approach capable of explaining the functioning of an economic system that features these three characteristics.

3.   AN ALTERNATIVE THEORETICAL APPROACH

The development of an alternative theory is discussed in the second part of this book, which will focus on the ideas of a group of 'heretical' economists such as Marx, Keynes, Schumpeter, Kalecki, Kaldor and Minsky. In order to develop what Keynes called a *Monetary Theory of Production*, a special emphasis will be placed on the need to revive the elements of Keynes's work that were neglected by the advocates of the Neoclassical Synthesis. We will show that Schumpeter's analysis of the role of credit is essential to explain Keynes's insights concerning: 1) the importance of uncertainty; 2) the principle of effective demand; 3) the importance of the process of wealth accumulation and of the phenomenon of speculation; and 4) the structural instability of modern market economies.

The third part of this book emphasizes two specific aspects of the endogenous nature of the current crisis. First, it shows how the same factors described by Schumpeter as characterizing the development of capitalist economies also explain economic systems' inherent instability and their tendency to be exposed to deep crises. Hyman Minsky is the contemporary economist who best analysed the endogenous nature of the crisis. Minsky's analysis highlights the limits of Bernanke's view whereby theoretical models reflect the characteristics of the historical period observed by scientists. As a result, in Bernanke's opinion, during an extended period of stability, the economists' choice to develop models ruling out the occurrence of economic crises was justified.[5] Nevertheless,

Bernanke's approach overlooks the fact that, as Minsky underlined, it is precisely during periods of 'fair-weather conditions' that the factors that will cause the next crisis are at work.[6]

Secondly, the last part of this book will point out that the endogenous nature of the current crisis does not imply that, like earthquakes, it is necessarily an unavoidable event. Recently, the equivalence between economic crises and earthquakes has been frequently used by economists to defend the category against the accusation of their alleged inability to anticipate what was going on: economic crises, like earthquakes, are not predictable. This metaphor is not at all convincing because, while earthquakes are natural events, economic crises are the outcome of social dynamics. This difference has major consequences. In fact, earthquakes are not only unpredictable but also inevitable. This means that the probability of their occurrence is completely independent of the theories developed by seismologists to explain their origin. This is not true for economic crises, as the likelihood of their occurrence is not at all independent of the way economists theorize the functioning of a market economy.

Chapter 8 will discuss how the elaboration of a theory whereby an economic crisis cannot occur increased the probability of the outbreak of the Great Recession in two ways. First, economists were led to completely underestimate the signs of instability that emerged during the period of the so-called Great Moderation. Second, the popularity of the mainstream theoretical approach fostered behaviours and choices that paved the way to the crisis.

The analysis of the nature of the current crisis is not only a matter of academic interest, but also has important consequences with regard to the definition of the policies needed to overcome it. The mainstream economists' conclusion that the crisis was determined by exogenous factors led them to advocate the implementation of the following policies: 1) a drastic reduction of public deficits and debts; 2) 'structural' reforms aimed at removing the constraints that inhibit the working of the price mechanism with the purpose of ensuring a smooth functioning of the markets, most especially the labour market; and 3) a remarkable increase in the banks' regulatory own capital, which would enable them to better counter the effects of a sudden reduction in their asset value in the future.

The third part of this book shows that the fundamental limitation of these policies consists in the fact that they are designed on the basis of the economic system described by the mainstream macroeconomic theory, in which, as was anticipated above, the contemporary crisis could not have happened. Paradoxically, these policies originate from the same theoretical model that contributed to cause the Great Recession. This contradiction can only be eliminated by developing policies that are consistent with the structural nature of the contemporary crisis. Therefore, the last chapter of this book outlines the characteristics of a set of policies aimed at achieving the two-fold objective of creating the conditions for a 'good life' and reducing the structural instability of contemporary economies.

4. STRUCTURE OF THE BOOK

This book is divided into three parts and nine chapters. The first chapter offers a brief description of the most important aspects of the financial crisis that erupted in 2007 and of the subsequent Great Recession. The second chapter provides a more detailed explanation of the origins of the crisis elaborated by mainstream economists, while the third emphasizes the contrast between these interpretations and the fundamental pillars of the orthodox theory of finance.

The fourth chapter opens the second part of the book, which accurately describes a theoretical framework that, drawing on the thought of Keynes and of other heretical economists, may offer a sound explanation of the structural nature of the current crisis. The fifth chapter shows how Keynes's and Schumpeter's theories clarify the relationship between monetary policy and credit supply which characterizes the first explanation of the causes of the crisis elaborated by mainstream economists. It also argues that Schumpeter's theory on the role of credit explains the importance of the Keynesian concept of uncertainty and the relationship between finance and risk that characterizes the second interpretation of the crisis formulated by conservative economists. The sixth chapter discusses the relationship between saving decisions and wealth accumulation, and the phenomenon of speculation. Keynes's analysis of speculation is key to defining the origins of the subprime mortgage crisis. Based on the evidence presented in the previous chapters, the seventh chapter explains the structural nature of the economic crises that characterize modern capitalist economies.

The third part of this book begins with the eighth chapter, which offers a description of the endogenous nature of the Great Recession, and an illustration of how the dissemination of neoliberal ideology in the 1970s helped to create the conditions for the development of the current crisis. The ninth and last chapter points out how the criticism of the traditional macroeconomic theory has important consequences in the definition of the policies needed to overcome the crisis.

NOTES

1. Ben Bernanke, for example, has claimed that: 'the recent financial crisis was more a failure of economic engineering and economic management than of what I have called economic science. ... I don't think the crisis by any means requires us to rethink economics and finance from the ground up' (Bernanke 2010b, p. 2). See also Taylor (2009), Chari (2010) and Cochrane (2011).
2. See Akerlof and Shiller (2009); Buiter (2009); Colander (2011); Colander et al. (2009); De Grauwe (2010); Fitoussi (2013); Galbraith (2014); Goodhart (2010); Harcourt and Kriesler (2011); Hodgson (2009); Kirman (2011); Krugman (2009, 2012); Laidler (2010); Lawson (2009); Leijonhufvud (2009, 2011); Palley (2012); Pasinetti (2011); Phelps (2009); Roncaglia (2010); Roubini and Mihm (2010); Sachs (2009, 2011); Skidelski (2009, 2011); Solow (2010); Spaventa (2009); Stiglitz (2011); Taylor (2010); Turner (2012, 2016).
3. See Palma (2009); Kates (2010); Krippner (2011); Leclaire et al. (2011); Bellamy Foster and McChesney (2012); Lin (2013); Gamble (2014); Cynamon et al. (2013); Mirowsky (2013); Bellofiore and Vertova (2014); Bougrine and Rochon (2015).
4. See, for example, Rajan and Zingales (2003a, 2003b, 2003c) and Blinder and Reis (2005).
5. 'Economic models are useful only in the context for which they are designed. Most of the time, including during recessions, serious financial instability is not an issue. The standard models were designed for these non-crisis periods, and they have proven quite useful in that context. Notably, they were part of the intellectual framework that helped deliver low inflation and macroeconomic stability in most industrial countries during the two decades that began in the mid-1980s' (Bernanke 2010b, p. 6). See also Caballero (2010) and Ascari (2011).
6. As noted by Borio (2011, p. 22): 'The processes that underlie financial instability have macroeconomic roots. That episodes of systemic financial distress are rare does not imply that we can live with two types of model, a fair-weather and stormy-weather one. That might be acceptable if the stormy weather was the result of outsize exogenous shocks. It is not, however, if, as argued here, the stormy weather is generated during fair-weather conditions; if, in other words, the boom does not just *precede*, but *causes* the bust.'

PART I

The Crisis and the Mainstream Theory

1. A brief description of the crisis

Instead of an aristocracy of the merely rich, we are moving to an aristocracy of the capable *and* the rich. The financial revolution is opening the gates of the aristocratic clubs to everyone. In this respect, the financial revolution is thoroughly liberal in spirit. Instead of capital, it puts the human being at the center of economic activity because, when capital is freely available, it is skills, ideas, hard work, and inescapably, luck that create wealth. (Raghuram Rajan and Luigi Zingales 2003c, p. 92)

The problem, or at least a significant part of it, is the rising political hegemony of the financial sector. ... The financial sector has increasingly been able to rig the rules to its own advantage. This has damaged not only the economy but the financial sector itself. (Luigi Zingales 2012, p. 49)

This chapter briefly describes the key characteristics of the contemporary crisis. The first characteristic is related to the place where the crisis originated. The second concerns the phenomenon that triggered it, that is, the substantial increase in delinquencies in a specific category of residential mortgages, namely, the so-called subprime mortgages. The third characteristic has to do with the evolution of the crisis since 2007.

1. THE OUTBREAK OF THE FINANCIAL CRISIS IN THE UNITED STATES

The financial crisis that caused the Great Recession erupted in the United States, the country with the world's most advanced financial system, a system that in recent decades had undergone an intense process of innovation and was taken as the benchmark that other countries should strive to replicate. The textbooks define the financial system as the complex structure of markets, institutions and instruments used to facilitate the transfer of funds from lenders to borrowers. It is a particularly dynamic structure due to innovations that change the features of the financial instruments, markets and intermediaries.

Economists have singled out different criteria that enable measurement of the degree of development of financial structures.[1] Rajan and Zingales (2003a, 2003b, 2003c) set a standard based on the concept of innovation, which takes on a central role in Schumpeter's work. Schumpeter (1912 [1949]) emphasizes that the fundamental characteristic of a capitalist economy is the process of change led by the innovations introduced by entrepreneurs. According to Rajan and Zingales, the degree of development of the financial system can be defined in relation to its ability to finance innovations. Hence, they claim that a financial system is highly sophisticated if it is capable of financing innovations, while it should be considered underdeveloped when it fails to fulfil this function.

To better understand the meaning of this classification, another aspect of Schumpeter's analysis should be taken into account. Schumpeter remarks that usually innovations are not introduced by existing companies, but by new subjects with special skills, other than those needed to manage an existing business. The introduction of an innovation breaks the equilibrium underpinning the normal trend of the economic process. An entrepreneur who is willing to introduce an innovation must therefore be ready to face resistance from those who, for social and economic reasons, oppose his choices. Recalling these elements of Schumpeter's analysis, Rajan and Zingales conclude that a developed financial system must be able to support new entrepreneurs by considering the characteristics of their investment projects independently of other elements, such as their family and personal relationships.[2]

Rajan and Zingales also believe that a financial system in which banks play a central role, known as a *relation-based financial system*, is a typical example of an underdeveloped financial system. In fact, in their opinion such a system is unable to finance innovations as banks tend to focus only on borrowers they know directly or that can offer sound guarantees. Moreover, given the relationships that they maintain with existing businesses, banks are less willing to finance innovations that could affect their customers' profitability. In contrast, a well-developed financial system, which Rajan and Zingales define as an *arm's length system*, is based on market relationships and is characterized by the presence of a multiplicity of subjects that can extend credit. According to Rajan and Zingales, in this type of system an entrepreneur-innovator without sufficient collateral has a better chance of getting a loan, since he can contact a larger number of potential lenders that will evaluate his investment project independently of each other.

The two authors underline that, due to the profound changes that had occurred since the 1980s, the American financial system represented an important example of an advanced financial structure that is highly suitable for financing innovations, while the financial systems of the European countries, still overly bank based, were typical examples of underdeveloped systems. Rajan and Zingales's analysis raises the question of how the financial crisis of 2007 could originate in the very system that was regarded as the most advanced in the world.[3]

2. THE CRISIS IN THE SUBPRIME MORTGAGE MARKET

The financial crisis erupted in the spring of 2007, when a major increase in default rates of residential mortgages, and particularly subprime mortgages, was recorded in the US housing market. In the United States there are two categories of residential mortgages, namely prime and non-prime mortgages. Prime mortgages meet certain conditions regarding the ratio between the loan amount and the value of the house (loan to value rate) and the ratio between the loan amount and the borrower's income (loan to income rate). Conversely, non-prime mortgages do not meet these conditions and are divided into three categories: Alt-A mortgages granted to borrowers who do not meet all the necessary criteria for receiving prime mortgages; Home Equity Line Of Credit (HELOC) mortgages, characterized by the assignment of a line of credit that cannot exceed a certain amount and must be used in a given timeframe; and finally subprime mortgages, granted to borrowers with low income and no capital endowment. Most of the subprime loans originated before the eruption of the crisis and comprised adjustable rate mortgages which, in accordance with the 2/28 or 3/27 formula, provided for the payment of interest rates that were so low as to be called *teaser loans* for the first two or three years, and the payment of much higher rates for the remaining 28 or 27 years of the contract. Another class of subprime mortgages that became notorious after the onset of the crisis consisted of loans offered to people with no income, no job and no assets (*ninja loans*).

The crisis occurred at the end of a period in which the US financial system had greatly increased the supply of mortgages. In six years, from the end of 2000 to the end of 2006, the number of mortgages more than doubled, reaching an astonishing value of 11 trillion dollars. The increase in supply was coupled with a significant deterioration in the quality of the loans. In fact, the share of non-prime mortgages increased from 14 per cent in 2001 to 48 per cent in 2006. Correspondingly, the share of subprime mortgages increased from 5 per cent in 2001 to 20.1 per cent in 2006 (Jaffee et al. 2009). This caused an unprecedented weakening of the mortgage market.

The drastic surge of defaults that triggered the crisis was linked to an increase in the federal funds rate, that is, the rate at which the Federal Reserve finances the US banking system, which affects the entire term structure of interest rates. After the stock market crash of 2000 and the terrorist attacks on the Twin Towers on 11 September 2001, the Federal Reserve slashed the federal funds rate. From a value of over 6 per cent in 2000, the rate dropped to 2 per cent in 2001 and 1 per cent in 2003. As in the early months of 2004 the recession seemed averted, the US monetary authorities began to progressively increase the federal funds rate, which reached 4 per cent in 2004 and 5.25 per cent in 2006. This drift explains the increase in defaults by borrowers, especially by those who, at the time when interest rates decreased, had signed adjustable rate loan agreements.

3. THE THREE PHASES OF THE CRISIS

The crisis broke out in the summer of 2007, when the effects of defaults by borrowers struck the financial institutions that were most involved in the mortgage market. The first dramatic case was that of the British bank Northern Rock, which in September 2007 was hit by a real bank run. Another striking episode involved Bear Stearns, one of the most import-ant American investment banks, which in the spring of 2008 did not go bankrupt thanks only to the intervention of the Federal Reserve.

During the first phase of the crisis, the monetary authorities were convinced that they were faced with a limited phenomenon that affected a significant but secondary segment of the financial system. However, the situation worsened in the summer of 2008, when the dramatic effects of the collapse of the mortgage market on the two major US mortgage agencies, Fannie Mae and Freddie Mac, were announced. These two institutions were also rescued by the US government. A few days later, the threat of insolvency hit another major US investment bank, namely Lehman Brothers. This time, contrary to its actions in the spring with the bailout of Bear Stearns, the US government did not intervene and let Lehman Brothers go bankrupt.

The bankruptcy of Lehman Brothers marked the beginning of the second phase of the crisis. It spread a deep uncertainty about the true conditions of banks and other financial institutions that paralysed the functioning of the interbank markets. This paralysis caused a remarkable rise in interest rates. The spread between the three-month interbank rate and the official rates charged by major central banks reached un-precedented levels. In just a few days, it increased from 87 to 364 basis points for the dollar, from 63 to 205 basis points for the euro, and from 75 to 215 basis points for the pound. In the United States, a few days after the collapse of Lehman Brothers, the government stepped in to save AIG, one of the world's largest insurance companies, while a reluctant Congress approved the TARP (Troubled Assets Relief Program), which provided for an allocation of 700 billion dollars to address the financial crisis.

The serious difficulties of the US financial system had severe repercussions in the economies around the world. Between 2007 and 2009, the world economy underwent the worst recession since the end of World War II. US per capita GDP recorded a decline of 7.2 per cent as compared with an average of 4.4 per cent experienced during previous recessions. Much greater decreases were observed in other countries such as Canada (–8.6 per cent), Italy (–9.8 per cent), Japan (–8.9 per cent) and Great Britain (–9.8 per cent) (Ohanian 2010).

Government interventions aimed at supporting the international financial system and mitigating the effects of the recession caused a significant deterioration in public finances. Thus, the third phase of the crisis began, and the default risk was no longer limited to banks but also affected sovereign states. The problem of sovereign debt became particularly severe in Eurozone countries. While in these countries the annual public deficit to GDP average ratio was 1.9 per cent in the 2000–2008 period, it rose to 6.3 per cent in 2009 and was 6.2 per cent in 2010. In Germany, the budget deficit to GDP ratio rose from an average of 2.3 per cent in 2000–2008 to 3.1 per cent in 2009 and 4.1 per cent in 2010; in France, it grew from 2.7 per cent in 2000–2008 to 7.5 per cent in 2009 and 7.1 per cent in 2010; in Italy the deficit to GDP average ratio increased from 2.9 per cent in the 2000–2008 period to 5.4 per cent in 2009 and 4.5 per cent in 2010; and finally, in Britain, it increased from 2.1 per cent in 2000–2008 to 11.5 per cent in 2009 and 10.1 per cent in 2010.

As from 2011, the growth of sovereign debts pushed the Eurozone countries to adopt austerity policies aimed at reducing their budget deficits. In March 2012, the EU countries, with the exception only of the UK and the Czech Republic, signed the Treaty on Stability, Coordination and Governance in the Economic and Monetary Union. A tax-related section of the Treaty, which became known as the *fiscal compact*, provides for the mandatory introduction of the constraint of a balanced budget and an automatically triggered correction mechanism at a national level. Moreover, countries with a government debt to GDP ratio exceeding 60 per cent are required to reduce the excess of the threshold value by one-twentieth per year.

4. SOME QUESTIONS

This brief review of the most important aspects of the Great Recession raises a number of questions. The first concerns the explanation of how the crisis could erupt in the country with the world's most advanced financial system. A system that, according to the analysis made by Rajan and Zingales, was the most appropriate to finance innovations and thus to facilitate the process of economic development. Residential mortgages can certainly not be considered as examples of innovation. It is therefore necessary to investigate the reasons why the American financial system began to provide mortgage loans instead of investing in innovations.

Secondly, it would be appropriate to establish the origin of the liquidity that allowed US banks to consistently expand their supply of mortgages. As pointed out above, in the 2000–2006 period, the sharp increase in mortgage supply was coupled with a marked deterioration in their quality. This raises a further question about the reasons that led banks to grant mortgage loans to families that were not able to pay them back. The fourth question concerns the behaviour of borrowers. Indeed, while banks unquestionably granted an excessive amount of subprime mortgages, borrowers, on their part, underwrote loan contracts that they could not reimburse. Thus, the obvious question is what caused these people to sign up for mortgages that they could hardly pay back given their low income.

The fifth question is about the impact of the collapse of the mortgage market on the entire financial system. What surprised economists and institutions was the fact that the crisis in the mortgage market spread to the financial system as a whole. The mechanisms whereby mortgage delinquencies threatened to cause the collapse of the entire financial system must therefore be clarified.

The last question regards the impact of the financial crisis on the levels of income and employment. There is no automatic link between a financial crisis and a recession. Over the last 40 years, several financial crises did not produce significant effects on real variables. Hence, we need to shed light on the reasons why this financial crisis had such bad consequences for production and employment rates. Bernanke (2012) tackled this issue by underlining that the subprime mortgage crisis implied a destruction of financial wealth equal to approximately 7000 billion US dollars, which is comparable to the loss caused by the stock market crash that occurred in 2000, when the dot.com bubble burst. In that case, however, despite a decrease in financial wealth of approximately 8000 billion dollars, no significant downturn in income and employment was recorded. Consequently, it is imperative to understand why the bursting of the housing bubble had such devastating effects on income and employment rates. The next chapter will discuss the answers provided to these questions by mainstream economists.

NOTES

1. See, for example, King and Levine (1993); Levine (1997, 2002, 2004); Rajan and Zingales (1998, 2003a, 2003b, 2003c); Wurgler (2000); Stulz (2001); Gorton and Winton (2002); Wachtel (2003); Capasso (2004); and Fergusson (2006).
2. 'In our view ... in a perfect financial system, it will be the quality of the underlying assets or ideas that will determine whether finance is forthcoming, and the identity of the owner ... will be irrelevant. Because our focus is on how easy it is to raise finance without prior connections or wealth, our measures of financial development will emphasize the availability of arm's length market finance ... we adopt the Schumpeterian view that a critical role of finance is creative destruction, and this is possible only if there is a constant flow of capital into new firms and out of old firms' (Rajan and Zingales 2003b, pp. 9–10).
3. For a critical analysis of Rajan and Zingales's arguments see Bertocco (2008).

2. Mainstream economists and the crisis

> Our view of the benefits of finance is inflated. While there is no doubt that a developed economy needs a sophisticated financial sector, at the current state of knowledge there is no theoretical reason or empirical evidence to support the notion that all the growth of the financial sector in the last forty years has been beneficial to society. In fact, we have both theoretical reasons and empirical evidence to claim that a component has been pure rent seeking. By defending all forms of finance, by being unwilling to separate the wheat from the chaff, we have lost credibility in defending the real contribution of finance. (Luigi Zingales 2015, p. 3)

Conservative economists see the contemporary crisis as an accidental phenomenon due to errors made by two subjects, namely public authorities – especially the Federal Reserve and the US government – and the US banking system. Mainstream economists have identified three separate explanations for the origins of the crisis that differ from one another depending on the culprit. The first explanation highlights the correlation between the crisis and the monetary policy implemented by the Federal Reserve. The second points to the choices made by the US banking system as the triggering factors. Finally, the last explanation, developed by Bernanke (2005, 2007a, 2010a), argues that the liquidity that allowed banks to expand their mortgage supply resulted from an excessive accumulation of savings in some areas of the world.[1]

1. THE FEDERAL RESERVE'S DECISIONS AND THE CRISIS

In order to define the correlation between US monetary policy and the crisis, it might be useful to first review how a central bank works. A central bank is the monopolistic producer of what textbooks call 'high-powered money' or 'monetary base', which, for the sake of simplicity, can be identified with the legal tender employed by the public as a means of payment and by the banks to build up their reserves. In modern economies, banks can obtain their monetary base by borrowing from the central bank, which, acting under monopoly conditions, fixes the price and quantity conditions at which it finances the banking system. The interest rate that the central bank applies to the transactions by which it funds the banking system is called the official or reference interest rate. By varying this parameter, the central bank influences the interest rates that banks pay on deposits and charge on loans and, more generally, the entire term structure of interest rates. (See, for example, Bank of England 1999; European Central Bank (ECB) 2004, 2010, 2011; Ryan-Collins et al. 2012; McLeay et al. 2014.)

Many economists believe that the responsibility for the crisis should be attributed to the choices made by the Federal Reserve as, after the collapse of the US stock market, due to the bursting of the dot.com bubble in 2000 and the terrorist attacks on the Twin Towers of 11 September 2001, it dramatically lowered the federal funds rate. The most renowned advocate of this view is John Taylor (2009), who presented a very effective description of the consequences of the excessively expansionary monetary policy adopted under Greenspan's chairmanship. Taylor measured the degree of expansiveness of US monetary policy using a tool that he himself developed in the 1990s, known as the Taylor rule.

This rule is the result of both a theoretical and an empirical analysis. In fact, one of the effects produced by the theoretical counterrevolution of the 1970s is the definition of the *modus operandi* of central banks. According to the new approach, central banks would have to give up the discretionary decision-making process that was adopted when the paradigm of the so-called Neoclassical Synthesis prevailed and act in conformity with a predetermined decision rule. A first example was proposed by Milton Friedman (1968), who predicated that monetary authorities should set, once and for all, the annual growth rate of the money supply.

The decision rule proposed by Taylor concerned the way the federal funds rate had to be fixed. Observing the behaviour of the Federal Reserve in the 1980s and 1990s, Taylor noted that the US monetary authorities had adjusted the federal funds rate in order to control both the inflation rate and the level of GDP. Upon analysing the data for that period, Taylor concluded that the Federal Reserve had followed a rule whereby the interest rate had to be increased when the inflation rate exceeded the target value fixed by the authorities, while it had to be lowered when GDP was below its potential level.[2]

Once the inflation target and the potential level of real income are known, the Taylor rule defines the correct interest rate level that should be fixed by the monetary authorities. Furthermore, the Taylor rule allows measurement of the gap between the actual behaviour of the monetary authorities and the behaviour that would be consistent with the rule's requirements. Figure 2.1 shows the gap between the values of the federal funds rate set by the Federal Reserve in the years before the outbreak of the crisis and those that should have been adopted according to the Taylor rule.

The figure shows two curves. The solid line, which starts from a value close to 6 per cent in 2000, then drops to 1 per cent between 2003 and 2004 and finally increases rapidly between 2004 and 2006, describes the historical values of the federal funds rate. The dotted line represents the interest rate values that the Federal Reserve should have set between 2001 and 2005 according to the Taylor rule. The distance between the two lines in Figure 2.1 shows the dimension of what Taylor considers the fundamental mistake made by the US monetary authorities.

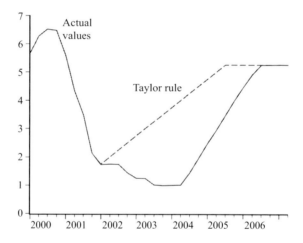

Source: Taylor (2009), p. 3.

Figure 2.1   Federal funds rate (real and counterfactual percentages)

In order to argue that the subprime crisis was caused by the decisions taken by the US monetary authorities, in addition to having an indicator that measures the degree of expansiveness of the monetary policy, it is necessary to demonstrate that there is a link between the Federal Reserve's over-expansionary monetary policy and the financial crisis. To investigate the existence of this correlation, Taylor (2009) built an indicator describing the boom and the collapse of the housing market. He also simulated the performance that this indicator would have had had the US monetary authorities followed the Taylor rule, adopted in the 1980s and 1990s.

The results of Taylor's analysis are summarized in Figure 2.2. The solid line represents the actual values of the real estate sector during the boom and the subsequent collapse of the housing market. The dotted curve, defined as counterfactual, illustrates the values that the indicator of the real estate sector would have recorded had the Federal Reserve followed a less expansionary monetary policy. In this case, according to Taylor's elaborations, the values of the real estate sector would have shown a much softer trend, without a real boom followed by a collapse.

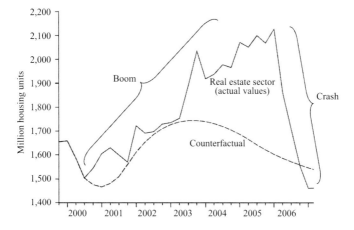

Source: Taylor (2009), p. 5.

Figure 2.2 The boom and the collapse of the real estate sector compared with the counterfactual hypothesis

Taylor's analysis certainly provides an answer to one of the questions posed at the end of the previous chapter, that is, the question concerning the origin of the funds that were used by the banks to expand their supply of mortgages. However, this is not enough to answer the other questions. For example, it is not clear why the banks which, according to Rajan and Zingales, operated in the world's most advanced financial system, used the funds obtained from the Federal Reserve to finance the purchase of houses by low-income families instead of funding investments by the most innovative companies. An answer to this question can only be provided by analysing the behaviour of the banking system in the years before the outbreak of the crisis.

2. THE AMERICAN BANKING SYSTEM AND THE CRISIS

The second explanation of the crisis developed by mainstream economists blames the American banking system for the excessive amount of
risk that it allegedly created. The expression 'creating risk' should not be
confused with 'taking on risks'. An insurance company that issues
policies covering the damages caused by an earthquake takes on the risk
associated with the need to pay the beneficiaries when an earthquake
actually occurs. However, with this transaction the insurance company
does not affect the probability of the actual occurrence of an earthquake.
In other words, it takes on a risk, but it certainly does not create it.
Conversely, with regard to the recent crisis, the US banking system is
accused of having created the risk that a financial meltdown might
actually occur because it expanded the supply of subprime mortgages,
thereby fuelling the formation of a bubble that ultimately burst and
produced catastrophic consequences.

The behaviour of the US banking system is attributed to two causes.
On the one hand, the policy adopted since the 1990s, first by the Clinton
administration and then by the Bush administration, to encourage low-
income American citizens to purchase their first home, and, on the other
hand, the profound structural transformation of the US banking system
since the early 1980s. In 1992, the US Congress ratified the Federal
Housing Enterprises Safety and Soundness Act with the aim of promoting home ownership by low-income families and minority ethnic groups.
This goal was achieved by employing two institutions, commonly known
as Fannie Mae and Freddie Mac, whose function was to buy real estate
mortgages with special requirements that were previously granted by
banks, financing these transactions by issuing securities on the market.
Pressures from the Clinton and Bush administrations led the two agencies
to ease the evaluation criteria of loans that could be secured or purchased,
thereby encouraging banks to expand the supply of mortgages, at the
expense of their quality (Rajan 2010).

The measures taken by the US government to support the financing of
home ownership by low-income families have often been regarded as the
response of the political class to the growing inequality in income
distribution, a social issue that has emerged with increasing evidence
since the 1980s. According to Rajan (2010), the strong aversion of the
American conservative party to policies aimed at levying taxes in order to
redistribute income among different social groups has prompted the US

government to address the problem of growing inequality by providing credit facilities to low-income families.

2.1 The Transformation of the Banking System

The banks' behaviour was influenced not only by the decisions of the US government, but also by a number of factors that have profoundly changed the characteristics of the American financial system in recent decades. The first of these factors is technology, and specifically the information and communications technology (ICT) revolution that makes it extremely easy to gather and process information on potential customers. The second element is the evolution of the theory of finance. During the 1950s and 1960s, Markowitz (1952), Tobin (1958), Sharpe (1964), Litner (1965) and Mossin (1966) developed the portfolio allocation theory, emphasizing the effects of the diversification process. In the 1970s, the work of Black and Scholes (1973), Merton (1973) and Cox et al. (1979) paved the way for the creation of complex financial instruments.

The third factor is the deregulation of the financial system and the liberalization of capital movements which, under the guidance of neo-liberal leaders such as Ronald Reagan and Margaret Thatcher, was intended to eliminate the control system that had been put in place after the Great Depression of the 1930s. The last factor is the profound modification of the remuneration system of bank managers. In fact, starting in the 1980s, the fixed-income compensation scheme has been gradually replaced by a variable system with bonuses based on the amount of profits generated for shareholders.

The combination of these elements has profoundly changed the banks' business model, resulting in a transition from the traditional model defined by the formula 'originate to hold' to a new 'originate to distribute' model. This transformation is crucial for understanding why banks created an excessive amount of risk in the years before the crisis.

To explain the differences between these two operational models, it should first be pointed out that finance is based on a form of credit–debit contract consisting in the exchange of a sum of money today against the promise of a larger sum in the future. Of course, it is possible that, for various reasons, this promise will not be kept. The risk inherent in this exchange causes the potential creditor to collect information on the debtor and the characteristics of the project that the latter plans to realize with the borrowed funds.

Economists have pointed out that, normally, the exchange on which finance is based occurs in a situation characterized by asymmetric information, since the lender has less information than the debtor regarding the manner in which the funds will be used and the factors that will determine the repayment of the loan. This situation hinders the exchange. A creditor who does not have sufficient information to assess the quality of the credit contract may decide not to grant the loan or else ask for higher interest rates. The latter, however, is not necessarily an effective solution, because it produces what economists call a process of adverse selection. In fact, high interest rates may discourage honest borrowers and attract those who, knowing they are not willing to repay the loan, promise to pay the high interest rates provided for in the contract.

In the 1970s, the seminal work of George Akerlof (1970) led to the development of a new theoretical approach, based on the idea that the primary function of financial intermediaries, most especially banks, was to overcome the problems associated with asymmetric information.[3] The role of banks was defined using the distinction between internal and external debt contracts. An internal debt contract is a loan agreement granted on the basis of information that is not publicly available and is collected by means of a direct relationship between the creditor and the debtor that allows the creditor to access confidential information on both the debtor and its projects. Conversely, an external debt contract is based on information that is publicly available, and which, therefore, does not imply a close relationship between the debtor and the creditor. The loans granted by the banks were considered to be a typical example of internal debt contracts (Fama 1985).

Economists believed that the key element that distinguished the banks from other financial intermediaries was the nature of their assets, which consisted primarily in loans granted on the basis of private information. Hence, loans were highly illiquid financial assets that could not easily be sold on the market (Goodhart 1987). The banks' business model was defined as 'originate to hold' to indicate that the banks retained until maturity the loans granted to families and businesses on the basis of privately collected information.

As mentioned above, this business model has changed radically in recent years. The immediate cause of this change was a higher availability of information due to the ICT revolution, which led to the development of companies specializing in gathering data on corporate activities (Rajan and Zingales 2003c, pp. 58–59). Due to the higher availability of information, the number of potential lenders increased as firms could get credit not only from local but also from more remote banks. Furthermore, the greater availability of information increased the liquidity of banks' loans, making them similar to external debt contracts based on publicly available information. Bank loans therefore became assets that could be sold on the financial markets. Banks gradually adopted a new operating model defined as 'originate to distribute', which allowed them to sell an increasing share of their originally illiquid assets on the market through a securitization process.

2.2 The Securitization Process

The securitization process led to a specialization of financial intermediaries. Let us take, for example, the case of a bank that operates according to the traditional 'originate to hold' model, providing loans for the purchase of residential properties. A bank of this type offers loan contracts by selecting potential borrowers and funds loan disbursements by issuing financial instruments, such as deposits or bonds, that meet the portfolio preferences of wealth holders. The bank thus performs two distinct functions: it provides credit to borrowers and, at the same time, it creates financial assets which are bought by the wealth holders.

The securitization process determined a division of labour between financial intermediaries, since the origination of credit and the creation of financial assets that can be accumulated by wealth holders are now performed by different institutions. A subject called the 'originator', for example a bank, grants the loans. As noted above, given the increasing availability of information, most of these loans feature the characteristics of external debt contracts and therefore can be sold on the market. Residential mortgages are certainly contracts of this kind, since all the information needed to calculate the borrowers' risk of default, such as household income, the location of the house to be purchased and its features, are easily available. After granting the mortgages, the originating bank may transfer them to another, legally independent, institution, known as a Special Purpose Vehicle (SPV). This institution finances the acquisition of the loans originated by the banks by issuing Asset Backed Securities (ABSs) or, in the specific case of the purchase of a package of residential mortgages, Mortgage Backed Securities (MBSs). These securities are then placed onto the market and purchased by wealth holders.

The division of labour between banks and SPVs is the foundation of what is known as structured finance, that is, the activity of grouping together (pooling) loans granted by banks, such as mortgages, consumer loans and leasing contracts, and their subsequent purchase by an SPV. The main advantage offered by the securitization process is that a vehicle company which acquires a large amount of mortgages granted by different banks, due to the effects of portfolio diversification, may issue financial assets with a lower risk profile as compared with that of the purchased mortgages (credit enhancement). Therefore, the division of labour between banks and SPVs allows an increase in the supply of derivative financial instruments, namely ABSs or MBSs, which, thanks to the benefits of diversification, have a low degree of risk, and may thus obtain a higher evaluation by credit-rating agencies.

The process by which derivative securities get a higher credit rating than that of the underlying loans can be illustrated by a simple example. Let us take two banks whose assets, for the sake of simplicity, each consist of a single credit, for example a mortgage, and let us further assume that these two credits have the same risk characteristics. Both banks can obtain an amount of 1 with a probability of 90 per cent when the borrower repays the loan and an amount of 0 with a probability of 10 per cent in the case of insolvency of the borrower. Therefore, default probability of the loans is equal to 10 per cent, which, according to the evaluation standards of the rating agencies, characterizes high-risk securities which receive a rating of BB (Coval et al. 2009). Thanks to the securitization process, a portfolio made of the two mortgages can be created and then purchased by a different subject, namely an SPV, which shall fund this financial transaction by issuing securities whose yield depends on the income generated by the new portfolio.

As a result of the diversification principle, the probability distribution of the expected income of the new portfolio is not equal to that of each of the two individual loans. Indeed, let us assume that the two banks granted a loan to two individuals who live in different areas and earn their income by working for different companies. We can therefore assume that the probability distributions of the expected income from the two loans are independent. This implies that the probability that both borrowers will default, and thus that the portfolio formed by the two loans will yield an income of 0, is 1 per cent (0.10×0.10). Furthermore, the portfolio will produce the following cash flows: 1) if none of borrowers defaults, the income generated by the portfolio will be equal to 2 with a probability of 81 per cent (0.9×0.9); 2) if both borrowers fail to repay their loans, the portfolio will produce an income of 0 with a probability of 1 per cent; and 3) if only one of the two borrowers defaults, the portfolio will generate a cash flow of 1 with a probability of 18 per cent ($100 - 81 - 1$).

To finance the purchase of the two loans, the SPV will issue securities that entitle the holder to receive cash flows consistent with those generated by the portfolio. For example, the SPV could issue two securities (tranching). The first, called the *senior* security, entitles the holder to receive a cash flow equal to 1 with priority over the other security, while the second, called the *junior* security, grants an income of

1 only if the holder of the senior security has already been repaid. The risk level of these two securities is very different. In fact, the necessary condition for the holder of the senior security to get an income of 1 is that the portfolio consisting of the two mortgages generates an income at least equal to 1. This will occur if none of the borrowers is insolvent and in the event that only one of them defaults. The probability that the portfolio will generate an income equal to 1 is therefore equal to 99 per cent (81 per cent in the case of no default, plus 18 per cent in the case of only one default), while the probability that it will produce an income of 0 is obviously 1 per cent. The senior security is of higher quality than the two individual mortgages. In fact, it will receive a credit rating of AAA if the policy followed by the rating agencies is to assign the highest rating to securities whose default probability does not exceed 1 per cent. The junior security, instead, allows the holder to earn an income of 1 only in the event that none of the borrowers is insolvent, which will occur with a probability of 81 per cent.

This example shows that the securitization process produces derivative financial instruments with characteristics that are profoundly different from those of the original debts. Let us assume, for the sake of simplicity, that the price of the two securities is equal to the weighted average of their expected returns. The price of the senior security will be equal to 0.99 (1 × 0.99 + 0 × 0.01), while the price of the junior security will be equal to 0.81 (1 × 0.81 + 0 × 0.18). Thanks to the portfolio consisting of the two loans, the SPV could issue two securities with an overall quotation of 0.99 + 0.81 = 1.80. As a result, 55 per cent (0.99/1.80) of the liabilities created by the SPV would obtain a credit rating of AAA.

As the number of mortgages in the SPV's portfolio grows, the default probability associated with the senior securities decreases further. Let us expand this example by adding a third mortgage with the same characteristics as the other two. In this case, the SPV can issue a senior security granting a cash flow of 1 with a default probability of 1 per 1000, which corresponds to the probability that all three borrowers become insolvent (0.1 × 0.1 × 0.1).[4]

Since the 1980s, the massive use of securitization techniques has produced a significant increase in the amount of issued securities with a credit rating of AAA granted by the rating agencies. When the housing bubble burst in mid-2007, about 60 per cent of all structured financial products had obtained a rating of AAA, a very high percentage if one considers that only 1 per cent of the securities issued by large corporations had achieved this rating (Coval et al. 2009). In the mid-2000s, the majority of economists and finance experts believed that the process of financial innovation accomplished in the previous three decades had made the financial system safer. Very few scholars questioned this conclusion. One of these was Raghuram Rajan, the author, along with Luigi Zingales, of a celebrated book (Rajan and Zingales 2003c) that a few years earlier had praised the positive effects produced by the evolution of the US financial system.

2.3   The Creation of an Excessive Amount of Risk by the Banking System

In August 2005, the annual conference organized by the Federal Reserve Bank in Kansas City at Jackson Hole was dedicated to the celebration of Alan Greenspan, the Chairman of the Federal Reserve, whose term of office, which had begun in 1987, would end on 31 January 2006. Rajan, who at that time was Director of Research of the International Monetary Fund, was asked to present a paper on the evolution of the financial system in the years of Greenspan's mandate.

While preparing his presentation, Rajan realized that the risk exposure of the large US banks had increased significantly over the previous years. In his report he emphasized the positive aspects of the evolution of the US financial system, but he also underlined that the financial innovation had also increased its fragility, and in his conclusions, Rajan (2006, pp. 521–522) did not exclude that a catastrophic crisis might occur. Rajan's arguments were strongly criticized because they did not seem in line with the celebratory nature of the Jackson Hole Conference. Later, however, thanks to his presentation, Rajan was celebrated as one of the few economists who, before 2007, publicly claimed that a disastrous crisis might actually happen.

The conclusions drawn by economists on the benefits of the securitization process were based on the assumption that the quality of the individual loans issued by banks would not change with the spread of innovative financial techniques. Rajan, instead, realized that this assumption was groundless. By giving the banks the opportunity to transfer their credits and the associated default risks, the securitization process had reduced the banks' incentive to scrupulously assess loan quality, thus generating a moral hazard issue, that is, a problem that occurs when a subject is in a position to take a risky decision and to earn profits while transferring future losses to other subjects. The spread of securitization techniques had encouraged banks to expand the amount of mortgages granted to subjects that would never be able to repay them. In fact, they gained profits from the fees collected on loans that were subsequently securitized. The incentive to expand the supply of mortgages was so strong that banks ended up creating what Rajan called a real 'iceberg of risk':

> Banks make returns both by originating risks and by bearing them [...] Banks cannot, however, sell all risks. They often have to bear the most complicated and volatile portion of the risk they originate. ... In fact, the data suggest that despite a deepening of financial markets, banks may not be any safer than in the past. Moreover, the risk they now bear is a small (though perhaps the most volatile) tip of an iceberg of risk they have created. (Rajan 2006, p. 502)

Rajan underlines that an important element accounting for the misuse of the securitization techniques by the banks is the profound change introduced in the compensation schemes of bank managers. In the 1950s and 1960s, the remuneration of bank managers was essentially fixed. The lack of competitiveness among banks and the importance of the relationship between banks and debtors for the extension of loans caused bank managers to act in an extremely conservative manner. When granting loans on the basis of privately collected information, their primary concern was to avoid wrong financing decisions that might jeopardize the bank's capital and trigger a flight of depositors. As Rajan put it, banking activity was considered boring and poorly paid (Rajan 2010; Admati and Hellwig 2013).

Since the 1980s, the situation has changed radically. The deregulation of financial systems and the technological revolution that facilitated the collection and processing of information on potential borrowers have led to a significant reduction in the heterogeneity that characterized the banking system. The evolution of the financial system resulted in the dominance of large universal banks. Legally established as public limited companies, banking conglomerates began to pursue the maximization of shareholders' value as their exclusive objective. This evolution was accompanied by a substantial change in the compensation system for bank managers. In order to align the goals of the managers with those of the shareholders, banks introduced a new remuneration scheme based on bonuses linked directly to the results obtained (Rajan 2006, p. 501). The remuneration of bank managers was defined by comparing their performance with that of their competitors. To earn large compensations, managers had not only to achieve high returns, but also such returns had to be higher than their competitors' as measured by an index called 'alpha'. Rajan pointed out that, due to this increasingly popular new remuneration structure, bank managers were more and more inclined to take on the so-called *tail risk*, that is, a risk associated with an event that has a very low probability of occurrence but, should it actually occur, has catastrophic consequences:

> What, then is a financial manager to do if she is an ordinary mortal – neither an extraordinary investor nor a great financial entrepreneur – and has no bright ideas on new securities or schemes to sell? The answer for many is to take on tail risk. [...] Suppose a financial manager decides to write earthquake insurance policies but does not tell her investors. As she writes policies and collects premiums, she will increase her firm's earnings. Moreover, because earthquakes occur rarely, no claims will be made for a long while. If the manager does not set aside reserves for the eventual payouts that will be needed (for earthquakes, though rare, eventually do occur), she will be feted as the new Warren Buffet: all the premiums she collects will be seen as pure returns, given that there is no apparent risk. The money can all be paid out as bonuses or dividends. Of course, one day the earthquake will occur, and she will have to pay insurance claims. Because she has set aside no reserves, she will likely default on the claims, and her strategy will be revealed for the sham it is. But before that, she will have enjoyed the adulation of the investing masses and may have salted away enough in bonuses to retire comfortably to a beach house in the Bahamas.[...] More generally, at times when financing is plentiful, so that there is immense competition among bankers and fund managers, the need to create alpha pushes many of them inexorably toward taking on tail risk. (Rajan 2010, pp. 138–139)

In their frantic search for high 'alpha' values, bank managers did not sell earthquake insurance policies. What they did, instead, was to grant mortgage loans to people who were not capable of repaying them. As long as there were no evident defaults, their profits and their compensations would increase. However, there is a substantial difference between the tail risk undertaken by an insurance company and that undertaken by banks. In fact, selling insurance policies does not influence the probability of occurrence of an earthquake in any way, while, in the case of subprime mortgages, the banks' behaviour increased the probability of a catastrophic collapse of the housing market and of the resulting financial crisis. With their decision to expand the supply of subprime mortgages, they actually *created* the risk that a disastrous financial meltdown might occur (Rajan 2010, p. 136).

To complete the analysis of the causes of the crisis, besides the banks' behaviour, it is necessary to explain the behaviour of many families that underwrote mortgage loans that, because of their low income, they would never be able to pay back. Undoubtedly, this unwise behaviour can partly be explained by the banks' ability to create loan typologies designed to appeal to low-income subjects through techniques that the case-law later stigmatized with the definition of 'predatory lending'. However, another factor fostered the demand for subprime mortgages, that is, an increasing expectation that housing prices would continue to rise. It was this widespread belief that also pushed low-income families to borrow from banks. As the housing demand grew, so did housing prices, which led to the self-fulfilment of the widespread expectation of an uninterrupted price surge on the real estate market, that is, to the development of a speculative bubble.

2.4 'This Time is Different': House Prices Will Continue to Rise

The concepts of speculation and speculative bubble, which have repeatedly been used to describe the characteristics of the financial crisis that broke out in 2007, can be illustrated by identifying two different market types. The first consists in traditional markets in which producers and consumers exchange goods that, once purchased, disappear from the market, as the buyer uses them directly. In these markets, the traditional law of supply and demand holds true. Speculative bubbles characterize markets of the second type, where goods, once purchased, can be traded countless times. Typically, in these markets the objects of exchange are durable goods such as residential properties or financial assets such as stocks or bonds. Those who decide to buy these kinds of assets do not necessarily want to hold them forever. In fact, they might gain a profit by selling such assets for higher prices in the future. Thus, the demand for assets traded on these markets depends on the expectations about their future prices. Consequently, the law of supply and demand does not apply and the formation of speculative bubbles is perfectly plausible.

Let us assume that the widespread expectations are for an increasing price of a specific asset. This will result in an increasing demand for such asset, which, in turn, will cause a surge in its price. In traditional markets, the price increase eliminates the imbalance between supply and demand. Conversely, in the second type of market, a price increase may lead to a further increase in demand, thus confirming the expectations of those who had bet on a price increase, thereby influencing also the expectations of other speculators. The spread of these expectations may result in a self-fulfilling prophecy, which may trigger a sustained rise in the asset price due neither to its production costs nor to its profitability.

Robert Shiller (2008), Nobel laureate in 2013, is probably the most renowned economist who used the concept of speculative bubble to explain the subprime mortgage crisis. He built an index of housing prices in the United States starting from 1890, which shows that, between 1996 and 2006, real housing prices rose by 85 per cent, that is, three times as much as the average increase recorded from 1890 to 1996. Shiller

observes that such increase is justified neither by the trend of construction costs nor by interest rate trends. He therefore concludes that, after
1996, the rise in housing prices has to be attributed to the growing
expectations of further and continued price increases, which were fuelled
by what he calls the tale of a 'new era' (Shiller 2008, p. 41), that is, a
myth about the reasons why the economy had entered a new era of
ever-increasing housing prices. Shiller points out that bubbles are a
recurring phenomenon in the history of economics. Every bubble is
always fuelled by widespread expectations about the increasing price of a
specific asset that are invariably disseminated through the tale of a new
era. What changes is only the content of the tale explaining why 'this
time is different', to use the title of a celebrated book by Carmen
Reinhart and Kenneth Rogoff (2009).[5] The dissemination of the message
that this time is different led many low-income families to believe that
the continuing increase in housing prices would enable them to repay the
old mortgage by subscribing a new loan for a larger amount.

2.5   From the Housing Bubble to the Financial Crisis: The Role of *Herd Behaviour*

In 2007, the housing bubble finally burst. This should not have come as a
surprise since no bubble can last indefinitely. Between 2007 and 2008,
the collapse of the subprime mortgage market caused a profound
financial crisis that culminated in September 2008 with the bankruptcy of
Lehman Brothers. This episode deeply shocked economists and traders
since, due to the securitization techniques, banks were supposed to
transfer the risks related to the subprime mortgages to other subjects.
With the outbreak of the crisis, it became clear that most of the securities
issued on the basis of the underlying mortgage loans were kept on the
banks' balance sheets. According to estimates by the Bank of England
and by the International Monetary Fund, in 2007 about 50 per cent of
ABSs and CDOs were still posted on the banks' balance sheets (Barucci
and Magno 2009, p. 148). At first glance, the banks' choice to hold a
significant portion of the assets resulting from the securitization of
subprime mortgages appears to make no sense, since they could not
ignore the poor quality of the loans. Rajan (2006, 2010) uses the concept
of *herd behaviour* to explain the reasons why banks resolved to buy
derivatives even though they knew that the housing bubble would
eventually burst.

   The concept of herd behaviour was developed by economists who
questioned the validity of the efficient financial markets theory according
to which no speculative bubble can ever happen. Bubbles cannot occur

because rational speculators would immediately take the profit opportunities that arise in case of discrepancy between the actual market price and the 'correct' value of a specific asset. The efficient market theory postulates that financial markets are driven by the choices of players who might be defined as 'professional speculators', whose decisions prevail over those of the so-called 'non-professional speculators', that is, players who are easily influenced by the tale of a 'new era'. However, studies conducted by the economists who developed the concept of herd behaviour have shown that, when faced with an overvalued asset, professional speculators may not find it profitable to sell it immediately or to sell it forward.[6]

In fact, even if they believed that the market price of an asset does not reflect its fundamentals, professional speculators might choose to bet on a further rise in market prices if they were convinced that the evaluation of non-professional speculators would prevail. In this case, professional speculators would abide by the behaviour of non-professional speculators and 'follow the herd'.[7] The gregarious attitude of professional speculators is justified by their desire to avoid the risk of incurring a loss while all the other players earn a profit. To dodge this risk, they are willing to give up the possibility of obtaining a profit when everyone else suffers a loss.[8]

In his presentation at the 2005 Jackson Hole Conference, Rajan emphasized that the remuneration system based on bonuses linked to the financial performance of their banks urged investment managers to adopt herd behaviours because, even when faced with huge discrepancies between market prices and the values consistent with the asset 'fundamentals', few of them would choose to fight the market trend.[9] Rajan observes that a major factor that contributed to the banks' herd behaviour was the attitude taken by the Federal Reserve. In fact, Alan Greenspan declared that the monetary authorities would not intervene to curb a sudden and substantial increase in financial asset prices because a speculative bubble can only be recognized when it bursts. Therefore, the Federal Reserve would only intervene to support market liquidity when the bubble actually burst. According to Rajan, the so-called 'Greenspan put' offered bank managers a strong incentive to adopt herd behaviours since they would enjoy the benefits of a continuous rise in asset prices while, thanks to the Federal Reserve's commitment to intervene, they would suffer limited losses should the bubble burst.

The fact that banks kept a high amount of derivative securities on their balance sheets exacerbated the effects of the bursting of the housing bubble on the financial system. The fair value accounting principle forced banks to immediately write-down their assets. This depreciation resulted in a corresponding reduction in the shareholders' equity and hence an increase in leverage. In order to restore an appropriate degree of leverage, banks could follow two strategies: increase their equity or deleverage by reducing the amount of securities held in their portfolios. Many banks opted for the second strategy and hence had to sell off even high-quality stocks. This caused a remarkable decline in their market value, which ended up in a generalized downward spiral of asset prices, with the involvement of several financial institutions that were not directly implicated in real estate speculations. The heavy losses incurred by banks explain why the bursting of the housing bubble, unlike the dot.com bubble, did cause a deep recession.[10] These losses resulted in a contraction of the credit supply, which led to a severe fall in aggregate demand and hence in the levels of income and employment.

3. THE GLOBAL SAVINGS GLUT AND THE CRISIS

The explanation of the origins of the crisis elaborated by Ben Bernanke (2005, 2007b, 2010a) aims to demonstrate that the liquidity that fuelled the housing bubble was not created by the Federal Reserve but was rather the result of an excess in global savings, especially in emerging Asian countries and oil-producing countries.

In April 2005, Bernanke issued a report, the objective of which was to explain the causes of the remarkable increase in the US trade deficit, which rose from $125 billion in 1996 (1.5 per cent of GDP), to $640 billion in 2004 (5.5 per cent of GDP), up to $812 billion in 2006 (6.2 per cent of GDP) (Bernanke 2007b).[11] Bernanke wondered whether the increasing US trade deficit was due to internal or external factors, that is, if the increase in the trade deficit was caused by the fall in the share of US savings from 16 per cent of GDP in 1996 to 14 per cent of GDP in 2006, or whether it was a result of the change in the saving and investment decisions made by the countries that recorded a growing trade surplus.

Bernanke rejected the first explanation since, if it were true, the lack of savings in the United States should have led to an increase in interest rates, while interest rates actually decreased in those years.[12] Therefore, he argued that the deterioration of the US trade balance was due to a change in the behaviour of countries that accumulated a significant trade surplus. According to Bernanke, the growing US trade deficit was due to an excess of savings recorded in emerging Asian countries and oil-producing countries. To endorse this thesis, Bernanke had to explain two points. First, he had to identify the factors that drove these countries to increase their propensity to save. Second, he had to clarify the mechanism by which a higher propensity to save in the rest of the world had led American households to reduce their propensity to save. As far as the first point is concerned, Bernanke identified three factors that pushed surplus countries to increase their propensity to save: 1) the financial crisis that hit the economies of many Asian countries in the 1990s, which led to a significant reduction in investment spending and to the adoption of policies aimed at accumulating huge dollar reserves; 2) a surge in oil prices; and 3) a major increase in the flow of savings from China boosted by a strong income growth and by a remarkable propensity to save among Chinese families.

Bernanke completed his explanation by identifying the mechanism whereby the accumulation of savings in emerging Asian countries led to a fall in the propensity to save in the United States. To this purpose, he stressed a causal link between the excess of global savings and the two bubbles that developed in the United States at that time. With regard to the dot.com bubble, Bernanke pointed out that, between 1996 and 2000, foreign savings flowed to the United States due to the prospect of earning high returns driven by the expectations spawned by the ICT revolution. Thus, the inflow of foreign capital fuelled the boom in the US stock market. The sharp rise of stock prices caused a significant increase in the financial wealth of US households, driving them to reduce their propensity to save. Therefore, the dot.com bubble is the first element that accounts for the lower propensity to save in the United States between 1996 and 2005.

In 2000, the collapse of the US stock market remarkably slowed the investment flow in the United States and in the rest of the world, while the propensity to save remained globally high. According to Bernanke, these elements caused a decline in interest rates that led US households to further reduce their propensity to save. So, while between 1996 and 2000 the lower propensity to save in the United States could be explained by the increased financial wealth of American families, after 2000 this phenomenon could be explained by the falling interest rates. Furthermore, the decline in interest rates increased the demand for loans, thereby fuelling the housing bubble. The surge in housing prices produced a wealth effect similar to that caused by the rise in the price of dot.com stocks, which further undermined the propensity to save among American families.

With his analysis, Bernanke intended to challenge the interpretation given by Taylor, who claimed that the responsibility for the crisis lay in the overly expansionary monetary policy adopted by the Federal Reserve. Bernanke's reply (2010a) was based on two points. First, he questioned the definition of the Taylor rule used to criticize the choices made by the

American monetary authorities. According to Taylor's definition, the Federal Reserve should have set the federal funds rate by taking into account the difference between the current inflation rate and its target value. Bernanke objected that the monetary authorities should fix the interest rate depending on their inflation expectations since the current inflation rate can be affected by accidental factors that cause only temporary changes in the price level. This may happen, for example, when a sudden increase in oil prices occurs. If the monetary authorities regarded these changes as temporary, there would be no reason to increase also the interest rates. Bernanke (2010a) showed that if the Taylor rule were applied on the expected inflation rate, there would be no significant difference between the actual interest rate values and those resulting from the Taylor rule.

In the second part of his reply, Bernanke offered an alternative explanation of the origin of the housing bubble as compared with Taylor's view. He blamed the excessive accumulation of savings in emerging Asian countries, especially in China. To endorse this thesis, Bernanke pointed out that the data collected for 20 developed countries show that 'countries in which current accounts worsened and capital inflows rose ... had greater house price appreciation over this period' (Bernanke 2010a, p. 7).

NOTES

1. The three explanations will be considered separately. Actually, many economists have explained the origin of the crisis by combining elements that appear in the three explanations identified above. See, for example, Mizen (2008), Bracke and Fidora (2008), Obstfeld and Rogoff (2009), Mayer-Foulkes (2009), Diamond and Rajan (2009), Rajan (2010), Catte et al. (2010) and Sa et al. (2011). See also the essays collected in Blinder et al. (2012) and Blanchard et al. (2012), and the works cited in Gorton and Metrik (2012) and Lo (2012).

2. This rule can be represented by the following equation:

$$r_t = 2\% + P_t + \alpha \, (P_t - P^*) + \beta(Y_t - Y^*).$$

r_t corresponds to the value of the federal funds rate controlled by the Federal Reserve in the current period; the 2 per cent figure refers to the value of the real interest rate that the monetary authorities consider correct when the levels of real income and of the inflation rate correspond to their targeted values. P_t indicates the actual level of the inflation rate in the current period; P^* represents the target value of the inflation rate set by the monetary authorities; Y_t is the actual value of real income, while Y^* indicates the target value of real income pursued by the monetary authorities. Finally, α and β are two positive parameters whose magnitude expresses the weight given by the monetary authorities to deviations of inflation and income from their respective target values. The equation shows that if the current values of inflation and income are equal to their respective target values, the Federal Reserve will set the level of the federal funds rate so as to reach a level of the real interest rate equal to 2 per cent. Conversely, the federal funds rate will be higher if the current inflation rate exceeds the target value, and will be lower if the current level of real income is under the level targeted by the monetary authorities.

3. 'Imperfect information about the probability of default ... gives rise to institutions – like banks – that specialize in acquiring information about default risk' (Blinder and Stiglitz 1983, p. 299). Stiglitz is probably the economist who has made the major contributions to this approach. See, for example, his Nobel lecture (Stiglitz 2002) and Stiglitz and Greenwald (2003).

4. Actually, the securitization process provided for the construction of portfolios made up of thousands of mortgages originated by various banks. Generally, these portfolios gave rise to the issuance of three distinct classes (tranches) of securities: the *senior* tranche consisting of the less risky securities; the *mezzanine* tranche, and finally, the *junior* tranche, composed of the most risky securities. In addition, the securitization process can be replicated again and again, for instance by creating portfolios made up of mezzanine and junior securities that allow the issuance of new derivative securities called CDOs (Collateralized Debt Obligations), or by building portfolios consisting of CDOs purchased through the issuance of other CDOs defined CDO squared, and so on.

5. '[T]he most commonly repeated and most expensive investment advice ever given in the boom just before a financial crisis stems from the perception that "this time is different". That advice, that the old rules of valuation no longer apply, is usually followed up with vigor. Financial professionals and, all too often, government leaders explain that we are doing things better than before, we are smarter, and we have learned from past mistakes. Each time, society convinces itself that the current boom, unlike the many booms that preceded catastrophic collapses in the past, is built on sound fundamentals, structural reforms, technological innovation, and good policy' (Reinhart and Rogoff 2009, p. xxxiv; see also Kindleberger 1978, Galbraith 1990, Chancellor 1999).

6. See, for example, Shleifer (2000), Shleifer and Vishny (2011) and Brunnermeier and Nagel (2004).

7. Shleifer (2000), Brunnermeier and Nagel (2004), Orléan (2009) and Cassidy (2009) argue that herd behaviours played a key role in the development of the dot.com bubble which burst in 2000.

8. As will be shown in the second part of the book, the concept of herd behaviour can be traced back to Keynes's analysis of the phenomenon of speculation presented in the *General Theory*.

9. 'The reason is that their horizon is limited. If the mispricing in stocks does not correct itself in a relatively short while, the investment manager will see an erosion of his customers as he underperforms. It takes a very brave investment manager with infinitely patient investors to fight the trend, even if the trend is a deviation from fundamental value' (Rajan 2006, p. 517).

10. 'In the case of dot-com stocks, losses were spread relatively widely across many types of investors. In contrast, following the housing and mortgage bust, losses were felt disproportionately at key nodes of the financial system, notably highly leveraged banks, broker-dealers, and securitization vehicles. Some of these entities were forced to engage in rapid asset sales at fire-sale prices, which undermined confidence in counterparties exposed to these assets, led to sharp withdrawals of funding, and disrupted financial intermediation, with severe consequences for the economy' (Bernanke 2012, p. 3).

11. For a critical analysis of Bernanke's interpretation see Lin (2013) and Bertocco (2014).

12. '[A] downward shift in the U.S. desired saving rate, all else being equal, should have led to greater pressure on economic resources and thus to increases, not decreases, in real interest rates' (Bernanke 2007b, p. 2).

3. The limits of the mainstream theory

[I]t is seriously misleading to discuss issues in terms of possible connections between 'the financial and real sectors of the economy', to use a phrase that appears occasionally in the literature on monetary economy. The phrase is misleading because it fails to recognize that the financial sector is a real sector. (Bennett McCallum 1989, p. 30)

The three explanations outlined in the previous chapter consider the crisis as an exogenous event, disconnected from the normal functioning of a market economy, caused by errors made by the Federal Reserve and the US banking system. The purpose of this chapter is to show that there is a sharp contrast between these explanations and the mainstream theory of money and finance. Indeed, the traditional theory describes an economic system in which catastrophic crises simply cannot occur. Within this analytical framework, monetary authorities have no reason to implement discretionary policies that cause major changes in interest rates, and banks are mere intermediaries that do not create risk.

We will see how the explanations of the origin of the crisis elaborated by mainstream economists are based on concepts and relationships that are not consistent with the macroeconomic theory developed since the 1970s. Taylor's explanation postulates the existence of a relationship between monetary policy and credit supply that is at odds with the mainstream theory of finance, which is based on the assumption that the supply of credit depends on saving decisions and not on the choices made by the monetary authorities. The second explanation, which focuses on the responsibilities of the US banking system, postulates a link between finance and risk that is completely inconsistent with the traditional interpretation of the functioning of the financial system. Finally, similarly to the first two explanations, the thesis of a global savings glut is also based on concepts, such as 'speculation' and 'speculative bubbles', that are not part of the dominant theory of finance, which emphasizes the causal relationship between saving decisions, credit supply and investment decisions.

1. MONEY AND CREDIT IN THE MAINSTREAM THEORY

The interpretations attributing the origin of the crisis to the decisions made by the US monetary authorities imply a close relationship between monetary policy and credit supply, although, according to the mainstream theory, monetary authorities control the quantity of money and not the credit supply. The traditional theory strictly separates the process of money creation from that of credit creation, and highlights the relationship between money supply and inflation, which is the core of the quantity theory of money. With the Keynesian theoretical revolution in the 20th century, the quantity theory of money was abandoned. Since the 1970s, thanks to the fundamental contributions of Milton Friedman and Robert Lucas, the monetarist counterrevolution has prompted economists to reaffirm the validity of this approach. The two American economists developed a new version of the quantity theory of money that offers an effective explanation of a phenomenon that had already been described by David Hume in 1752, that is, the difference between the short- and long-term effects of a change in the amount of money (see Lucas's Nobel lecture, 1996).

The mainstream theory considers money and credit as two distinct phenomena by clearly separating the process of money creation from the process of credit creation. This point is emphasized by Friedman and Schwartz (1982) in their reply to the criticisms raised by Keynesian economists against the quantity theory of money. More specifically, they point out that the opponents of the quantity theory of money often confuse the money market with the credit market and consequently misperceive the prices established on those two distinct markets. After pointing out that the fundamental function of money is to be a medium of exchange, Friedman and Schwartz conclude that the price of money is the amount of goods that can be purchased with a unit of currency. Hence, the price of money is the reverse of the price level: if the price level doubles, the price of money is halved. Like any other price, the price of money also depends on its supply and demand. According to the law of supply and demand, an increase in the quantity of money will result in a reduction in the price of money and thus an increase in the general price level. Conversely, the price of credit is the interest rate. Any imbalance between credit supply and demand will be eliminated by a change in the interest rate and not by a change in the general price level. According to the traditional theory, monetary authorities control the quantity of money, and hence the price of money, but not the supply of credit, which depends on the saving decisions. Taylor's explanation is totally in contrast with the mainstream theory of money because it describes a system in which monetary authorities control the supply of credit, that is, an economy where the supply of credit is independent of saving decisions.

2. THE MAINSTREAM THEORY OF FINANCE

2.1 Saving Decisions, Credit Supply and Asymmetric Information: The Irrelevance of the Credit Market

The mainstream theory defines the phenomenon of finance by emphasizing the close links between saving decisions and credit supply on the one hand, and between investment decisions and credit demand on the other hand. The interest rate is the price that strikes a balance between credit demand and supply, and, therefore, between investment and saving decisions. The close link between saving decisions and credit supply enables mainstream economists to explain why a change in credit supply has no effect on aggregate demand, and hence on the general price level. In fact, an increase in credit supply results from the savers' decision to reduce their consumption. All other conditions being equal, this behaviour will result in a decline in interest rates that, in turn, will drive businesses to increase their investments. Therefore, the level of aggregate demand will remain unchanged, since higher investments will offset lower consumption.

According to the mainstream theory, the presence of financial institutions, such as banks, is justified by the dissociation between saving and investment decisions. In other words, financial intermediaries exist because those who decide to save are not the same subjects who want to expand their capital assets.[1] The dissociation between saving and investment decisions introduces an element of fragility into the system, as the debtor may fail to fulfil his promise to pay back what he borrowed. Consequently, savers are forced to gather information on the characteristics of the investment projects to be funded and of potential borrowers. As outlined in the second chapter, economists have applied the conclusions of information economics, which are based on the seminal work of George Akerlof (1970), to the credit market.

When the traditional theory describes the operating mechanisms of a generic market, it implicitly assumes that both the buyer and the seller perfectly know the characteristics of the exchanged goods. Akerlof, however, studied the dynamics of a market in which buyers and sellers do not share the same information and showed that the presence of asymmetric information has a significant impact on the characteristics of the market equilibrium. First, he remarks that when buyers are not capable of assessing the quality of goods, then goods with different qualities will be exchanged at the same price in the same market. For example, let us take two groups of second-hand cars, one of good quality and one of poor quality (the so-called lemons), and let us assume that the sellers perfectly know the quality of their cars. If the buyers are not capable of recognizing the quality of a second-hand car, then all the cars will be exchanged for the same price.

Akerlof argues that, in a situation where asymmetric information is available, the owners of high-quality cars are penalized because the price they can obtain is lower than that they would get were the information available perfectly symmetrical. At the same time, the owners of 'lemons' will profit from a higher selling price. This situation favours the appearance of subjects specializing in the evaluation of the quality of second-hand cars, for example mechanics acting as intermediaries between buyers and sellers. Being able to recognize the quality of second-hand cars, they neutralize the effects of asymmetric information. Consequently, the two groups of cars will be sold at different prices, as would be the case in a market characterized by the availability of perfect information.

Akerlof's analysis has been applied to the credit market since it can be easily assumed that this market is also characterized by asymmetric information. Similarly to the example of the second-hand car market, two groups of debtors can be hypothesized: good-quality creditors with a high probability of paying back their loans, and poor-quality debtors with a low probability of paying back their debts. Should perfect information be available, savers-creditors would apply different conditions to the two groups of borrowers, charging a higher interest rate to riskier borrowers and a lower interest rate to high-quality borrowers. However, in a situation of asymmetric information, the same interest rate will be charged to all debtors, thereby penalizing borrowers of higher quality, while low-quality debtors would benefit from this situation. As in the case of second-hand cars, the effects of asymmetric information can be eliminated by introducing an intermediary specializing in the evaluation of the borrowers' quality. According to the mainstream theory, financial intermediaries, such as banks, play the same role as a mechanic in the second-hand car market.

Stiglitz and Weiss (1990 [1995]) illustrate the role of banks in a situation of asymmetric information by referring to an agricultural economy in which the object of credit is corn that can be used as seeds in plots of land with different productivity characteristics:

> The need for credit arises from the discrepancy between individual's resource endowments and investment opportunities. This can be seen most simply if we imagine a primitive agricultural economy, where different individuals own different plots of land and have different endowments of seed with which to plant the land. (For simplicity we assume that seed is the only input.) The marginal return to additional seed on different plots of land may differ markedly. National output can be increased enormously if the seed can be reallocated from plots of land where it has a low marginal product to plots where it has a high marginal product. But this requires *credit*, that is, some farmers will have to get more seed than their endowment in return for a *promise* to repay the loan in the next period, when the crop is harvested. Banks are the institutions within this society for screening the loan applicants, for determining which plots have really high marginal returns, and for monitoring, for ensuring that the seeds are actually planted, rather than, say, consumed by the borrower in a consumption binge. (Stiglitz and Weiss 1990, pp. 91–92)

This example shows how the concept of finance used in the mainstream theory perfectly applies to an economic system in which, as in the case of an agricultural economy, only few goods are produced. Economists have described this economic system by developing theoretical models that assume that only one good is produced. Classical economists, especially Smith and Ricardo, considered an economic system in which only corn is produced and the amount of unconsumed corn can be used as an investment good, namely as seeds or as payment to workers hired for producing capital goods such as spades or ploughs.

Böhm-Bawerk (1884 [2005]) illustrated his interest rate theory by referring to a fishing economy in which only fish is produced. He observed that the production of a community of fishermen would increase considerably by shifting from a fishing technique that involves only the use of labour – where fishermen simply collect the fish left behind on the seashore by the receding tide – to a more sophisticated fishing technique that involves the use of capital goods such as, for example, fishing nets and boats. These capital goods can be built provided that a portion of the catch is saved in order to pay the workers employed to produce nets and boats. Böhm-Bawerk pointed out that households would be encouraged to save in order to receive a flow of interest paid by entrepreneurs, who would be able to pay interest thanks to the higher productivity achieved by using capital goods in the fishing activity.[2]

With an economic system featuring these characteristics, it is easy to explain why mainstream economists developed theoretical models that only consider saving and investment decisions and overlook the credit market. In fact, in the world depicted by mainstream economists, credit demand and supply are a mere reflection of saving and investment decisions. Bennett McCallum clearly explains the reasons why his analysis focuses on the money market and neglects the credit market:

> [c]an it be sensible to discuss monetary economics with little attention devoted to the workings of financial markets? [...] The question's answer is ... fairly straightforward. It rests basically on the fact that in making their borrowing and lending decisions, rational households (and firms) are fundamentally concerned with goods and services consumed or provided at various points in time. They are basically concerned, that is, with choices involving consumption and labor supply in the present and in the future. But such choices must satisfy budget constraints and thus are precisely equivalent to decisions about borrowing and lending – that is, supply and demand choices for financial assets. Thus, for example, a household that chooses to consume this year in excess of this year's income, equivalently chooses to borrow (or to draw down its assets) to the required extent. Consequently, there is no need to consider *both* types of decisions explicitly. The practice adopted in this book is to focus attention on consumption/saving decisions rather than on borrowing/lending decisions, letting the latter be determined implicitly. [...] From the perspective just expressed, it is seriously misleading to discuss issues in terms of possible connections between 'the financial and real sectors of the economy', to use a phrase that appears occasionally in the literature on monetary policy. The phrase is misleading because it fails to recognize that the financial sector *is* a real sector. (McCallum 1989, pp. 29–30)

To eliminate the credit market from the theoretical analysis means to completely neglect the risks of default. This approach is reasonable in the context of a corn economy, such as that analysed by classical economists, or in Böhm-Bawerk's fishing economy. In fact, in these economies entrepreneurs can obtain the resources needed to repay the loans thanks to the productivity of the land or the enhanced productivity of the fishing activity conducted with the use of boats and nets. Moreover, the presence of intermediaries, such as banks, ensures that the saved corn or fish will be used to finance the farmers owning the most fertile plots of land or the most skilled fishermen. In these economic systems, savings determine the volume of investments and thus the capital stock on which the process of economic growth depends. This relationship is the foundation of the mainstream growth theory.[3]

2.2   Bank Money and the Mainstream Theory: Wicksell's Analysis

In the previous pages, we assumed that the amount of money in the economic system coincided with the legal tender issued by central banks. However, in contemporary economies another type of money can be identified, namely bank deposits. Therefore, in modern market economies, the quantity of money is an aggregate formed by two components: legal tender and bank money consisting of deposits. The presence of bank money leads to a reconsideration of the relationship between money and credit described above. In fact, in an economic system in which money consists only of legal tender, the process of money creation controlled by monetary authorities can be clearly separated from the process of credit creation, which depends on saving decisions. Yet, in a system where bank money is used, the separation between money and credit does not hold anymore, as banks may extend credit by creating new money. Already in the late nineteenth century, Knut Wicksell noted that in an economy that employs bank money, the separation between money and credit tends to disappear because demanding money signifies demanding means of payments created by the banking system, and hence borrowing from banks. He believed that the separation between the concepts of money demand and money supply should also be eliminated, as banks could meet the demand for credit-money by creating new money:

> However much 'money' is demanded in the banks, they can pay it out without danger of insolvency, since they do nothing about it, but enter a few figures in their books to represent a loan granted or a deposit withdrawn; the cheques and orders drawn against these must necessarily come back into the banks within a few days, and are credited to the depositors as a deposit paid in or a debt paid off. Supply and demand of money have in short now become one and the same thing. (Wicksell 1898 [1958], p. 76)

Wicksell maintains that the use of bank money does not alter the structure of the economic system, which essentially remains that of the corn economy described by classical economists or of Böhm-Bawerk's fishing economy. The only change introduced by Wicksell is a new version of the quantity theory of money to be applied to a world in which bank money is employed.[4] In fact, Wicksell points out that in a world where most payments are made with bank money it is unreasonable to conclude that the general price level depends on the amount of legal tender created by the central bank. It will rather depend on the overall quantity of money. Since bank money is created through credit agreements, Wicksell concludes that its amount will depend on the price at which it is offered, that is, on what he calls the *rate of interest on money*, namely the rate charged by banks on loans that must be paid by those who demand money from the banking system. A low rate of interest on money causes a high demand for bank credit, which feeds the creation of new bank money, thereby leading to an increase in the general price level. Similarly, a high monetary interest rate causes a fall in the general price level.

Wicksell underlines that the definition of a high or low monetary interest rate must be specified with reference to what he calls the *natural rate of interest*. The natural interest rate is the rate determined in an economic system in which savers and businesses directly exchange capital goods in kind, without using money. For instance, the natural interest rate can be thought of as the rate that, within the context of a corn economy, brings the amount of corn offered by savers in balance with the amount of corn demanded by entrepreneurs willing to use it either as seeds or as a means to pay the workers employed in the production of spades or ploughs. Since the saved corn is handed over to entrepreneurs through a credit agreement, in such a system the capital market in which the saved corn is exchanged coincides with the credit market.

Wicksell also notes that, in an economy characterized by the use of bank money, the capital market and the credit market do not coincide. In fact, the demand for credit does not consist in the entrepreneurs' demand for corn but rather in the demand for money made to banks, which will fulfil such demand by creating new money. The interest rate observed on the credit market is the rate of interest on money.[5] This rate, however, is not the only relevant interest rate in the system. Wicksell argues that the natural rate of interest plays a key role as it represents the reference towards which the level of the monetary interest rate converges.

To explain this conclusion, Wicksell considers two distinct cases. In the first case, the two rates are identical and the use of bank money does not alter the workings of the system as compared with an economy in which capital goods are exchanged in kind. The money market where banks meet the entrepreneurs' demand for credit by creating new money coincides with the capital market, as the new money created by the banks allows entrepreneurs to purchase exactly the amount of corn saved by households.[6] In the second case, the two interest rates diverge. The gap between the two rates will cause an imbalance between the demand for purchasing power by entrepreneurs and the supply of resources saved by households. If, for example, the monetary interest rate is lower than the natural interest rate, there would be an excessive creation of money by the banks, which would result in a demand for capital goods in excess of the available supply and, hence, in a higher general price level. Conversely, if the interest rate on money is higher than the natural rate, the demand for capital goods would be lower than supply, thus leading to a fall in the general price level. In Wicksell's view, inflation and deflation are the phenomena that indicate an imbalance between the two interest rates.

Wicksell states that the discrepancies between the two interest rates are determined by changes in the natural rate of interest due to fluctuations in the propensity to save among households or in the propensity to invest on the part of businesses. The banking system is not able to directly detect these fluctuations, because the natural rate of interest is not materially observable. Therefore, both monetary authorities and banks will only realize that there is such imbalance between the two interest rates by observing the change in the general price level, and they will intervene by changing the monetary interest rate in order to restore a condition of price stability.

Wicksell's analysis also allows the application of the mainstream theory of finance to an economic system characterized by the use of bank money, that is, a system in which banks can provide credit by creating new money. Also in this case, banks continue to play their vital role as intermediaries between savers and businesses, since the rate of interest on money converges towards the value of the natural rate of interest that still depends on saving and investment decisions. Therefore, the phenomenon of finance continues to be tied to the fundamental concepts of savings and investment. This explains why, a few decades after Wicksell, Milton Friedman (1968; Friedman and Schwartz 1982) continued to define the interest rate as the price of credit and not as the price of money. It also explains why textbooks of macroeconomics and finance still regard banks as mere intermediaries that lend out resources that were previously collected from savers.

Rajan's explanation of the origin of the crisis, based on the reasons why the US banking system created an 'iceberg of risk', is not consistent with the traditional theory of finance. In fact, while it acknowledges that banks can expand credit by creating new money, this theory also considers banks as mere intermediaries that allocate previously collected savings. According to the traditional theory of finance, banks cannot create risk because, as illustrated by the asymmetric information approach, their function consists in reducing the risk that saved resources are allocated to incapable entrepreneurs. Similarly to Akerlof's (1970) mechanics working in the second-hand car market, the banks' task is to distinguish between good and bad borrowers.

Wicksell's work has profoundly influenced the supporters of the Austrian school and their explanation of the origins of the contemporary crisis. More specifically, they believe that the discrepancy between the natural and the monetary interest rates, which is allegedly at the root of the contemporary crisis, was caused by the monetary authorities' political decision to support the economic growth process in a historical period characterized by a shortage of savings.[7] However, this argument overlooks the fact that Wicksell's theory is the theoretical foundation of the strategy adopted in recent years by the central banks of the Western countries, a strategy aimed at guaranteeing price stability through a monetary policy rule based on controlling the interest rate (see, for example, Woodford 2003; ECB 2004, 2011). Until the outbreak of the crisis, no one had questioned the actions taken by central banks, since inflation rates in the Western countries were consistent with the targeted objective. Therefore, it is difficult to identify the reasons why monetary authorities, which should have been perfectly aware of the fact that they could not use their policies as tools to increase the growth rate of the Western economies, abused their power to create money in such a way as to cause a catastrophic crisis.

Bernanke's view on Wicksell's theory is particularly interesting. As anticipated earlier (see Chapter 2, note 12), in order to develop the 'saving glut' hypothesis, Bernanke used the Wicksellian concept of the natural rate of interest, arguing that it is determined by the interaction between saving and investment decisions. A few years later, Bernanke (2013) changed his mind. When he describes the Fed's behaviour in the aftermath of the crisis, he recognizes that monetary authorities can indeed control both short-term and long-term interest rates. Bernanke recalls that the Federal Reserve reacted immediately at the first signs of the crisis by cutting the federal funds rate from over 5 per cent to a level between 0 and 25 basis points in December 2008. Since short-term rates could not be reduced any further, the Fed then pursued the goal of reducing long-term rates through unconventional measures, that is, so-called 'quantitative easing', consisting in large-scale asset purchases:

> Why were we buying these securities? [...] [b]y purchasing Treasury securities ... we effectively lowered the interest rate of longer-termed Treasuries and GSE [Government-Sponsored Enterprises] securities as well. Moreover, to the extent that investors no longer having available Treasuries and GSE securities to hold in their portfolios, to the extent that they are induced to move to other kinds of securities, such as corporate bonds, that also raises the prices and lowers the yields on those securities. And so the net effect of these actions was to lower yields across a range of securities ... instead of focusing on the short-term rate, we were focusing on longer-term rates. But the basic

logic of lowering rates to stimulate the economy is really the same. (Bernanke 2013, p. 104)

By recognizing that the Fed can control both short-term and long-term interest rates, Bernanke implicitly considers a system in which the Wicksellian concept of a natural rate of interest does not apply and where interest rates and credit supply are independent of saving decisions.

3. BANK MONEY, WEALTH AND SPECULATION

Wicksell's analysis allows an explanation of the relationship between monetary policy and credit supply, which is central in the interpretation that attributes the responsibility for the contemporary crisis to the excessively expansionary monetary policy adopted by the Federal Reserve. However, it does not provide a meaning to the relationship between finance and risk, nor does it explain the phenomenon of speculation. The three explanations of the causes of the crisis described in the second chapter are all based on concepts such as speculation and speculative bubbles that are at odds with contemporary theoretical models.

The phenomena of speculation and speculative bubbles can only be defined by considering an economic system characterized by the presence of markets in which assets are bought and sold based on expectations about their future price. As will be explained in the following pages, the importance of these markets emerges in an economic system in which the concept of wealth is relevant. The meaning of wealth can be easily understood if one thinks of contemporary economic systems. The wealth of an individual comprises all the financial assets and durable goods (e.g. residential and land properties) owned by such individual at a given time. Over time, wealth can vary depending on the flow of savings. When an individual decides to save part of his income, he adds new financial assets or new durable goods to his pre-existing wealth. The relationship between saving decisions and wealth is hard to explain in the world described by the mainstream theory, where money represents a mere 'veil' and savings are defined in real terms as the quantity of goods that, once produced, have not been consumed. However, if savings consist of unconsumed corn, it is unrealistic to assume the existence of a wealth accumulation process by which an individual continues to pile up a growing quantity of corn, thereby adding, from year to year, the new flow of savings to those accumulated previously. Conversely, it is reasonable to suppose the existence of a physiological limit to the amount of corn that individuals wish to accumulate.

Mainstream economists' analysis of speculative bubbles is indeed contradictory. As Rajan's analysis demonstrates, they recognize that bubbles develop in speculative markets in which the law of supply and demand does not hold.[8] However, they also continue to support a theory of money and finance that can apply only in what we have called a corn economy, that is, in an economy in which the process of wealth accumulation and the presence of speculative markets cannot be explained.

4. TWO CONCLUSIONS

The mainstream theory describes an economic system with three key features. First, it is an economy in which the quantity theory of money elaborated on the basis of Friedman's and Lucas's works holds. Second, it is an economy with the characteristics of a corn economy. In such an economy, banks are financial intermediaries fulfilling a function similar to that carried out by mechanics in second-hand car markets described by Akerlof. Wicksell's distinction between the natural and the monetary interest rate shows that the use of bank money does not alter the structure of this economic system. Finally, in the economic system depicted in the mainstream theory, the process of wealth accumulation and the phenomenon of speculation are not relevant. In other words, this economic system consists only of markets in which the law of supply and demand holds, and where the price system can always ensure a full employment balance.

In an economic system with these characteristics, a crisis such as that triggered by the collapse of the subprime mortgage market could never occur. In fact, in such a system neither the central bank nor the banking system could ever make the mistakes attributed to them in the explanations of the origins of the crisis described in Chapter 2. The Federal Reserve, perfectly aware of the ineffectiveness of the monetary policy, would have no reason to adopt an expansionary monetary policy bringing the monetary interest rate below the level of the natural rate. Nor could the banking system, whose function in a corn economy is to select the most creditworthy borrowers, suddenly begin to finance entrepreneurs who were unable to produce corn.

The inability to explain the origins of the crisis through the lens of the traditional theory is confirmed by the fact that the explanations elaborated by the conservative economists, illustrated in the second chapter, are based on concepts and relationships that are at odds with the principles of the orthodox theory of money and finance. According to these explanations: 1) the financial system determines the supply of credit, which is therefore independent of saving decisions; 2) the financial system can create risk; and 3) the speculation and speculative bubble phenomena are relevant.

The distance between the fundamental propositions of the dominant theory and the concepts used by mainstream economists to explain the origins of the crisis suggest two conclusions. The first is that the mainstream theory is completely unable to explain the workings of modern economies. The second conclusion concerns the need to develop a different theoretical model, one that allows an analysis of an economic system with the characteristics emerging from the explanations of the origin of the crisis elaborated by mainstream economists. The second part of this book will show that such a theory can be built starting from the thinking of heretical economists such as Marx, Keynes, Schumpeter, Kalecki, Kaldor and Minsky.

NOTES

1. 'It is easy to imagine a world in which there is a high level of saving and investment, but in which there is an unfavorable climate for financial intermediaries. At the extreme, each of the economy's spending units – whether of the household, business, or government variety – would have a balanced budget on income and product account. For each spending unit, current income would equal the sum of current and capital expenditures. There could still be saving and investment, but each spending unit's saving would be precisely matched by its investment in tangible assets. In a world of balanced budgets, security issues by spending units would be zero, or very close to zero. The same would be true of the accumulation of financial assets. Consequently, this world would be a highly uncongenial one for financial intermediaries; the saving–investment process would grind away without them' (Gurley and Shaw 1956, pp. 257–258).

2. 'Let us imagine … a tribe of people who live by fishing and who are entirely without capital. They catch their fish on the seashore by seizing with their bare hands such fish as are stranded in the pools left behind by the receding tide. A workman of this tribe catches and consumes 3 fish a day. If he had a boat and net he could catch 30 fish a day instead of 3. But he cannot construct those implements because their construction would cost him a month's time and labor, and during that interval he would have nothing to live on. And so in order not to starve he must continue his wretched and unskilled system of fishing. Now [let us suppose that] someone lends him 90 fish on condition that he promise to pay back 180 fish one month later. Our man agrees to the transaction, provides his subsistence out of the borrowed fish for one month and in the meantime constructs a boat and net with which in the following month he catches 900 fish instead of 90. From these he cannot only repay the stipulated amount of 180 fish but also retain a sizable net gain for himself' (Böhm-Bawerk 1884 [2005], pp. 280–281).

3. See, for example, Pagano (1993), King and Levine (1993), Levine (1997, 2002, 2004), Gorton and Winton (2002), Wachtel (2003) and Barro and Sala-i-Martin (2004).

4. For a critical analysis of the Wicksellian theory of loanable funds see Bertocco (2013b).

5. 'It is said that what is lent in reality is not money but real capital; money is only an instrument, a way of lending capital, and so on. But this is not strictly true; what is lent *is* money and nothing else; liquid real capital, in the form of goods, is bought and sold with the money, but is not lent. Negotiation concerning the level of interest on loans is conducted with the owners of the money, not with the owners of the real capital' (Wicksell 1898 [1958], p. 83).

6. '[I]f capital was lent in kind, there would undoubtedly develop, through the supply of and demand for the available capital, a certain rate of interest on the lending market, which would be the natural rate of interest on capital in the strictest sense. If the actual rate of interest on money corresponds with this figure, the intervention of money will cause no change in the economic equilibrium; money transactions are then only the particular form taken by what, theoretically speaking, could just as well have been effected without the intervention of money' (Wicksell 1898 [1958], pp. 84–85).

7. See, for example, Salin (2009), Desai (2010) and Horwitz and Luther (2011).

8. See, for example, Santos and Woodford (1997), Barlevy (2007), Wang and Wen (2012) and Cheng et al. (2014).

PART II

An Alternative Theoretical Approach

4. Keynes and the monetary theory of production

In my opinion the main reason why the problem of crises is unsolved … is to be found in the lack of what might be termed a monetary theory of production. […] Accordingly I believe that the next task is to work out in some detail a monetary theory of production, to supplement the real-exchange theories which we already possess. (John M. Keynes 1933a [2013c], pp. 408–411)

1. WHICH KEYNESIAN THEORY?

The conclusion that the mainstream theory cannot explain the workings of modern economies is certainly not new. In fact, it is shared by a large group of 'heretical' economists, including Marx, Keynes, Schumpeter, Kalecki, Kaldor and Minsky. In the second part of this book, we will present a theoretical model, alternative to the traditional one, which makes reference to Keynes's thinking and to other heretical economists. In the first chapter of his major work, Keynes explains that he entitled his book *The General Theory of Employment, Interest and Money* to underline the limits of the classical theory,[1] which, in his opinion, applies to a system whose characteristics 'happen not to be those of the economic society in which we actually live, with the result that its teaching is misleading and disastrous if we attempt to apply it to the facts of experience' (Keynes 1936 [2013a], p. 3). Keynes underlines that the classical theory can be applied only to a situation of full employment and argues that modern economies are characterized by big fluctuations in output and employment that cannot be avoided through the flexibility of wages:

the contention that the unemployment which characterises a depression is due to a refusal by labour to accept a reduction of money-wages is not clearly supported by the facts. It is not very plausible to assert that unemployment in the United States in 1932 was due either to labour obstinately refusing to accept a reduction of money-wages or to its obstinately demanding a real wage beyond what the productivity of the economic machine was capable of furnishing. (Keynes 1936 [2013a], p. 9)

57

Keynes's lesson can be summarized in two points. First, he intended to develop a new theory that could explain the reasons why a market economy is subject to strong fluctuations in the levels of income and employment. Secondly, he identified fiscal and monetary instruments that could be used to reduce these fluctuations. In Keynes's view the elaboration of a new theory leading to a deep and final departure from the principles of the classical theory was much more important than the prescription of specific monetary and fiscal policies aimed at overcoming a crisis.[2] Nevertheless, in the years following the publication of the *General Theory*, economists have largely neglected the elements of Keynes's analysis that marked a break from the traditional theory. The process of removal of the revolutionary content of Keynes's theoretical approach occurred in two phases.

The first dates back to the 1950s and 1960s, when scholars accepted an interpretation of Keynes's thinking that resulted from a compromise between Keynesian and neoclassical economists. On the one hand, the former acknowledged that a market economy in which price adjustments are working perfectly cannot be exposed to crises. On the other hand, the latter recognized that, in the real world, some forms of rigidity could prevent the effective functioning of price adjustments, thereby causing high levels of unemployment. Neoclassical economists therefore accepted the principle that, under these conditions, Keynesian policies could effectively replace the price adjustment mechanism.

This interpretation of the *General Theory*, which has become known as the Neoclassical Synthesis, reduced Keynes's theoretical approach to a special case of the traditional theory applying to situations in which prices were not perfectly flexible. By focusing on Keynesian policies and by accepting the thesis that the presence of unemployment should be attributed to price and wage rigidities, economists completely neglected the arguments developed by Keynes to explain that a market economy is subject to deep fluctuations in income and employment even in the presence of perfectly flexible prices and wages.

The second phase of the detachment from Keynes's thinking occurred in the 1970s, when the phenomenon of stagflation emerged. In fact, this phenomenon could not be explained by the prevailing model, such the Neoclassical Synthesis based on the Phillips curve. Doubts about the validity of the then dominant paradigm were reinforced by the criticisms raised by Milton Friedman and Robert Lucas. At different times, they showed that Keynesian policies were effective only if one assumed that workers suffered from a 'monetary illusion'. Friedman and Lucas showed that if workers did not suffer from a monetary illusion, Keynesian policies could not be effective. This criticism led economists to abandon the Neoclassical Synthesis model and to accept a new version of the neoclassical theory based on a seemingly incontrovertible argument: if Keynesian policies were ineffective, then income and employment necessarily depended on market forces, and the only effective policies were those aimed at eliminating the barriers to the unfettered action of these forces. In a world in which these market forces can work perfectly, the price adjustment mechanisms ensure full employment and no crises can possibly occur.

The current crisis calls for a rediscovery of the analysis of income and employment fluctuations developed by Keynes, which has been largely neglected in the last 80 years.

2. KEYNES AND THE CONCEPT OF A MONETARY ECONOMY

Keynes aimed at developing a general theory that could account for the factors leading to economic crises and to the income and employment fluctuations observed in the real world. In Keynes's view, economic crises are monetary phenomena. In fact, he points out that money is the essential element explaining the fluctuations in income and employment that characterize contemporary economies. Keynes emphasizes that the inability of the classical theory to explain economic crises stems from the way in which it describes the phenomenon of money. According to the classical theory, money is a medium of exchange, that is, a tool that facilitates exchanges as compared with a barter economy. Keynes plainly rejects this approach because it leads to the consideration of money as a neutral instrument only, since it does not affect the structure of the economic system, which essentially remains that of a barter economy.[3]

Keynes instead uses the expression *monetary economy* to indicate an economic system in which the presence of money profoundly modifies the nature of exchanges and the features of the production process as compared with a barter economy. To emphasize this point, he replaces the classification based on the distinction between a barter economy and a monetary economy with a classification that separates a *real-exchange economy* from a *monetary economy*. What differentiates these two economies is not the use of money, but the effects generated by the presence of money. In a real-exchange economy, the use of money does not change the structure of the economic system, which essentially remains that of a barter economy. Conversely, in a monetary economy, money deeply affects the structure of the economic system:

> An economy, which uses money but uses it merely as a neutral link between transactions in real things and real assets and does not allow it to enter into motives or decisions, might be called – for want of a better name – a *real-exchange economy*. The theory which I desiderate would deal, in contradistinction to this, with an economy in which money plays a part of its own and affects motives and decisions and is, in short, one of the operative factors in the situation, so that the course of events cannot be predicted, either in the long period or in the short, without a knowledge of the behaviour of money between the first state and the last. And it is this which we ought to mean when we speak of a *monetary economy*. (Keynes 1933a [2013c], pp. 408–409)

Keynes argues that the classical theory can only explain the functioning of a real-exchange economy and that its failure to emphasize the endogenous nature of economic crises is due to the fact that it considers money as a neutral element, namely as a 'veil' behind which the real forces that govern the economic system are at work. He points out that, in order to develop a sound explanation of the functioning of modern economies and of the economic crises, the reasons for the non-neutrality of money must be explained.[4] Keynes concludes his analysis by illustrating his commitment to developing what he defines as a *monetary theory of production*, that is, a theory that can explain crises based on the concept of non-neutrality of money:

> In my opinion the main reason why the problem of crises is unsolved … is to be found in the lack of what might be termed a *monetary theory of production*. [...] Accordingly I believe that the next task is to work out in some detail a monetary theory of production, to supplement the real-exchange theories which we already possess. At any rate that is the task on which I am now occupying myself, in some confidence that I am not wasting my time. (Keynes 1933a [2013c], pp. 408, 411)

Keynes explains the difference between the barter economy described by the traditional theory and the monetary economy in which 'we actually live' by using two formulas adopted by Marx. These formulas separate the 'simple circulation of commodities' expressed by the sequence Commodities (C) – Money (M) – Commodities (C') from the 'circulation of money as capital' represented by the sequence Money (M) – Commodities (C) – Money (M') which typically characterizes the workings of a capitalist economy.[5]

The first sequence describes an economic system with two fundamental features. First, the production of goods is the essential condition for demanding other goods. Second, money is no more than a tool allowing the costs of exchanges to be cut compared with a barter economy. These characteristics perfectly match Adam Smith's description of a market economy. In fact, Smith argued that an economic activity stems from 'a certain propensity in human nature … the propensity to truck, barter, and exchange one thing for another' (Smith 1776 [1981], p. 25). This propensity leads every individual to specialize in the production of a specific type of good in order to exchange it for other goods, thereby relying on other people's selfishness rather than on their goodwill:

> It is not from the benevolence of the butcher, the brewer, or the baker that we expect our dinner, but from their regard to their own interest. We address ourselves, not to their humanity, but to their self-love, and never talk to them of our own necessities, but of their advantages. (Smith 1776 [1981], p. 27)

The price system is the 'invisible hand' that ensures coherence between private and public interests.[6] In such an economic system, characterized by the presence of small producers, such as butchers, brewers and bakers, supply creates its own demand. In other words, Say's Law holds, since the production of goods is the necessary condition to demand and obtain other goods.

Keynes was very clear when he stated that an economic system of this kind does not reflect the system in which we actually live. The M–C–M' sequence identifies two fundamental characteristics of what Keynes defined as a monetary economy. First, it suggests that in contemporary economies the goal of economic activities is not to produce goods but to obtain money, that is, the production of goods is the tool that allows the accumulation of money. This sounds like an obvious truth: an entrepreneur is not interested in accumulating unsold commodities, but in making money by selling commodities in exchange for money. Nevertheless, when comparing two different economic systems characterized by the sequences defined by Marx, it is necessary to explain why the accumulation of money is a goal only for entrepreneurs acting in a monetary economy and not for Adam Smith's bakers, butchers and brewers. Therefore, we must specify why in a monetary economy the ultimate goal of the economic activity is to accumulate money and not to produce goods. This point will be dealt with in Chapter 6.

Second, the M–C–M' sequence shows that the availability of money is the necessary condition to produce commodities. This is not what happens in a real-exchange economy, where the production of goods is the prerequisite for obtaining the money needed to buy other goods. The M–C–M' sequence shows that in modern economies money is not just a means of exchange, but is the fundamental tool for producing goods. The relationship between money and production of goods, which is the first link in the M–C–M' sequence, raises two issues. The first consists in defining the process of money creation: if the availability of money is the necessary condition for producing goods, then it is important to specify the characteristics of money and of the process of money creation. The second issue consists in defining the characteristics of the process of goods production, as, unlike what happens in a real-exchange economy, in a monetary economy money is required in order to produce goods.

By analysing the M–C–M' sequence, we will show that a monetary economy features the same characteristics that emerge from the explanations of the origin of the crisis elaborated by Taylor, Rajan and Bernanke. We will show that Keynes's monetary economy is a system where: 1) the supply of credit is independent of saving decisions; 2) the financial system can create risks; and 3) speculative markets, and the phenomena of speculation and asset bubbles, are relevant. To illustrate these points, we first need to consider the work of another great heretical economist, that is, Joseph Schumpeter.

3. KEYNES, SCHUMPETER AND THE CHARACTERISTICS OF MONEY

Joseph Schumpeter is the other great economist of the first half of the twentieth century who emphasized the limits of the traditional theory. He draws a distinction between a *pure-exchange economy* and a *capitalist economy*. The orthodox theory describes a pure-exchange economy based on private property, the division of labour and free competition. Like Keynes, Schumpeter stresses that this kind of economy does not reflect the economic system in which we actually live.

Schumpeter identifies two distinctive features of a capitalist economy. The first concerns the process of change. A pure-exchange economy is a static system that tends to reproduce itself in an essentially unchanged manner over time. The only forms of change are those affecting the amount of goods produced, or those concerning non-social elements such as weather conditions or extra-economic events such as wars. According to Schumpeter, the process of change that characterizes a capitalist economy is caused by the innovations introduced by entrepreneurs.[7] Schumpeter identifies five different cases of innovation: 1) production of new goods; 2) introduction of new methods of production of existing goods; 3) opening of new markets; 4) emergence of new sources of raw materials; and 5) reorganization of an industrial sector that can lead to the creation or the destruction of a monopoly.

To emphasize the differences between a capitalist economy and a barter economy, Schumpeter introduces the concepts of growth and development. He applies the term 'growth' to the economic system described by the traditional theory, in which the changes observed over time only concern the production volume. Such changes may depend on demographic dynamics or on differences in the propensity to save. Schumpeter (1939 [1964], p. 61) introduces the term 'development' to indicate 'changes in the economic process brought about by innovation, together with all their effects, and the response to them by the economic system'.

The second element that characterizes a capitalist economy is the role of money. Schumpeter remarks that the classical theory describes an economy that, despite the use of money, preserves the structure of a barter economy.[8] To contrast this view, Schumpeter points out that money is a crucial element of the process of change that the traditional theory cannot explain. Hence, Schumpeter felt the need to develop a new theory based on a heresy regarding the definition of the role of money, that is, 'the heresy that [in a capitalist economy] money … perform[s] an essential function, hence that processes in terms of means of payment are not merely reflexes of processes in terms of goods' (Schumpeter 1912 [1949], p. 95).

Both Schumpeter and Keynes feel the need to develop a new theory to highlight the crucial role of money in the economic system. While Schumpeter emphasizes the fundamental role played by money in the process of change that characterizes capitalist economies, Keynes underlines the relationship between money and economic crises and thus the role played by money in explaining the fluctuations of income and employment that characterize a monetary economy. We will show that Schumpeter's analysis is essential to explain Keynes's insights concerning: 1) uncertainty; 2) the principle of effective demand; 3) the phenomenon of speculation; and 4) the structural instability of a monetary economy.[9]

Both Schumpeter and Keynes underline that the money used in modern economies has specific characteristics that reflect those of bank money. According to Keynes, a monetary economy is characterized by the use of fiat money, that is, money which has no intrinsic value and whose production cost expressed in terms of labour can be assumed to be zero. In his *General Theory*, Keynes leads the reader to identify money with the liabilities of the central banks and to overlook bank money. However, he recognized this omission in his reply to the criticisms of the *General Theory* raised by the advocates of the *loanable funds theory*. These criticisms urged Keynes to explicitly consider the issues of investment financing and the process of money creation through which banks finance enterprises. He underlines that banks can fulfil the demand for credit by creating new money and highlights the link between money and credit rather than the link between saving decisions and credit supply.[10] The presence of bank money is an essential element of post-Keynesian monetary theory. (See for example: Palley 2002; Rochon and Rossi 2003, 2013; Bertocco 2001, 2005, 2010, 2013b.)

Schumpeter considers bank money such an essential element of a capitalist economy that he claims no capitalist economy would exist without bank money.[11] As was pointed out in the third chapter, neo-classical economists, following Wicksell, also recognize that banks are not mere intermediaries since they can extend credit by creating money. But there is a substantial difference between Keynes and Schumpeter on the one side, and Wicksell and mainstream economists on the other side. In fact, Keynes and Schumpeter see the presence of bank money as a fundamental element that explains the profound differences between the barter economy described by the traditional theory and the economic systems in which we actually live. Conversely, Wicksell and the contemporary mainstream economists believe that the use of bank money does not alter the basic structure of the economic system and, hence, they consider bank money as a neutral instrument.

This profound difference is confirmed by the fact that Wicksell and mainstream economists illustrate the functioning of an economy in which bank money is employed by using the concept of natural rate of interest which characterizes a real-exchange economy, that is, a system similar to a corn economy. In a corn economy, saved resources correspond to the flow of corn that was produced and not consumed and are offered to businesses to be used as a means of production. In this context, the natural interest rate is the price that balances the demand and supply of saved resources. By introducing the concept of natural rate of interest, Wicksell and mainstream economists point out that the structure of the economy in which we currently live, and in which bank money is used, does not differ from the structure of a corn economy.

Keynes's and Schumpeter's analyses differ significantly from Wicksell's theoretical framework. In fact, they both reject the concept of natural interest rate and emphasize the monetary nature of the interest rate. In the *General Theory*, Keynes distances himself from what he had written a few years earlier in the *Treatise on Money*, in which he used the Wicksellian concept of natural interest rate.[12] Schumpeter, too, sharply criticizes the Wicksellian theory of two interest rates.[13]

Keynes's and Schumpeter's criticisms of the Wicksellian concept of natural interest rate reflect their beliefs that: 1) the workings of the economic system in which we live cannot be described by using a theoretical model that describes a barter economy; and 2) it is necessary to elaborate an alternative theory to explain the functioning of Keynes's monetary economy and Schumpeter's capitalist economy.

4. THE NATURE OF THE FIRM IN A REAL-EXCHANGE ECONOMY

In a real-exchange economy, to produce goods it is not necessary to have money available. Each individual produces goods thanks to his/her special skills. Conversely, the M–C–M' sequence characterizing a monetary economy shows that the availability of money is a necessary condition for producing goods. This relationship can be easily explained by considering an economic system in which large corporations produce goods by employing a large number of workers who receive money as their wages. In this case, having money available is fundamental for producing goods since entrepreneurs need to hire the necessary workforce. This observation should lead us to conclude that it is impossible to analyse a production process based on large enterprises through a theoretical model that applies to an economic system made up of small producers.

In fact, mainstream economists believe that the presence of large corporations does not change the structure of the economic system, which remains that of a barter economy. This conclusion is based on Coase's (1937) seminal work on the nature of enterprises. Coase remarks that economists view the economic system as a structure in which the activity of a multitude of subjects is coordinated through the price system, which allows the allocation of scarce resources to alternative uses. He observes that this approach is incorrect because there are places, made up of enterprises, in which economic transactions are not coordinated by the price system but by an alternative mechanism, namely the entrepreneur-coordinator.[14] Consequently, Coase wonders what might be the reasons for the emergence of firms in a market economy. He concludes that the existence of enterprises and entrepreneurs is justified by the presence of transaction costs.[15]

Therefore, the presence of companies and entrepreneurs does not alter the structure of the economic system as compared with that of a barter economy. An enterprise is a form of organization that reduces the transaction costs that would emerge in an economic system made up only of individual producers. This conclusion is further confirmed by Coase's criticism of the explanations justifying the existence of enterprises based on the concept of the division of labour. The most popular example describing the effects of the division of labour is that of the pin factory (pinmaker) used by Adam Smith at the beginning of his most famous work. Coase does not accept this explanation since, in his opinion, the existence of the pin factory does not depend on the advantages deriving from the workers' specialization. The price system could indeed co-ordinate the activities of the workers who perform the various phases of the pin production process while operating in many small workshops. The existence of the pin factory is actually justified by the presence of transaction costs.

The kind of entrepreneur who emerges from Coase's analysis is not significantly different from the wage earners employed by the enterprise. The entrepreneur is simply a subject who compares the transaction costs with the organizational costs generated by the enterprise. This conclusion is also confirmed by Coase's criticism of Frank Knight (1921) [1964], who explains the role of the entrepreneur and of the enterprise by introducing the concept of uncertainty.[16] Coase states that Knight 'would appear to be introducing a point which is irrelevant to the problem we are considering' (Coase 1937, p. 392).

Following Coase's insights, an economic system comprising large enterprises could be dealt with in the same way as an economic system made up of small producers whose activities are coordinated by the price system. We can thus conclude that, if the role of enterprises is that described by Coase, the relationship between money and production, which is the first link in the M–C–M' sequence, continues to be irrelevant. In fact, in his analysis Coase completely neglects the role of money.

Conversely, both Keynes and Schumpeter believed that money is a key element in explaining the characteristics of the production process in capitalist economies. The relationship between money and production, which will be discussed in the next chapter, will allow us to describe two of the features of modern market economies that emerge from the explanations of the origin of the crisis elaborated by mainstream econo-mists: 1) the independence of credit supply from saving decisions; and 2) the relationship between finance and risk.

NOTES

1. In Keynes's terminology, the classical theory is what is now commonly known as neoclassical theory. Following Keynes, in the remaining part of this book, the term 'classical theory' will therefore be used to refer to the neoclassical theory and its various developments.

2. 'I am more attached to the comparatively simple fundamental ideas which underlie my theory than to the particular forms in which I have embodied them. [...] This that I offer is ... a theory of why output and employment are so liable to fluctuation. It does not offer a ready-made remedy as to how to avoid these fluctuations and to maintain output at a steady optimum level. But it is, properly speaking, a theory of employment because it explains *why*, in any given circumstances, employment is what it is. Naturally I am interested not only in the diagnosis, but also in the cure; and many pages of my book are devoted to the latter. But I consider that my suggestions for a cure, which, avowedly, are not worked out completely, are on a different plane from the diagnosis. They are not meant to be definitive; they are subject to all sorts of special assumptions and are necessarily related to the particular conditions of the time. But my main reasons for departing from the traditional theory go much deeper than this. They are of a highly general character and are meant to be definitive' (Keynes 1937a [2013d], pp. 211, 221–222).

3. 'The distinction which is normally made between a barter economy and a monetary economy depends upon the employment of money as a convenient means of effecting exchanges – as an instrument of great convenience, but transitory and neutral in its effect. It is regarded as a mere link between cloth and wheat, or between the day's labour spent on building the canoe and the day's labour spent on harvesting the crop. It is not supposed to affect the essential nature of the transaction from being, in the minds of those making it, one between real things, or to modify the motives and decisions of the parties to it. Money, that is to say, is employed, but is treated as being in some sense *neutral*' (Keynes 1933a [2013c], p. 408).

4. '[T]he conditions required for the 'neutrality' of money ... are, I suspect, precisely the same as those which will insure that crises *do not occur*. If this is true, the real-exchange economics, on which most of us have been brought up and with the conclusions of which our minds are deeply impregnated ... is a singularly blunt weapon for dealing with the problem of booms and depressions. For it has assumed away the very matter under investigation. [...] I am saying that booms and depressions are phenomena peculiar to an economy in which ... money is not neutral' (Keynes 1933a [2013c], pp. 410, 411).

5. Marx 1867–1894 [1992], Book I, Chapter 4, and Book II, Chapter 1. On this point see Dillard (1984), Aoki (2001), Bellofiore (2005) and Sardoni (2011, 2013).

6. '[E]very individual [...] generally ... neither intends to promote the public interest, nor knows how much he is promoting it ... he intends only his own gain; and he is in this, as in many other cases, led by an invisible hand to promote an end which was no part of his intention. Nor is it always the worse for the society that it was no part of it. By pursuing his own interest, he frequently promotes that of the society more effectually than when he really intends to promote it' (Smith, 1776 [1981], p. 456).

7. 'Unlike other economic systems, the capitalist system is geared to incessant economic change. Its very nature implies recurrent industrial revolutions which are the main sources of the profit and interest incomes of entrepreneurs. [...] Whereas a stationary feudal economy would still be a feudal economy, ... stationary capitalism is a contradiction in terms' (Schumpeter 1943 [1951], pp. 178–179).

8. In the economic system described by the classical theory, 'money only performs the function of a technical instrument, but adds nothing new to the phenomena. To employ a customary expression, we can say that money thus far represents only the cloak of economic things and nothing essential is overlooked in abstracting from it' (Schumpeter 1912 [1949], p. 51).

9. Several economists have emphasized the desirability of integrating the Keynesian theory of income determination with Schumpeter's theory of economic development. For example, see Minsky (1986b, 1993), Goodwin (1993), Morishima (1992), Vercelli (1997), Bertocco (2007, 2009b), Dosi (2012), Dosi et al. (2010) and Mazzucato and Wray (2015).

10. '[T]he banks hold the key position in the transition from a lower to a higher scale of activity. If they refuse to relax, the growing congestion of the short-term loan market or of the new issue market, as the case may be, will inhibit the improvement, no matter how thrifty the public purpose to be out of their future incomes. On the other hand, there will

always be *exactly* enough ex post saving to take up the ex post investment and so release the finance which the latter had been previously employing. The investment market can become congested through shortage of cash. It can never become congested through shortage of saving. This is the most fundamental of my conclusions within this field' (Keynes 1937c [2013d], p. 222).

11. '[C]apitalism [is] defined by three features of industrial society: private ownership of the physical means of production; private profits and private responsibility for losses; and the creation of means of payments – banknotes or deposits – by private banks. The first two features suffice to define private enterprise. But no concept of capitalism can be satisfactory without including the set of typically capitalistic phenomena covered by the third' (Schumpeter 1943 [1951], p. 175). Hodgson (2015) has developed a definition of capitalism which, like that of Schumpeter, emphasizes the fundamental role of bank money.

12. 'In my *Treatise on Money* I defined what purported to be a unique rate of interest, which I called the *natural rate* of interest – namely, the rate of interest which, in the terminology of my *Treatise*, preserved equality between the rate of saving (as there defined) and the rate of investment. I believed this to be a development and clarification of Wicksell's "natural rate of interest". ... I am now no longer of the opinion that the concept of a "natural" rate of interest, which previously seemed to me a most promising idea, has anything very useful or significant to contribute to our analysis' (Keynes 1936 [2013a], pp. 242–243).

13. 'The roots of this idea reach very far into the past. ... Its role in the thought of our own time is due to the teaching of Knut Wicksell and the work of a brilliant group of Swedish and Austrian economists. For us, however, there is no such thing as a real rate of interest, except in the same sense in which we speak of real wages: translating both the interest and the capital items of any loan into real terms by means of the expected variation in an index of prices. ... But nominal and real rates in this sense are only different measurements of the same thing. ... Hence, the money market with all that happens in it acquires for us a much deeper significance than can be attributed to it from the standpoint just glanced at. It becomes the heart, although it never becomes the brain, of the capitalist organism' (Schumpeter 1939 [1964], pp. 101–102).

14. 'Outside the firm, price movements direct production, which is co-ordinated through a series of exchange transactions on the market. Within a firm, these market transactions are eliminated and in place of the complicated market structure with exchange transactions is substituted the entrepreneur-co-ordinator, who directs production. It is clear that these are alternative methods of co-ordinating production. Yet, having regard to the fact that if production is regulated by price movements, production could be carried on without any organisation at all, well might we ask, why is there any organisation?' (Coase, 1937, p. 388).

15. 'The main reason why it is profitable to establish a firm would seem to be that there is a cost of using the price mechanism. [...] It is true that contracts are not eliminated when there is a firm but they are greatly reduced. A factor of production (or the owner thereof) does not have to make a series of contracts with the factors with whom he is co-operating within the firm, as would be necessary of course, if this co-operation were as a direct result of the working of the price mechanism. For this series of contracts is substituted one. [...] The contract is one whereby the factor, for a certain remuneration (which may be fixed or fluctuating) agrees to obey the directions of an entrepreneur *within certain limits*. The essence of the contract is that it should only state the limits to the power of the entrepreneur. Within these limits, he can therefore direct the other factors of production' (Coase 1937, pp. 390–391).

16. 'There might be managers, superintendents, etc., for the purpose of coordinating the activities of individuals. But under conditions of perfect knowledge and certainty such functionaries would be laborers merely, performing a purely routine function, without responsibility of any sort, on a level with men engaged in mechanical operations' (Knight 1921 [1964], pp. 267–268).

5. Finance and risk

> Monetary Analysis introduces the elements of money on the very ground floor of our analytical structure and abandons the idea that all essential features of economic life can be represented by a barter-economy model. Money prices, money incomes, and saving and investment decisions bearing upon these money incomes, no longer appear as expressions ... of quantities of commodities and services and of exchange ratios between them: they acquire a life and an importance of their own, and it has to be recognized that essential features of the capitalist process may depend upon the 'veil' and that the 'face behind it' is incomplete without it. (Joseph Schumpeter 1954 [1994], p. 278)

As was illustrated in the previous chapter, in order to explain the relationship between money and production, that is, the first link in the M–C–M' sequence, it is necessary to specify: 1) what characterizes the production process in a monetary economy versus the process described by the mainstream theory; and 2) the money creation process. As is well known Keynes underlines that, in a monetary economy, the production process is carried out under conditions of uncertainty. In this chapter, we will see that Keynes's and Schumpeter's analyses allow us to consider uncertainty as a consequence of the presence of money. In other words, their analyses stress the monetary nature of uncertainty and lead to the explanation of the relationship between finance and risk used by Rajan to explain the origins of the current crisis.

The first part of this book showed that Rajan's thesis clearly clashes with the tenets of the mainstream theory of finance whereby the financial system does not create risk. Banks are indeed mere intermediaries collecting saved resources in order to transfer them to entrepreneurs. Because of their ability to evaluate the characteristics of entrepreneurs and their investment projects, banks do not create risk. On the contrary, they reduce the risk that savers misallocate their resources to incompetent or dishonest entrepreneurs. Rajan's analysis is not only inconsistent with the principles of the mainstream theory, but also poses a challenge to Keynesian economists, who developed an explanation of the origins of the current crisis by replacing the concept of risk with the Keynesian notion of uncertainty (see, for example, Skidelsky 2009, 2011; Palley

2012; Argitis 2013; Asensio 2013–2014). However, Keynesian economists generally regard uncertainty as an exogenous given fact, as a
dimension that does not depend on the presence of bank money. Since
Rajan's interpretation provides that the banking system can create risk,
Keynesian economists should wonder whether uncertainty is indeed an
exogenous given fact, or whether the financial system can 'create
uncertainty'. In other words, Rajan's work should urge Keynesian
scholars to investigate whether finance can be considered as a key factor
to explain the importance of uncertainty.

In this chapter the causal relationship between money, finance and
uncertainty is defined by considering: 1) the relationship between investment decisions and uncertainty; and 2) the relationship between bank
money and investment decisions.

1. INVESTMENT DECISIONS AND UNCERTAINTY

1.1 The Concept of Uncertainty

Keynes blames the classical theory for completely neglecting the dimension of uncertainty and for considering only an abstract economy in
which decisions are taken in conditions of certainty. He notes that the
absence of uncertainty characterizes economic systems based on consumption decisions, in which investment decisions are irrelevant, that is,
economic systems such as agricultural economies, which produce only
few goods that are immediately consumed. In contrast, in monetary
economies, investments play a fundamental role:

> The whole object of the accumulation of wealth is to produce results, or
> potential results, at a comparatively distant, and some times at an *indefinitely*
> distant, date. Thus the fact that our knowledge of the future is fluctuating,
> vague and uncertain, renders wealth a peculiarly unsuitable subject for the
> methods of the classical economic theory. This theory might work very well
> in a world in which economic goods were necessarily consumed within a
> short interval of their being produced. But it requires, I suggest, considerable
> amendment if it is to be applied to a world in which the accumulation of
> wealth for an indefinitely postponed future is an important factor; and the
> greater the proportionate part played by such wealth-accumulation the more
> essential does such amendment become. (Keynes 1937a [2013d], p. 213)

Keynes's statement that the classical theory describes a world without
investments seems excessive since investments are actually made also in
the economy described by the classical theory. In fact, in a corn economy

investments consist in the share of the harvest used as seed or as wage for the workers employed in the production of spades and ploughs in order to increase the system's productivity. Therefore, what distinguishes the two economies is not the presence of investments, but their features. The fundamental difference between an investment in a monetary economy and an investment in a corn economy is the degree of certainty with which an entrepreneur may foresee the future results of his decisions. According to Keynes, the investments that characterize a monetary economy are made under conditions of uncertainty. He explains that he uses the term 'uncertainty' to underline that there are no objective criteria that would allow an entrepreneur to make a reliable estimate of the future results of his investment decisions. In other words, in a monetary economy future economic results cannot be expressed in probabilistic terms:

> By 'uncertain' knowledge, let me explain, I do not mean merely to distinguish what is known for certain from what is only probable. The game of roulette is not subject, in this sense, to uncertainty; nor is the prospect of a Victory bond being drawn. Or, again, the expectation of life is only slightly uncertain. Even the weather is only moderately uncertain. The sense in which I am using the term is that in which the prospect of a European war is uncertain, or the price of copper and the rate of interest twenty years hence, or the obsolescence of a new invention, or the position of private wealth owners in the social system in 1970. About these matters there is no scientific basis on which to form any calculable probability whatever. We simply do not know. (Keynes 1937a [2013d], pp. 213–214)

Conversely, in the economic system described by the classical theory, investments are made under conditions of certainty and the entrepreneur can predict the results of his decisions in probabilistic terms. In fact, in the world described by classical economists, as emphasized by the C–M–C' sequence, the economic activity consists in the production of goods, and the availability of goods is a necessary condition to demand other goods. This is an economy made of small producers, such as Smith's butchers, brewers and bakers, in which an entrepreneur plans an investment by comparing its costs, which equal the amount of real resources needed for the production of a specific good, with its prospective results, which consist in the quantity of goods produced. This comparison is carried out in conditions of certainty because the relationship between used resources and produced goods is determined by the existing technology. Hence, an investment decision only requires technical skills. In a corn economy, a technician can calculate the increase in future production achievable by using a given quantity of corn either as seed or as wages paid to the workers employed for the manufacturing of spades or ploughs.

Of course, such economy may also feature factors preventing the entrepreneur from obtaining the amount of expected corn. However, such factors are of a non-economic nature and may include, for instance, extremely adverse weather conditions or socio-political events such as the outbreak of a war. Leaving these factors aside, it must be concluded that in a corn economy investment decisions are made in conditions of certainty. The situation is totally different if one looks at investment decisions made in a monetary economy. In a capitalist economy, enterprises are not simple organizations reducing transaction costs. In fact, as Schumpeter pointed out, their fundamental function is to introduce innovations. The Schumpeterian concept of innovation allows us to explain the relationship between investment decisions and uncertainty that characterizes a monetary economy.

1.2   Investment Decisions, Innovations and Uncertainty

In the *General Theory*, Keynes provided some examples to illustrate the relationship between investment decisions and uncertainty, which clarify the link between investment decisions and innovations:

> The outstanding fact is the extreme precariousness of the basis of knowledge on which our estimates of prospective yield have to be made. Our knowledge of the factors which will govern the yield of an investment some years hence is usually very slight and often negligible. If we speak frankly, we have to admit that our basis of knowledge for estimating the yield ten years hence of a railway, a copper mine, a textile factory, the goodwill of a patent medicine, an Atlantic liner, a building in the City of London amounts to little and sometimes to nothing; or even five years hence. (Keynes 1936 [2013a], pp. 149–150)

The uncertainty of the future yield of an investment, be it the construction of a railway or an Atlantic liner, or the production of a new medicine, can be explained by referring to the characteristics of innovations. Schumpeter underlines that innovations are not introduced as a consequence of a demand for new goods by consumers but as a result of decisions made by entrepreneurs. While in the barter economy described by the traditional theory needs are given facts and the production process allows their fulfillment, in capitalist economies the causal relationship between consumer needs and productive processes is reversed. Needs are not exogenously given facts but are continuously influenced by the innovations introduced by entrepreneurs. Schumpeter illustrates this argument very effectively:

> Railroads have not emerged because any consumers took the initiative in displaying an effective demand for their service in preference to the services of mail coaches. Nor did the consumers display any such initiative wish to have electric lamps or rayon stockings, or to travel by motorcar or airplane, or to listen to radios, or to chew gum. The great majority of changes in commodities consumed has been forced by producers on consumers who, more often than not, have resisted the change and have had to be educated up by elaborate psychotechnics of advertising. (Schumpeter 1939 [1964], p. 47)

The use of the Schumpeterian concept of innovation makes it relatively easy to explain why, in a monetary economy, investment decisions are made under conditions of uncertainty. In fact, in such a context it cannot be assumed that entrepreneurs-innovators will be able to sell their entire production, since their monetary proceeds depend on the reaction of the consumers to the innovation, on their ability to influence consumer behaviours, and on the purchasing power of households at the time when the innovation is introduced.

While in the economy of small producers described by the traditional theory every good becomes money since its production is the necessary condition to buy other goods, in a monetary economy goods are not money. In fact, they can be transformed into money only if they are sold in exchange for money. The goal of an entrepreneur is not to produce, for example, cars in order to barter them in exchange for other goods, but to sell them in exchange for money. Therefore, the results of an entrepreneur's investment decisions are the monetary proceeds that he will obtain by selling the products made thanks to his investment. If the entrepreneur cannot sell what he has produced, his revenues would amount to zero, despite the existing manufactured cars.

Schumpeter makes a distinction between the production of already existing goods and the introduction of innovations, and he associates the terms 'enterprise' and 'entrepreneur' with the latter.[1] He also remarks that special skills are needed to introduce innovations, as the decisions made by the entrepreneur-innovator change the structural characteristics of the economic system. Therefore, the entrepreneur-innovator is forced to plan his activity in an attempt to anticipate the possible reactions of a world that does not yet exist.[2] Schumpeter (1912 [1949], p. 66) thus concludes that usually innovations are introduced by new people who are not running existing businesses. A few years later, Keynes introduced the concept of *animal spirits* to illustrate the distinguishing features of entrepreneurs who take investment decisions in conditions of uncertainty.[3]

Keynes uses Marx's formulas described in Chapter 4 to emphasize the differences between investment decisions characterizing a real-exchange economy and a monetary economy. In a barter economy, the entrepreneur's decision-making criterion consists in comparing the amount of goods initially invested in the production process with the quantity of produced goods. In contemporary capitalist economies, however, entrepreneurs are not interested in the amount of produced goods, but in the amount of money obtained from sales proceeds:

> The classical theory supposes that the readiness of the entrepreneur to start up a productive process depends on the amount of value in terms of product which he expects to fall to his share; i.e. that only an expectation of more *product* for himself will induce him to offer more employment. But in an entrepreneur economy this is a wrong analysis of the nature of business calculation. An entrepreneur is interested, not in the amount of product, but in the amount of *money* which will fall to his share. He will increase his output if by so doing he expects to increase his money profit, even though this profit represents a smaller quantity of product than before. (Keynes 1933b [2013g], p. 82)

By using the C–M–C' sequence, Keynes argues that an entrepreneur operating in the economy described by the classical theory will only hire a new worker if this generates an increase in the production of goods higher than or at least equal to the amount of goods corresponding to the new worker's salary. This decision-making criterion perfectly applies to economic systems that can be described by models based on the assumption that only one good is produced, as Adam Smith's and David Ricardo's corn economy or Böhm-Bawerk's fishermen economy. Conversely, Keynes uses the M–C–M' sequence to emphasize that entrepreneurs acting in a monetary economy do not evaluate the results of their investment decisions on the basis of the amount of produced goods, but on the basis of the monetary proceeds obtained from the sale of the produced goods.

Obviously, in a real-exchange economy costs and revenues can be also expressed in monetary terms. However, there is a substantial difference between these two types of economies. In a real-exchange economy, the entrepreneur's profits can be expressed in real terms by comparing the amount of goods used as means of production and the quantity of goods obtained at the end of the production process. In this case, monetary values actually are no more than a 'veil'. On the other hand, in a monetary economy profits cannot be defined in terms of quantities of goods. In fact, revenues do not coincide with the amount of goods produced or the monetary value of production; rather, they correspond to the monetary value of the quantity of goods sold in exchange for money.

Keynes contrasts the monetary values with the quantities of goods to underline that, in a monetary economy, the nature of an entrepreneur's revenues is completely different from the nature of revenues in a corn economy. In a capitalist economy, monetary values are not a mere 'veil' hiding the real factors determining an entrepreneur's profits. They are indeed the only elements that allow an entrepreneur to decide whether or not he should make an investment. In Keynes's world, investments and production decisions do not create the conditions that generate an equivalent demand for goods, and the results of an investment can be defined only on the basis of expected monetary revenues.

2. BANK MONEY AND INVESTMENT DECISIONS

2.1 Bank Money and Innovations

This section will analyse the monetary nature of uncertainty. More specifically, it will show that the use of a specific type of money, namely bank money, is a necessary factor to explain the implementation of a large number of investment projects and the importance of uncertainty (see Bertocco 2013a, 2013b). To explain the link between money and uncertainty, it is useful to start from Schumpeter's analysis of the fundamental role played by bank money in capitalist economies. First, Schumpeter points out that, in general, innovations are introduced by 'new men' capable of acting in conditions of uncertainty who, unlike those running existing businesses, do not control the basic production factors, that is, labour and land. Secondly, he assumes that innovations are implemented in conditions of full employment.[4] This hypothesis clashes with Keynes's theoretical framework, as will be further discussed in the following pages. According to Schumpeter, in a situation of full employment, innovations can be introduced only if new entrepreneurs can take control of part of the available productive resources away from existing businesses. Schumpeter remarks that it is unreasonable to imagine some form of direct exchange between the owners of existing businesses and the new entrepreneurs, as 'in principle, a loan of the services of labor and land by workers and landlords is not possible' (Schumpeter 1912 [1949], p. 96).

Schumpeter explains that entrepreneurs-innovators can take away control of production factors from existing businesses thanks to bank money. In fact, by expanding the supply of credit, banks provide new purchasing power to entrepreneurs-innovators, thereby allowing them to demand labour services. This demand adds to the demand of existing businesses and hence triggers an increase in the level of wages. This is how entrepreneurs-innovators take some of the production factors away from existing businesses in order to use them for innovations (Schumpeter 1912 [1949], pp. 106–109).

Therefore, the phenomenon of credit based on the creation of money by the banking system is an essential element of the process of change typical of capitalist economies. Without banks and credit, the presence of a consistent flow of investments and the development process of capitalist economies could not be explained.[5] Schumpeter (1912 [1949], p. 102) underlines that an entrepreneur 'can only become an entrepreneur by previously becoming a debtor'. To emphasize the importance of bank money, Schumpeter claims that his theory is based on the heretical conjecture that the development process that characterizes a capitalist economy does not depend on saving decisions but rather on the presence of entrepreneurs-innovators and on the bankers' willingness to finance them through the creation of money (Schumpeter 1912 [1949], pp. 66–69).

Keynes and Schumpeter share the view that, in modern economies, investment decisions do not depend on saving decisions. Investments are only feasible through the process of money creation triggered by the banking system. It can be demonstrated that this conclusion does not depend on Schumpeter's assumption regarding full employment of available productive resources. On the contrary, as will be discussed in greater detail in Chapter 7, by recognizing the fundamental role of bank money in the implementation of investments-innovations, an effective explanation of income and employment fluctuations and of Keynes's principle of effective demand can be provided.

2.2 An Example

The following example illustrates the relationship between bank money and investment decisions. This example is built on the hypothesis that, as suggested by Schumpeter, 'development … arise[s] out of a position without development' (Schumpeter 1912 [1949], p. 64). Let us take a corn economy and assume that there comes an entrepreneur who, following his animal spirits, plans to build a railway.[6] The aim of this example is to show that, in a monetary economy, it would be impossible to build a railway without bank money.

Let us also assume that this corn economy can rely on a workforce of 1400 units and that each worker's productivity, given the existing technology, is equal to 10 quintals of corn per unit of time. Let us further assume that the price of a quintal of corn is equal to one unit of money and that the wages paid to workers, equal to 5 units of money, are completely used to buy corn for the sustenance of workers' families. As Keynes emphasized, in such an economy, an entrepreneur's decision to hire an additional worker is taken by comparing costs and revenues in real terms, that is, in terms of quantities of corn. Since in real terms the workers' productivity is higher than their cost, all 1400 available workers will be employed. In fact, by employing the whole of the existing workforce, the entrepreneurs will obtain 14 000 quintals of corn (1400 × 10) against a total cost of 7000 quintals (1400 × 5), which corresponds to the amount of corn consumed by the workers. This means that the entrepreneurs will make a profit of 7000 quintals of corn.

For the sake of simplicity, let us now assume that the entrepreneurs' consumption is equal to zero and that their profits are saved to be used for future investments. For example, the 7000 quintals of corn accounting for the entrepreneurs' profits could be used as seed or to pay a certain number of workers hired to manufacture spades or ploughs in order to increase the productivity of agricultural labour, and thus to obtain a higher quantity of corn in subsequent periods.

As shown in the example of Stiglitz and Weiss mentioned in section 2.1 of Chapter 3, a corn economy, due to the asymmetric distribution of information between savers and investors, may also feature a dissociation between saving and investment decisions, which would justify the presence of banks. Let us now assume that there comes an entrepreneur who plans to build a railway by employing, for example, 400 workers, whose salaries correspond to 2000 quintals of corn (400 × 5). Since this amount is only a fraction of the farmers' savings, building the railway seems possible also without the creation of new money by banks, which could act as mere intermediaries. Banks could simply lend the 2000 quintals of corn collected from the savers to the entrepreneur who wants to build the railway instead of allocating them to others for manufacturing spades or ploughs.

In fact, it is difficult to reach a credit agreement of this type, since it is not clear what the debtor will have to return to the creditor. As the entrepreneur-innovator does not produce corn, he cannot assume the commitment to repay the creditor in real terms. Thus, the credit agreement allowing the construction of the railway must be concluded in monetary terms, and the entrepreneur-innovator assumes the commitment to return money to the subject, the banks, which are able to supply credit by creating new money. This credit agreement is very different from that referred to as a corn economy by Stiglitz and Weiss in the example reported in section 2.1 of Chapter 3. In that case, as was discussed above, investment decisions are taken by comparing costs and revenues in terms of the quantity of goods consumed and produced. This decision criterion is not applicable to the construction of a railway. Obviously, it would still be possible to define costs and investment results in quantitative terms. The costs actually consist of the corn consumed by the workers employed in the construction of the railway, while the results of the investment can be measured in terms of miles of track and numbers of locomotives and wagons. However, these parameters do not allow an entrepreneur to decide whether or not he should build the railway. In principle, one could imagine that there are people who are willing to build a railway after comparing the expected results in terms of tracks and locomotives with the costs expressed in terms of corn. For example, there may be an eccentric individual who wishes to leave a mark on the Earth or simply impress his friends, but he could hardly be called an entrepreneur, and no banks would ever be willing to finance his project.

In fact, an entrepreneur is not interested in building the railway as if it were a monument to himself. He rather wishes to obtain a monetary income higher than the costs incurred, in order to make a monetary profit by selling transportation services. Therefore, an entrepreneur will take the decision to build the railway by comparing the monetary values concerning, on the one hand, the cost of wages to be paid to the workers he wishes to employ, and, on the other hand, the expected revenues from the sale of the train tickets. These monetary values are not a simple 'veil'. On the contrary, they are the only element on which the entrepreneur-innovator who wants to build a railway and the banker who is in a position to finance his investment project will base their decisions.

The monetary revenues expected by the entrepreneur willing to build a railway are uncertain in Keynesian terms. They depend on whether consumers will accept the innovation introduced in the transportation sector. This will depend, on the one hand, on the ability of the entrepreneur-innovator to convince consumers to use the railway, and, on the other hand, by the purchasing power at their disposal, which will depend on the level of wages. More generally, sales proceeds are a function of the level of aggregate demand, which will only be established after the railway is constructed.

The above arguments suggest that the credit agreement between a bank and an entrepreneur who wants to build a railway has to be established in monetary terms. The bank will actually lend money and not corn, and the entrepreneur will undertake to repay the bank by using money, since his revenues are obtained only in monetary form. Actually, train tickets are not paid with corn since the workers employed in the construction of the railway do not produce corn. Moreover, the goal of the entrepreneur is not to make a profit in real terms. If it were so, he would hire the available workers for the production of corn and not for the construction of a railway.

There is another element that corroborates this conclusion. Indeed, in a monetary economy farmers who produce corn also have to take their decisions by comparing monetary values and not quantities of corn. In fact, their final goal is not to produce goods, and their profit will not be the amount of produced corn in excess of the quantity that they initially used as a means of production. Their profit will depend on the monetary incomes gained by selling their corn production, and also these monetary proceeds, as those of the entrepreneur who wants to build the railway, are uncertain. In fact, farmers take production decisions based on their expectations on the amount of corn they will be able to sell. This amount depends on the number of employed workers, and thus also on the investment decisions of the entrepreneur-innovator who wants to build the railway.

It is unrealistic to assume that farmers will hire all the available 1400 workers just because their productivity of 10 quintals of corn is higher than their wages, which equal 5 quintals of corn. Farmers are not interested in earning a profit of 7000 quintals of corn. What they want is a monetary profit from the sale of corn. Consequently, they define the number of workers to be hired based on the amount of corn that they expect to produce in order to fulfil the overall estimated demand by the workers and their families. As every employed worker demands a quantity of corn equal to his wage, the total demand for corn will depend on the overall number of employed workers. If all the available work-force of 1400 workers were to be employed, the farmers would have to fulfil an overall demand of corn of 7000 quintals. Since each worker employed in the production of corn produces 10 quintals, 700 workers will suffice to meet the overall demand corresponding to the employment of 1400 workers. The farmers' production decision is taken in conditions of uncertainty because it is based on a forecast of the overall number of employed workers. This number depends on the presence of entrepreneurs-innovators who, similarly to the entrepreneur who wants to build a railway, are willing to employ the remaining 700 workers in order to realize their investment projects.

This example shows that it is unrealistic to imagine that, in a monetary economy, a flow of savings made of goods, such as corn, will allow for the construction of a railway or for the development of other similar investments thanks to the intermediation of banks. In such an economy, investments-innovations are actually financed through the money created by banks. Therefore, the presence of bank money is a necessary condition for the execution of large investments with the characteristics of the innovations described by Keynes and Schumpeter, that is, investments associated with the dimension of uncertainty.

Following Minsky's thinking, it can be said that the credit agreement between the banker and the entrepreneur involves an exchange of certainty, namely the amount of labour used to build the railway, for the uncertainty associated with the amount of monetary proceeds that could be obtained through the sale of train tickets (Minsky 1982, p. 20). In a monetary economy, uncertainty is not independent of the presence of money. Thus, far from being an exogenous phenomenon, uncertainty is a consequence of the use of money. In other words, uncertainty has a monetary nature.

The relationship between bank money, investment decisions, innovations and uncertainty emerging from Keynes's and Schumpeter's analysis is an essential element in the definition of the link between finance and risk used by mainstream economists to explain the origins of the contemporary crisis. To complete the analysis of this link, other distinctive aspects of a monetary economy need to be investigated.

3.   THE CHARACTERISTICS OF A MONETARY ECONOMY

The relationship between money and production described above introduces another distinctive feature of a capitalist economy. In the mainstream theory, the economic system is made up of small producers, that is, homogeneous subjects taking their decisions under conditions of certainty. As a consequence, in a real-exchange economy there is no significant difference between workers and entrepreneurs who act under conditions of certainty. Conversely, a capitalist economy is a heterogeneous system in which the figure of the entrepreneur, driven by his animal spirits, is totally different from that of the wage earner.[7]

As the supply of money is a necessary condition to start the production process, it is crucial to take the process of money creation into account.

The analysis of the process of bank money creation highlights the relationship between money and credit, which is another significant feature of a monetary economy.

3.1 The Relationship between Money and Credit in a Monetary Economy

As was discussed in Chapter 3, the traditional theory clearly separates the process of money creation from the process of credit creation. The supply of money depends on the monetary authorities' decisions, while the supply of credit depends on saving decisions. Conversely, Keynes's and Schumpeter's analysis emphasizes the link between money creation and credit creation. In fact, in a monetary economy the supply of credit by the banking system implies the creation of new money. Schumpeter strongly emphasized the monetary nature of credit. He defined the credit market as the 'money market'. Schumpeter (1912 [1949], p. 125) indeed remarked that the main actors of the money market are not savers and businesses, but entrepreneurs and bankers who create the purchasing power needed to carry out investments.

The criticism of the traditional theory of credit is a recurring element in Schumpeter's writings. In his *History of Economic Analysis*, he illustrates the key elements of his theory of credit by questioning the traditional theory accepted by the vast majority of economists. Schumpeter points out that, according to the traditional theory, banks are mere intermediaries, while the real creditors are the savers who deposited their money. Thus, in the traditional theory the nature of credit is independent of the presence of banks; the phenomenon of credit precedes the appearance of banks, whose presence does not alter the nature of credit (Schumpeter 1954 [1994], p. 1113).

Schumpeter criticized especially the version of the classical theory of credit developed by Edwin Cannan, who, in an article written in 1921, defended the traditional theory of bank deposits by stressing that their nature does not differ from that of a deposit of real assets. To illustrate this point, he compared bank deposits with railway cloakrooms. In Cannan's view, in both cases the term 'deposit' means the action of placing an object, be it money or bags, with some person or institution for safe custody. Cannan recognizes that there is an obvious difference between these two operations, since the banker who received a sum of money on deposit can lend out a part of it, while the cloakroom attendant certainly cannot lend a bag left in his custody. However, Cannan sees this as a minor difference, which must not hinder the recognition of the fundamental element shared by the two deposits: in both cases, it is impossible to lend an amount of money or bags greater than the deposited amount. In other words, both the banker and the cloakroom attendant are mere intermediaries whose lending capacity is constrained by the amount of deposits.

To criticize Cannan's conclusion, Schumpeter (1954 [1994], p. 1114) compares the characteristics of the receipts issued by the banker and by the cloakroom attendant. Both are credit instruments that entitle the holder to receive back what was previously deposited. However, Schumpeter notes that there is a substantial difference between these two pieces of paper. Indeed, the receipt issued by the cloakroom attendant is not a good substitute for the deposited bag, since it cannot be used instead of the bag to carry objects. If the depositor needs the bag, he has to go to the cloakroom in order to get it back. With a bank deposit, things are totally different because the receipt issued by the bank is a good substitute for the deposited gold or legal tender. In fact, here the depositor can use the receipt obtained from the bank as a means of payment. Consequently, when an individual deposits gold or legal tender, he does not give up on the possibility of using the money, since he can use the receipt issued by the bank to make payments, while the deposited money can simultaneously be spent by those who obtained a loan from the bank.

What should be added to Schumpeter's analysis is that in a modern monetary economy banks do not need to collect deposits to create money. In fact, when they finance businesses, they can create money by crediting their accounts with a certain amount of deposits, as, for example, John Hicks (1967) pointed out when describing the stages of the evolution of the banking system. The significant aspect of Schumpeter's analysis consists in showing that bank money is a key element of the development process that characterizes capitalist economies. Furthermore, Schumpeter points out that the spread of bank money reverses the relationships between deposits and loans that characterize the theoretical framework of the neoclassical tradition.[8]

The relationship between bank money, investments and saving decisions is at the core of the analysis of another great economist belonging to the generation following that of Keynes and Schumpeter: Nicholas Kaldor, whose works originated the modern theory of endogenous money. Like Schumpeter, Kaldor states that the distinctive feature of contemporary economies is the process of change. More specifically, he argues that the fundamental task of economic theory is to explain the ongoing transformation of economic systems due to the adoption of technologies characterized by increasing returns that reduce production costs (Kaldor 1982, 1985). Kaldor points out that the presence of bank money and the creation of money by banks play a fundamental role in the development of capitalist economies, as they allow for investments that otherwise would never have been made (see Bertocco 2001, 2010). The Appendix to this chapter shows that many economic historians have highlighted the role of bank money in the process of development triggered by the industrial revolution.

3.2 The Monetary Nature of Profits, Capital and Interest Rate

As was previously discussed, in a monetary economy, entrepreneurs take their production decisions by comparing expected monetary revenues and costs. Far from being a mere 'veil', these quantities are the actual drivers of production decisions. Schumpeter underlines this point by supporting the need to abandon

> the idea that all essential features of economic life can be represented by a barter-economy model. Money prices, money incomes, and saving and investment decisions bearing upon these money incomes, no longer appear as expressions … of quantities of commodities and services and of exchange ratios between them: they acquire a life and an importance of their own, and it has to be recognized that essential features of the capitalist process may depend upon the 'veil' and that the 'face behind it' is incomplete without it. (Schumpeter 1954 [1994], p. 278)

This implies that profits can be defined only in monetary terms. The monetary nature of profits is another element that distinguishes a monetary economy from a real-exchange economy. According to the mainstream theory, money is a 'veil' and profits can be defined in terms of quantities of corn. Keynes points out that the entrepreneur's results cannot be defined in terms of amounts of product and that his final objective is the attainment of a monetary profit.[9] Similarly, Schumpeter (1912 [1949], p. 128) states that '[e]ntrepreneurial profit is a surplus over costs. From the standpoint of the entrepreneur, it is the difference between receipts and outlay in a business.' Schumpeter uses this definition to emphasize that profits are not the result of land productivity, as is the case with corn production, but a typical outcome of the development process, and hence of capitalist economies.[10]

Underlining the monetary nature of profits also means recognizing the monetary nature of capital. According to the mainstream theory, capital consists of physically available means of production such as spades, ploughs or fishing nets and boats. Schumpeter argues that this definition applies to any economic system and hence it does not characterize the special features of a capitalist economy. In order to emphasize the fundamental importance of bank money, Schumpeter defines capital as the amount of money available to entrepreneurs for implementing innovations.[11]

Finally, as anticipated in Chapter 4, Keynes and Schumpeter reject the Wicksellian concept of natural rate of interest, and consider the interest rate as a purely monetary phenomenon. In the economy described by the neoclassical theory, the interest rate stems either from the productivity of the labour employed in the production of corn or, in the case of Böhm-Bawerk's fishing economy, from the productivity of the boat fishing activity. These productivity gains allow the rewarding of savers for their abstention from consumption. Conversely, in a monetary economy, the interest rate is not the reward for abstaining from consumption, but the premium paid to those who create money.[12]

3.3 Innovations, Endogeneity of Needs and the Social Function of Banks

Keynes's analysis of investment decisions under conditions of uncertainty and Schumpeter's emphasis on the role of innovations emphasize another structural feature of a monetary economy. In fact, the principle of consumer sovereignty, which characterizes a real-exchange economy, does not apply in a monetary economy. In the former, the purpose of production is to provide goods in order to satisfy a given set of needs that remains unchanged over time. In the latter, the introduction of innovations changes the set of consumers' needs continuously.

The crucial role of innovations in a monetary economy leads to an emphasis on the key role of the banking system and, more generally, of finance. By creating new money, banks enable the entrepreneur-innovator to control the productive factors that, according to Schumpeter, basically consist of the workforce needed to realize innovations. Therefore, banks perform a crucial social function as they take decisions that can change the way of living of an entire society. Another element that emphasizes the role of banks is the fact that, in a monetary economy, entrepreneurs who borrow money from the banking system can fail since their investment decisions are taken in conditions of uncertainty. Although this may sound obvious, we should not forget that, as was discussed in Chapter 3, in the economy described by mainstream economists, businesses cannot fail because investment decisions are taken under conditions of certainty. In a monetary economy, the banking system plays a dual role. On the one hand, it creates 'risk' by providing credit through the creation of new money. On the other hand, it allows the spread of the consequences of the risk of failure across society. Schumpeter underlines that the risk of default is not borne by entrepreneurs-innovators since they do not use their own resources, but by society as a whole, which, through banks, gives them control over the workforce.[13]

To highlight the role of banks, it is worth recalling that Keynes compares the attitude of an entrepreneur-innovator endowed with animal spirits with the attitude of an explorer preparing an expedition to the South Pole. Schumpeter's writings show that there is a significant difference between the entrepreneur-innovator and the explorer. In fact, while the presence of bank money allows the transfer of risks arising from the introduction of an innovation to the entire economic system, in the case of an expedition to the South Pole the explorer cannot transfer the risk of losing his life to society as a whole.

Schumpeter underlines the banks' social functions by comparing their role in a capitalist economy with the role of the central authority, that is, the planning authority, in a socialist economy. In a planned economy, the means of production are publicly owned and therefore it is the central authority that decides how to allocate them. Conversely, in a capitalist economy, where the productive factors are controlled by private individuals, the role of the central planning authority is played by banks, which create new money in order to allow the entrepreneurs-innovators to take away the control of the necessary means of production from existing businesses (Schumpeter 1939 [1964], p. 86).

Having assigned such an important role to banks, Schumpeter felt it necessary to define strict rules for the conduct of the banking activity. First, while bankers must investigate the personality of entrepreneurs and the characteristics of the investment projects to be financed, they should not participate in any way in the business profits. Therefore, bankers' remuneration should consist only in the interest charged on the granted loans. Second, bankers must be completely independent of the financed businesses and of the political power (Schumpeter 1939 [1964], pp. 90–92). It goes without saying that Schumpeter's rules for the conduct of banking activity are profoundly different from those in place during the decades before the crisis erupted in the summer of 2007.

4. CONCLUSIONS

This chapter has analysed the relationship between money and the production process, which is the first link in the M–C–M' sequence. This analysis has shed light on some distinctive aspects of a monetary economy, namely: 1) production decisions are taken under conditions of uncertainty; 2) the availability of money is a necessary condition that allows entrepreneurs to produce goods by employing labour; 3) the introduction of innovations makes the concept of consumer sovereignty inapplicable; 4) the distinction between employers and workers is relevant and affects income distribution; and 5) profits, capital and interest rates are monetary variables, and monetary quantities are not a mere 'veil' but the very core of the economic agents' decisions.

This analysis leads us to conclude that a monetary economy possesses the first two characteristics emerging from the explanations of the origin of the crisis elaborated by mainstream economists: 1) the supply of credit is independent of saving decisions; and 2) the financial system creates 'risk'. The description of the characteristics of a monetary economy should now be completed by analysing the relationship between the production of goods and money, which is the second link in the M–C–M' sequence. This analysis, outlined in the next chapter, allows us to explain the presence of speculative markets and the importance of speculation.

NOTES

1. 'The carrying out of new combinations we call "enterprise"; the individuals whose function it is to carry them out we call "entrepreneurs". ... [I]t is the carrying out of new combinations that constitutes the entrepreneur' (Schumpeter 1912 [1949], pp. 74–75).
2. '[O]utside these accustomed channels the individual is without those data for his decisions and those rules of conduct which are usually very accurately known to him within them. Of course he must still foresee and estimate on the basis of his experience. But many things must remain uncertain, still others are only ascertainable within wide limits, some can perhaps only be "guessed". In particular this is true of those data which the individual strives to alter and of those which he wants to create. [...] Carrying out a new plan and acting according to a customary one are things as different as making a road and walking along it' (Schumpeter 1912 [1949], pp. 84–85).
3. '[A] large proportion of our positive activities depend on spontaneous optimism rather than on a mathematical expectation, whether moral or hedonistic or economic. Most, probably, of our decisions to do something positive, the full consequences of which will be drawn out over many days to come, can only be taken as a result of animal spirits – of a spontaneous urge to action rather than inaction, and not as the outcome of a weighted average of quantitative benefits multiplied by quantitative probabilities. Enterprise only pretends to itself to be mainly actuated by the statements in its own prospectus, however candid and sincere. Only a little more than an expedition to the South Pole, is it based on an exact calculation of benefits to come' (Keynes 1936 [2013a], pp. 161–162). On the concepts of uncertainty and animal spirits in Keynes's writings see A. Dow and S. Dow (2011), O'Donnell (2013) and Carabelli and Cedrini (2014).
4. '[W]henever we are concerned with fundamental principles, we must never assume that the carrying out of new combinations takes place by employing means of production which happen to be unused. In practical life, this is very often the case. There are always unemployed workmen, unsold raw materials, unused productive capacity, and so forth. [...] As a rule the new combinations must draw the necessary means of production from some old combinations – and for reasons already mentioned we shall assume that they *always* do so, in order to put in bold relief what we hold to be the essential contour line.

The carrying out of new combinations means, therefore, simply the different employment of the economic system's existing supplies of productive means' (Schumpeter 1912 [1949], pp. 67–68).

5. '[W]e define the kernel of the credit phenomenon in the following manner: credit is essentially the creation of purchasing power for the purpose of transferring it to the entrepreneur, but not simply the transfer of existing purchasing power. The creation of purchasing power characterises, in principle, the method by which development is carried out in a system with private property and division of labor. By credit, entrepreneurs are given access to the social stream of goods before they have acquired the normal claim to it. […] Granting credit in this sense operates as an order on the economic system to accommodate itself to the purposes of the entrepreneur, as an order on the goods which he needs: it means entrusting him with productive forces. It is only thus that economic development could arise. … And this function constitutes the keystone of the modern credit structure' (Schumpeter 1912 [1949], p. 107). On this point see De Vecchi (1995).

6. The building of a railway is one of the examples routinely used by Schumpeter to illustrate the discontinuities produced by the introduction of innovations (Schumpeter 1912 [1949], pp. 62–63).

7. Braudel (1977) has pointed out that the figure of the entrepreneur distinguishes a market economy, which in his definition corresponds to Keynes's real-exchange economy, from a capitalist economy. Braudel emphasizes that a 'market' economy consists of homogeneous subjects like the bakers, the brewers and the butchers of Adam Smith's analysis. They perform equivalent activities out of which they obtain similar incomes. In a market economy, exchanges, which take place locally, are not dominated by subjects with a monopoly power and they give rise to modest and predictable profits. Instead, a capitalist economy is characterized by a high degree of heterogeneity due to the presence of individuals who have a monopolistic power. Braudel observes that in pre-industrial economies these individuals are the great merchants involved in long-distance trade. The activities of merchants differed from the traditional forms of exchange typical of market economies since they could gain a dominant position that, for example, allowed them to directly influence the activity of manufacturing units through the purchase of specific products, such as wool or wheat, by means of forward contracts. (See also Mulgan 2013.)

8. Schumpeter argues that the mechanism of bank money creation 'alters the analytic situation profoundly and makes it highly inadvisable to construe bank credit on the model of "existing funds" being withdrawn from previous uses by an entirely imaginary act of saving and then lent out by their owners. It is much more realistic to say that the banks "create credit", that is, that they create deposits in their act of lending, than to say that they lend the deposits that have been entrusted to them. And the reason for insisting on this is that depositors should not be invested with the insignia of a role which they do not play. The theory to which economists clung so tenaciously makes them out to be savers when they neither save nor intend to do so; it attributes to them an influence on the "supply of credit" which they do not have. The theory of "credit creation" not only recognizes patent facts without obscuring them by artificial constructions; it also brings out the peculiar mechanism of saving and investment that is characteristic of full-fledged capitalist society and the true role of banks in capitalist evolution' (Schumpeter 1954 [1994], p. 1114).

9. 'The firm is dealing throughout in terms of sums of money. It has no object in the world except to end up with more money than it started with. That is the essential characteristic of an entrepreneur economy' (Keynes (1933b) [2013g], p. 89).

10. 'Without development there is no profit, without profit no development. […] The size of profit is not as definitely determined as the magnitude of incomes in the circular flow. In particular it cannot be said of it, as of the elements of cost in the latter, that it just suffices to call forth precisely the "quantity of entrepreneurial services required". Such a quantity, theoretically determinable, does not exist' (Schumpeter 1912 [1949], p. 154).

11. '*Capital* […] does not consist of any definite category of goods, of any definable part of the existing supply of goods. […] [C]apital defined so as to consist of goods belongs to every economic organisation and hence is not suitable for characterising the capitalistic

one [...]. *We shall define capital, then, as that sum of means of payment which is available at any moment for transference to entrepreneurs.* [...] In the carrying out of new combinations, however, money and its substitutes become an essential factor, and we express this by describing them as capital. Thus, according to our point of view, capital is a concept of development to which nothing in the circular flow corresponds' (Schumpeter 1912 [1949], pp. 116–117, 122). See Hodgson (2015, Chapter 7).

12. Schumpeter emphasizes that the entrepreneur-innovator will be able to pay this premium thanks to the profits he will obtain through the realization of his innovative investment project. Hence, the interest rate is a result of profits, and ultimately of the development process of capitalist economies: 'Thus without development ... there would be no interest' (Schumpeter 1912 [1949], p. 174).

13. 'The entrepreneur is never the risk bearer. [...] The one who gives credit comes to grief if the undertaking fails. [...] [E]ven if the entrepreneur finances himself out of former profits, ... the risk falls on him as capitalist ... not as entrepreneur. Risk-taking is in no case an element of the entrepreneurial function' (Schumpeter 1912 [1949], p. 137).

APPENDIX BANKS AND THE INDUSTRIAL REVOLUTION: GERSCHENKRON'S ANALYSIS

Economic historians use a classification similar to that introduced by Marx in order to distinguish the characteristics of two different economic systems that are chronologically separated by the extraordinary watershed represented by the industrial revolution. The changes brought about by the industrial revolution are described very effectively by Karl Polanyi (1944 [2001]), who considers the introduction of machines as the key to understanding the characteristics of the economic system that emerged with the industrial revolution. He points out that the industrial revolution profoundly changed the motivations underlying any economic activity. While in the pre-industrial economies the basic goal of economic activities was the population's subsistence, after the industrial revolution the main objective of economic activities became the achievement of a profit through monetary exchanges:

> The transformation implies a change in the motive of action on the part of the members of society; for the motive of subsistence that of gain must be substituted. All transactions are turned into money transactions, and these in turn require that a medium of exchange be introduced into every articulation of industrial life. All incomes must derive from the sale of something or other, and whatever the actual source of a person's income, it must be regarded as resulting from sale. No less is implied in the simple term 'market system'. (Polanyi 1944 [2001], pp. 43–44)

The role of bank money and, more generally, of the financial system in the process of transformation of the economic system triggered by the industrial revolution has been analysed in many works produced by economic historians. Basically, there are two different theories. According to the first theory, the financial system has played an essentially passive role in the transformation of Western economies, since 'financial institutions ... [grew] more or less spontaneously as the need for their services ar[ose] – a case of demand creating its own supply. This view is associated with the notion that financial service ... is a passive, permissive, or facilitating agent, rather than a factor of production' (Cameron 1967, p. 1).

According to the second theory, the financial system played an active role in influencing the early evolution of Western economies. An important advocate of this thesis is Alexander Gerschenkron (1962). He criticizes the analysis based on the concept of 'primitive accumulation' according to which the beginning of the industrialization of a country must necessarily be preceded by the accumulation of an adequate amount of capital. Gerschenkron, instead, stresses the fundamental role played by banks in the industrialization of continental European countries such as Germany, France and Italy.

Gerschenkron remarks that the concept of primitive accumulation implies that the development process of every country has followed a substantially homogeneous path, characterized by a phase of capital accumulation followed by a phase where 'the tocsin of the industrial revolution was to summon [capital] to the battlefields of factory construction' (Gerschenkron 1962, p. 33). Although Gerschenkron recognizes that the economic development of various European countries presents common elements, he underlines that, compared with England, the industrialization processes in countries such as Germany, France and Italy showed significant differences. More specifically, Gerschenkron observes that the industrialization process in England was more gradual and hence slower than in countries where the industrial revolution took off later. This difference is explained by the fact that the underdeveloped countries could benefit from the experience of the industrialized countries as they could immediately introduce the most technologically advanced production facilities. In specific production sectors, this implied the construction of huge factories, for instance blast furnaces. This is why the industrialization process of the relatively underdeveloped countries was faster and more intense than in England (Gerschenkron 1962, p. 44).

Gerschenkron points out that if the argument based on the concept of primitive accumulation were valid, at the beginning of their industrialization processes the underdeveloped countries should have accumulated a much greater stock of capital than that available to England when its industrial revolution took off. In other words, an underdeveloped country should have had much more capital than England at the beginning of the industrial revolution. This conclusion clashes with the historical evidence: 'There is little doubt that in reality the opposite seems to have taken place' (Gerschenkron 1962, p. 45).

The second limitation of the approach based on the concept of primitive accumulation concerns the definition of capital. This approach considers capital in terms of unconsumed goods that are accumulated in order to be used as production factors. As was previously pointed out, this concept can be applied to a corn economy or to Böhm-Bawerk's fishing economy. Conversely, Gerschenkron (1962) uses a definition of capital similar to that used by Schumpeter. By distinguishing between wealth and capital, he stresses that wealth can contribute to the industrialization process only if it transforms into purchasing power available to entrepreneurs.[1] He also claims that the accumulation of wealth is neither a necessary nor a sufficient condition for industrialization because the purchasing power required to make investments can also be created by the banking system. According to Gerschenkron, this is what happened in the continental European countries that experienced the industrialization process after England:

> [I]n the more backward countries on the European continent, neither the size of previous accumulations nor the sympathy with industrial development was consonant with the much greater capital requirements of a delayed industrialization. The focal role in capital provision in a country like Germany must be assigned not to any original capital accumulation but to the role of credit-creation policies on the part of the banking system. It is true that the banks also collected and passed on to entrepreneurs both current savings and some previously created assets that could be converted into claims on current output, but this is much less significant. (Gerschenkron 1962, p. 45)

Note

1. 'It is easy to say that a wealthy country will find it easier to launch the period of rapid industrialization. As an abstract statement such a proposition is unexceptionable. In historical reality, however, simple availability of wealth will be helpful for industrialization only if it is assembled in the hands of the people who either will be willing to invest it in industrial ventures themselves or, alternatively, are willing and able to pass it on in one form or another to those who are immediately engaged in industrialization. In any case, it must be wealth in a form which either directly or through some financial transformation is capable of being so passed on. One can think of many historical cases where wealth, even though potentially available in an appropriate form, will not in fact reach the industrial entrepreneurs. [...] In short, there is no assurance at all that previously accumulated wealth will in fact be made available for industrial investment finance' (Gerschenkron 1962, pp. 39–40).

6. Saving decisions, wealth and speculation

> Of the art of acquisition then there is one kind which by nature is a part of the management of a household, in so far as the art of household management [provides] such things necessary to life, and useful for the community of the family or state, as can be stored. They are the elements of true riches; for the amount of property which is needed for a good life is not unlimited. […] There is another variety of the art of acquisition which is commonly and rightly called an art of wealth-getting, and has in fact suggested the notion that riches and property have no limit. (Aristotle, *Politics*, pp. 11–12)

> [T]he act of saving implies … a desire for 'wealth' as such, that is for a potentiality of consuming an unspecified article at an unspecified time. (John M. Keynes 1936 [2013a], p. 211)

This chapter focuses on the relationship between production decisions and accumulation of money, which is the second link in the M–C–M' sequence. To explain the significance of this relationship, the nature of savings in a monetary economy must first be specified. As was illustrated in the previous chapter, investment decisions in such an economic system are profoundly different from those described by the mainstream theory. This chapter will show that saving decisions also differ from those defined by the orthodox theory. While the economy described by mainstream economists is characterized by the causal relationship between saving and investment decisions, what is key in a monetary economy is the relationship between saving decisions and wealth accumulation.

1. MONEY, SAVINGS AND WEALTH

1.1 Money and Savings

As was discussed in the third chapter, the causal relationship between saving and investment decisions described by the traditional theory applies to an economic system that resembles a corn economy. In such an economy, savings are the result of the corn producers' decision to refrain from consuming the entire corn production in order to produce a larger quantity of corn in the future. In this economy investment decisions can be taken either by the same individuals who decide to save corn or by other individuals. In the latter case, the saved resources are transferred to investors by means of a credit agreement providing for the payment of an interest. The presence of money does not alter the characteristics of the phenomenon of finance, as credit is only a 'veil' hiding real decisions concerning the amount of savings and investments.

While in a corn economy saving decisions drive investment decisions, in a monetary economy a causal relationship can be identified between saving decisions and the wealth accumulation process. In fact, in a monetary economy savers receive their income in the form of money. Thus, each individual can choose whether to use his income to buy goods or to save a share of his income and accumulate money.

In a monetary economy, money is not a simple veil, because saving money is not the same as saving, for example, corn. In both cases, the act of saving implies refraining from consuming part of the disposable income. However, these decisions differ in two ways. First, in a corn economy, savings consist in the unconsumed portion of the corn production. Therefore, to consume means to destroy potential production resources; indeed, only saved corn can be used to undertake investments. This conclusion does not hold in a monetary economy where the decision to consume, which is still an alternative to the decision to save a portion of the disposable income, does not involve the destruction of money, that is, the destruction of the means for implementing investment decisions. Unlike what happens in a corn economy, in a monetary economy the decision to allocate part of the monetary income to consumption does not affect the amount of money that can be used by the entrepreneurs for their investments. Keynes emphasized that saving decisions are not the only channel through which money flows to entrepreneurs planning to carry out investments. According to Keynes, consumption decisions can also be a source of funds to entrepreneurs. There are no obvious reasons to conclude that only saved money can be made available to businesses for their investments.[1]

The second difference concerns the importance of the relationship between saving decisions and wealth accumulation. In fact, this relationship has no meaning whatsoever in a corn economy since corn is a perishable good that cannot be stored indefinitely. Furthermore, even if corn could actually be preserved over time, the decision to accumulate it would break the relationship between saving and investment decisions that characterizes the mainstream theory, thereby blocking investments. This is not true in a monetary economy because money can be preserved indefinitely. Furthermore, the characteristics of a real-exchange economy described by the C–M–C' sequence do not allow us to explain any relationship between saving decisions and wealth. A corn economy is a static system with the same characteristics as an agricultural economy where few goods are produced and are used to fulfil the essential needs of households. It is reasonable to assume that an economy of this type is characterized by a physiological limit to the total amount of goods that individuals wish to accumulate. Indeed, a farmer would never wish to accumulate an infinite amount of corn, nor would a craftsman wish to pile up an endless amount of tables.[2]

The desire to accumulate unlimited money and wealth that characterizes individuals in a monetary economy can be explained by assuming that they have unlimited needs and hence that the principle of insatiability of needs applies. If needs are insatiable, resources are necessarily scarce. The importance of the principle of insatiability of needs can be explained by the relationship between bank money, investment decisions and uncertainty described in Chapter 5. In fact, in a monetary economy the introduction of innovations continually influences consumers' needs. This process accounts for the presence of consumers with insatiable needs and scarce resources, whose goal is to accumulate wealth via their saving decisions.

Wealth can be defined as the total amount of money and other financial and real assets owned by an economic agent at a certain point in time. Therefore, wealth is the purchasing power that can be used at any future time in order to buy any desired good. Keynes emphasized the relationship between wealth and saving decisions and pointed out that, when an individual decides to save part of his income, he does not contemporarily choose to purchase a particular good or service in the future, but only to accumulate a certain amount of purchasing power:

> An act of individual saving means – so to speak – a decision not to have dinner to-day. But it does *not* necessitate a decision to have dinner or to buy a pair of boots a week hence or to consume any specified thing at any specified date. [...] The act of saving implies ... a desire for 'wealth' as such, that is for a potentiality of consuming an unspecified article at an unspecified time. (Keynes 1936 [2013a], pp. 210–211)

Frank Hahn (1982) postulated that the choice to accumulate money can only be justified in an economic system in which the dimension of uncertainty is relevant. An individual accumulates money because he does not know the quality and the quantity of goods that he will want to buy in the future. This condition of uncertainty becomes relevant in an economic system in which needs are not given. Hahn observes that in a world where each individual knows exactly how to employ his income at any present and future time, there is no need to accumulate money.[3] The Keynesian models developed in the 1950s and 1960s do consider the concept of wealth but, quite surprisingly, neglect the relationship between wealth and saving decisions.[4]

1.2 Wealth in Pre-industrial Economies

At first glance, it may seem surprising to claim that the concept of wealth is relevant only in modern economies. Actually, pre-industrial economies were also characterized by the presence of immensely rich individuals and extreme inequalities in the distribution of wealth (see Goldsmith 1987).

More than 2000 years ago, Aristotle even imagined a society in which goods were produced not in order to fulfil people's needs but to accumulate money. More specifically, he identified two different economic systems: one based on the production of 'such things necessary to life, and useful for the community of the family or state' (Aristotle, p. 11), and the other a system where the production of goods is aimed at accumulating money and wealth. Aristotle used the term 'economics' to indicate the study of a system based on family units forming small communities in which they exchange goods that satisfy basic needs. A system like this is clearly subject to the principle of satiety of needs. With reference to the possession of 'such things useful for the community of the family or state', Aristotle stated that 'the amount of property which is needed for a good life is not unlimited' (Aristotle, p. 11).

Aristotle then used the term 'chrematistics' to identify an economic system in which the introduction of money is followed by a growing desire to accumulate money through trade. He observed that the economic system based on 'chrematistics' is governed by the principle of insatiability of needs. This distinction between 'economics' and 'chrematistics' anticipated what Marx, acknowledging his debt to Aristotle, described by using the Commodities (C) – Money (M) – Commodities (C') and Money (M) – Commodities (C) – Money (M') sequences.

However, there are at least two significant differences between wealth in Aristotle's world and wealth in a monetary economy. The first concerns the specific economic decisions that allow the accumulation of money and wealth. Aristotle identified the source of wealth accumulation in trade, which does not consist in the simple exchange of goods, based on use values, which would be typical of a barter economy, but in the exchange of goods aimed at gaining a profit in monetary terms.[5] Conversely, in the monetary economy described by Marx, Keynes and Schumpeter, the accumulation of wealth is triggered by the introduction of innovations. More specifically, in a monetary economy, the process of wealth accumulation is fuelled by savings flows resulting from investment-innovation decisions funded with the money created by the banking system. The second difference lies in the fact that, unlike Aristotle's economic system, contemporary monetary economies are characterized by a significant relationship between wealth and capital.

1.3   Wealth and Capital

The definition of capital provided in the previous chapter was consistent with Schumpeter's concept whereby capital is the amount of purchasing power available to the entrepreneur-innovator to make an investment. A monetary economy features a well-developed financial system that facilitates the transformation of wealth into capital. In *Lombard Street* (1873) [2009], Walter Bagehot pointed out that having a well-developed financial system was a big advantage for England, compared with France and Germany, in its industrialization process (see North and Wiengast 1989; Martin 2013).

In a monetary economy, investments can be financed not only through the creation of new money by the banks, but also by using existing money accumulated by wealth owners. In fact, businesses can finance their investments by issuing shares or bonds that will be underwritten by wealth holders in exchange for money. The presence of well-developed financial markets allowing for the transformation of wealth into capital is an essential element that distinguishes a capitalist economy from the economy described by Aristotle. Historically, bond markets were established to facilitate the funding of state debts, which mainly consisted in war costs. The origins of these markets date back to a period between the fourteenth and fifteenth centuries. In the late seventeenth century, the 'Glorious Revolution' in Great Britain represented a fundamental turning point for the further development of these markets, as it produced not only important political effects, but also significant economic consequences. The reform of the laws ruling the issuance of Great Britain's national debt indeed transformed the debt of the Crown, which was once guaranteed by the sovereign's properties, into a public debt backed by the state's ability to obtain future revenues through taxes.

The issuance of bonds by the British government resulted in the creation of a relatively safe and attractive alternative to the accumulation of money. In the eighteenth century, the British market for government bonds experienced a significant expansion. In fact, while the British public debt amounted to 75.6 million pounds in 1748, it increased to 247.9 million pounds in 1793. Between 1793 and 1815, in the period of the Napoleonic wars, the British national debt tripled, reaching 745 million pounds, that is, twice the amount of Great Britain's GDP. The development of the government bond market then favoured the issuance of corporate bonds. A similar process took place also in the United States and in many other countries (see Baskin and Miranti 1997).

The relationship between wealth and capital illustrated in these pages is consistent with the concept of liquidity described in the Radcliffe Report in the 1950s, which is at the root of Nicholas Kaldor's monetary theory. Kaldor uses the concept of liquidity developed by the Radcliffe Committee to criticize the quantity theory of money, which postulates a direct relationship between the amount of money, the level of aggregate demand and the general price level. Kaldor states that, in an economy with a developed financial system, spending decisions, and especially investment decisions, are not affected by the amount of circulating money, but by the economic agents' 'whole liquidity position', which can be defined as the ability to obtain money, for example by selling real or financial assets, or through a loan granted by the banking system.[6]

2.   WEALTH AND SPECULATION

The concept of wealth described in the previous paragraph is crucial for explaining the importance of the phenomenon of speculation, which is central to all the explanations of the origin of the crisis elaborated by mainstream economists, even though it is completely neglected in the traditional macroeconomic models. Keynes, however, devotes a considerable part of his *General Theory* to analysing speculative phenomena. He remarks that, in a monetary economy, every individual who receives a monetary income has to take two decisions. The first concerns the allocation of such income between savings and consumption. Thus, to save means to accumulate money and, more generally, to accumulate wealth. Once an income allocation decision is taken, every individual must choose the composition of his wealth. In his *General Theory*, Keynes considers two alternatives to money in the composition of the wealth holder's portfolio, namely long-term bonds and shares.

A monetary economy is characterized by the presence of markets where long-term bonds and shares can be continually traded. The importance of these markets can be explained by recalling that, in this economic system, investments have the same characteristics as Schumpeter's innovations. In Keynes's and Schumpeter's world, large industrial companies finance their investments with new money created by banks and with the issuance of long-term bonds or shares. In the economy described by the traditional theory, in which small producers manufacture only few goods for the satisfaction of a set of exogenously given needs, the presence of such markets is difficult to explain. Keynes emphasizes this point by distinguishing two historical phases: in the first, enterprises were owned and managed by a single individual, while in the current phase the ownership and management of enterprises fall into separate domains, and bonds and shares are traded in markets developed for this specific purpose.[7] In the works following the publication of the *General Theory*, Keynes distinguishes two phases in the process of investment financing. In the first phase, businesses fund investments through bank lending, while in the second phase they substitute bank lending with long-term financing forms.[8]

The choice of a specific wealth composition will depend on the expected future return of the different assets. An individual deciding on the composition of his wealth must estimate the future price and the future yield of instruments representing an alternative to money. In other words, in a monetary economy a wealth holder becomes a speculator. In the *General Theory*, Keynes contrasts the concept of 'speculation' with the concept of 'enterprise'. With the term 'enterprise' he describes the activity of an entrepreneur evaluating the opportunity to undertake an investment, such as the construction of a railway, based on the expected future revenues that could be generated by such investment. Keynes suggests 'to appropriate the term *speculation* for the activity of forecasting the psychology of the market' (Keynes 1936 [2013a], p. 158).

To fully understand the meaning of Keynes's definition of speculation, it is worth recalling that he identifies two separate categories of speculators. The first consists of the 'professional' speculators, that is, individuals who have the necessary information and skills to properly assess the present situation and the prospective returns of a company. The second category of speculators consists of 'a large number of ignorant individuals [...] who do not manage and have no special knowledge of the circumstances, either actual or prospective, of the business in question' (Keynes 1936 [2013a], pp. 153–154). The existence of these two groups of speculators is essential to define the characteristics of prices that are determined in the financial markets. In theory, the prices of shares and bonds correspond to the present value of their future revenues. However, Keynes remarks that this would be true only if the evaluations of professional speculators were to prevail, but this is rarely the case.

The fundamental factor that justifies this conclusion is the fact that the expectations on the future value of financial assets, as well as those on the future performance of an investment-innovation, are formulated under conditions of uncertainty. The distinction between ignorant and professional speculators makes no sense in traditional markets, where there is no uncertainty. In the world described by Adam Smith, ignorant butchers, bakers or brewers, that is, individuals incapable of doing their job, would not survive. Furthermore, not even the presence of asymmetric information can justify the structural presence of ignorant subjects. In the famous example of the second-hand car market described by Akerlof (1970), information asymmetries between buyers and sellers favour the emergence of subjects, such as mechanics, who specialize in the assessment of second-hand cars. In this market, it is impossible to introduce a distinction between professional and ignorant mechanics, that is, mechanics who are unable to assess the quality of used cars, as the latter would soon disappear from the market.

After introducing the distinction between ignorant and professional speculators, Keynes explains that it is not at all obvious that financial markets are driven by the choices of professional speculators. In fact, the choices made by ignorant speculators, which are influenced by 'factors which do not really make much difference to the prospective yield' (Keynes 1936 [2013a], p. 154), might well prevail. According to Keynes, the prices formed in the financial markets are the result of a 'convention'. With this expression Keynes wanted to emphasize that the prices of financial assets may reach values that are very far from those consistent with a professional evaluation of the prospective yield of a business. Moreover, the prices of financial assets may also be very unstable and vary depending on factors that influence the expectations of ignorant speculators, even though they may not have any impact on the future returns of a business.[9]

The potential prevalence of conventional evaluations affects the behaviour of the professional speculators as they may decide to act not on the basis of their informed and knowledge-based estimates of a company's future performance, but according to their expectations of how the mass of ignorant operators will evaluate the company's situation. Professional speculators will thus specialize in foreseeing the 'psychology of the market'.[10] Keynes describes the behaviour of professional speculators with the metaphor of the beauty contests published in the newspapers of his time. Those contests invited readers to choose among a hundred pictures of women's faces not the one deemed prettier according to the reader's own judgement, but the one they thought would be chosen by the majority of the contest participants. The 'conventional evaluations' and the attempt of the 'professional' speculators to predict the 'psychology of the market' can push the prices of financial assets very far from the fundamental levels. In other words, they can generate a speculative bubble.

To explain this statement, it is necessary first to pinpoint the reasons why, with market prices that, for example, are much higher than those based on the fundamentals, professional speculators do not sell the overvalued assets before their market prices collapse. If they behaved this way, the market prices would drop and no speculative bubble would develop. Keynes remarks that it is difficult for professional speculators to make this choice because, if their estimate of the 'psychology of the market' leads them to believe that the market price of overvalued securities will continue to rise, they will have to follow the behaviour of the market and continue to buy those securities, even though they are aware of their excessive value. A professional speculator can act on the basis of his evaluations only if he is in a position to bear the short- and medium-term losses linked to his investments.[11] Keynes also notes that an investor who must continuously account for the performance of his activity to his shareholders cannot easily take decisions on the basis of long-term expectations.[12]

The easiest choice for a professional speculator is to follow the other operators' behaviour, that is, to 'follow the herd', for it is worse to obtain poorer results than those achieved by others when others are successful, and thus to fail alone, than to achieve a lonely success. According to Keynes, '[w]orldly wisdom teaches that it is better for reputation to fail conventionally than to succeed unconventionally' (Keynes 1936 [2013a], p. 158). As was illustrated in the second chapter, a few decades later, Rajan used Keynes's arguments, without quoting him, to explain why bank managers, despite the fact that they were aware of the overvaluation of housing prices, continued to 'follow the herd' by betting on a continuous increase of real estate prices.

Finally, Keynes underlines that the behaviour of professional speculators who specialize in forecasting the 'psychology of the market' can lead to a situation where speculation prevails over entrepreneurship, thus generating catastrophic results:

> Speculators may do no harm as bubbles on a steady stream of enterprise. But the position is serious when enterprise becomes the bubble on a whirlpool of speculation. When the capital development of a country becomes a by-product

of the activities of a casino, the job is likely to be ill-done. The measure of success attained by Wall Street, regarded as an institution of which the proper social purpose is to direct new investment into the most profitable channels in terms of future yield, cannot be claimed as one of the outstanding triumphs of *laissez-faire* capitalism – which is not surprising, if I am right in thinking that the best brains of Wall Street have been in fact directed towards a different object. (Keynes 1936 [2013a], p. 159)

3. SATIETY, INSATIABILITY AND SCARCITY: THE CONTRADICTIONS OF THE MAINSTREAM THEORY

The concepts of wealth and speculation analysed in this chapter apply to a monetary economy governed by the principle of insatiability, in which resources are scarce since the needs of the economic agents are unlimited. The relationship between insatiability and scarcity unveils a profound contradiction in the mainstream theory. In fact, the concept of scarcity is a pillar of the traditional theory, which accepts Lionel Robbins's famous definition of economics as 'the science which studies human behaviour as a relationship between ends and scarce means' (Robbins 1932, p. 15). The contradiction lies in the fact that mainstream economists, while recognizing the importance of the concept of scarcity, accept a theoretical model that applies to economic systems, such as a corn economy, that are ruled by the principle of satiety. This contradictory attitude can be illustrated by looking at the comments made by 'mainstream economists' to a famous essay published in 1930, in which Keynes wondered what the economic situation of 'his' grandchildren would look like in 2030. The significant aspect of this paper is that Keynes elaborated his predictions considering an essentially classical theoretical model, that is, a model based on the principle of satiety of needs.

Making forecasts for an economic system governed by this principle is rather simple. If one assumes that there is a given and immutable set of goods that satisfy the needs of the population, the only innovations that can be introduced in the system are those aimed at increasing the productivity of the workforce employed for the production of these goods. So, with time, the system will reach a state where the population will be able to produce all the necessary goods by working only a few hours per week. In other words, the system will reach what classical economists called 'stationary state'.

According to classical economists, from Adam Smith to John Stuart Mill, the stationary state is a desirable achievement. Adam Smith did not identify the process of economic development with a continuous and unlimited growth of production. He rather regarded this process as a means to free the population of a country from misery. In the mid-nineteenth century, when the effects of the industrial revolution in England were already evident, John Stuart Mill's position was even more explicit.[13] Following the classical approach, in 1930 Keynes made a very clear prediction: over a hundred years, the economic system would reach a virtuous stationary state, that is, a condition in which the economic problem will have been solved.

Mainstream economists correctly explained the reasons for Keynes's forecast error by pointing out that he had completely overlooked the importance of the process of change caused by the continuous introduction of innovations that characterizes modern economies. Mainstream economists' criticism thus emphasizes the limits of the classical model used by Keynes in his essay published in 1930. However, it is surprising that, at the same time, mainstream economists neglect Keynes's later works, in which he declared the need to develop a monetary theory of production based on the concepts of investment and innovation, namely the concepts that they use to criticize the conclusions of Keynes's earlier writings.

3.1   Keynes and the Economic Possibilities of 'His' Grandchildren

The Great Depression of the 1930s led Keynes to develop a new theory in order to explain the endogenous nature of the crisis. Nevertheless, his essay of 1930 still reflected his classical approach. Robert Skidelsky reports that the first version of this work dates back to 1928, when Keynes gave a lecture to the students of Cambridge. Two years later, he reworked the text of the conference to include some considerations on the Great Depression. Keynes's reflections on the crisis of the 1930s are surprising, since he strongly criticizes the pessimistic attitude of those who interpreted the events following the Wall Street crash of 1929 as a sign of the traumatic end of the development of capitalistic economies. Like today's mainstream economists on the eve of the current crisis, he considers the economic turmoil of the 1930s as an accident that will soon pass.[14] Keynes therefore harshly criticizes those who believed that radical changes were required in order to overcome the crisis.[15]

The difference from contemporary economists lies in the way in which Keynes justifies his position. Today, few economists would dare to argue that the current crisis is only a passing event and that the economic system is on a path of development that, within a few years, will bring humanity to reach a condition in which hard work will no longer be required to produce the goods necessary for a dignified life. Nonetheless, as recalled by Skidelsky and Skidelsky (2012), at the beginning of the crisis of the 1930s, Keynes used these arguments to convince an audience of students who were sceptical of capitalism and fascinated by the experience of Soviet communism that 'capitalism, too, was a utopian project – a more effective utopian project than communism, because it was the only efficient means to the abundance which would make possible a good life for all' (Skidelsky and Skidelsky 2012, p. 15).

To achieve this goal, Keynes shifted his attention to the long-term scenario. In fact, he considered the crisis as a sideshow, and therefore wondered: 'What can we reasonably expect the level of our economic life to be a hundred years hence? What are the economic possibilities of our grandchildren?' (Keynes 1930 [2013b], p. 322). He answered this question having in mind the process of economic development that unfolded from the industrial revolution onwards, which he believed to depend on the introduction of innovations that greatly increased the workforce's productivity. Keynes thus concluded that:

> in the long run … *mankind is solving its economic problem.* I would predict that the standard of life in progressive countries one hundred years hence will be between four and eight times as high as it is today. […] This means that the economic problem is not – if we look into the *future –the permanent problem of the human race.* (Keynes 1930 [2013b], pp. 325–326)

Keynes's forecast is based on the key assumption that the economic system is governed by the principle of the satiety of needs. Actually, he recognizes the existence of two distinct types of needs: absolute needs to which the principle of satiety applies, and relative needs which are dominated by the principle of insatiability. In Keynes's view, absolute needs are prevalent, while relative needs are secondary as they concern a limited number of individuals whose behaviour cannot change the essence of his predictions.[16] In order to enhance the credibility of his prophecy, in the second part of the essay Keynes argues, with his unconventional and provocative streak, that humanity will have to prepare itself to live in a new world in which working will no longer be necessary. According to Keynes, to avoid traumatic changes it would be appropriate for humanity to continue performing some sort of productive activity for some time after reaching the stationary state.[17] Economists, whose role is doomed to become unnecessary, have the task to prepare humanity for a future without work, a future in which their function will not be that of doctors and researchers who aim at discovering the secrets of life, but that of technicians, as for example dentists, using their abilities to free people from a nagging unease.[18]

3.2   Keynes's Wrong Predictions and the Characteristics of a Monetary Economy

More than 80 years after the publication of his visionary essay, it is easy to evaluate Keynes's predictions. Economists agree that only half of those predictions have proved to be correct. While the average income of the population in developed countries has actually increased in line with Keynes's forecast, the average working time has showed no trend towards a reduction as Keynes expected.[19]

The common explanation for Keynes's forecast error is that he underestimated the importance of relative needs and thus the relevance of the principle of insatiability. In fact, human beings are characterized by an inborn desire to constantly improve their living conditions. Innovations are the instrument for expanding people's needs, providing responses to the endless pursuit of a higher level of satisfaction. Innovations may contribute to increasing the living standards in different ways. First, by offering goods of higher quality (see Frank 2008). Of course, this also applies for goods that fulfil absolute needs, such as, for instance, the quality of food, which can improve unlimitedly.[20] Second, innovations allow the production of goods that satisfy what Keynes called 'relative needs', or, to use a more modern terminology, 'positional' or 'Veblen goods', that is, goods purchased to signal the social position of an individual. Harrod introduced the concept of 'oligarchic goods', namely goods whose availability is structurally limited, for example paintings by the great masters of the past, holidays in pristine places or houses built in exclusive resorts.[21]

In conclusion, contemporary economists believe that Keynes's wrong predictions stemmed from his underestimation of the importance of the instinct of humanity to continuously improve its living conditions, and thus from the misperception of the fundamental role played by the process of innovation in modern market economies. Pecchi and Piga (2008) observe that Keynes emphasized the negative qualities of capitalism, such as greed and love for money, thereby overlooking the fact that an entrepreneur is often motivated not only by the desire to earn a profit, but above all by the desire to create something new, as is the case with scientists who devote their lives to research. The two authors describe a kind of entrepreneur who resembles Keynes's entrepreneur in the

General Theory, in which he recognized the role of entrepreneurship and the importance of the entrepreneur-innovator and of his animal spirits.

After 1930, the contents of Keynes's work started to differ deeply from the position of classical economists. In fact, Keynes not only introduced the figure of the entrepreneur-innovator and recognized the importance of entrepreneurship, but he also profoundly changed his view on economic crises. From 1933 onwards, starting with the preliminary drafts of the *General Theory*, Keynes began to consider economic crises as a structural phenomenon of modern monetary economies.

NOTES

1. Keynes expressed these concepts by criticizing the way the Committee of Statistical Experts of the League of Nations had analysed the process of capital formation: 'According to the Committee funds for investment can only become available either from prior saving or from dishoarding and credit expansion. [...] The Committee have overlooked the fact that spending releases funds just as much as saving does, and that these funds when released can then be used indifferently for the production either of capital goods or of consumption goods. [...] Money which is spent on prior consumption flows into the same pool of available funds as money which is saved' (Keynes 1939 [2013d], pp. 572–573).

2. This view is consistent with the conclusions of anthropological studies showing that in prehistoric subsistence economies the accumulation of wealth was not a significant phenomenon. Sahlins (1966 [2006]), for example, applies the concept of *affluent society* introduced by John K. Galbraith to the primitive societies of hunters and gatherers. On this topic see also Polanyi (1944 [2001]).

3. 'The most serious challenge that the existence of money poses to the theorist is this: the best developed model of the economy cannot find room for it. The best developed model is, of course, the Arrow–Debreu version of a Walrasian general equilibrium. A world in which all conceivable contingent future contracts are possible neither needs nor wants intrinsically worthless money. ... [A] minimal requirement for a theory of a monetary economy is that the latter should have trading at every date. [We will christen] such economies *sequence economies*. [...] The step to sequence economies has quite decisive consequences for economic theory; for if there are transactions at every date, then the agent must also, in making his plans at any date, form expectations about market conditions at future dates. [...] One of Keynes's claims to the title of great economist is that he saw this more clearly than any of his predecessors had done – and, indeed, more clearly than many of his successors. One of the dangers, for instance, of the IS–LM tradition is that it leads easily to a neglect of expectational variables, and scores of textbooks testify to the confusion that results. In any case: no monetary theory without sequences, and no sequences without expectations' (Hahn 1982, pp. 1–3).

4. Among the leading economists who support the Neoclassical Synthesis, one notable exception is James Tobin, who, in his Nobel lecture, recognized the need to develop models specifying this relationship: 'Although households are simultaneously saving to accumulate wealth, the IS–LM model contains no specific saving functions describing in what forms they wish to accumulate it. [...] The unwelcome implication is that wealth-owners and savers, in formulating their portfolio demands, ignore the fact that they are at the same time saving to augment their wealth' (Tobin 1982, p. 187).

5. As Polanyi remarked, Aristotle's merit lies in the fact that he defined the concepts of profit and wealth, while living in a pre-capitalistic society: 'Only a genius of common sense

could have maintained, as he did, that gain was a motive peculiar to production for the market, and that the money factor introduced a new element into the situation, yet nevertheless, as long as markets and money were mere accessories to an otherwise self-sufficient household, the principle of production for use could operate' (Polanyi 1944 [2001], p. 56).

6.   'Though we do not regard the supply of money as an unimportant quantity, we view it as only part of a wider structure of liquidity in the economy. … It is the whole liquidity position that is relevant to spending decisions and our interest in the supply of money is due to its significance in the whole liquidity picture. [...] The decision to spend thus depends upon liquidity in the broad sense, not upon immediate access to the money. [...] The spending is not limited by the amount of money in existence but it is related to the amount of money people think they can get hold of, whether by receipts of income (for instance from sales), by disposal of capital assets or by borrowing' (Radcliffe Report, quoted in Kaldor 1982, p. 8).

7.   'Decisions to invest in private business of old-fashioned type were, however, decisions largely irrevocable, not only for the community as a whole, but also for the individual. With the separation between ownership and management which prevail to-day and with the development of organized investment markets, a new factor of great importance has entered in, which sometimes facilitates investment but sometimes adds greatly to the instability of the systems. In the absence of security markets, there is no object in frequently attempting to revalue an investment to which we are committed. But the Stock Exchange revaluates many investments every day and the revaluations give a frequent opportunity to the individual … to revise his commitments. It is as though a farmer, having tapped his barometer after breakfast, could decide to remove his capital from the farming business between 10 and 11 in the morning and reconsider whether he should return to it later in the week' (Keynes 1936 [2013a], pp. 150–151).

8.   'The entrepreneur when he decides to invest has to be satisfied on two points: firstly, that he can obtain sufficient short-term finance during the period of producing the investment; and secondly, that he can eventually fund his short-term obligations by a long-term issue on satisfactory conditions' (Keynes 1937c [2013d], p. 217).

9.   'A conventional valuation which is established as the outcome of the mass psychology of a large number of ignorant individuals is liable to change violently as the result of a sudden fluctuation of opinion due to factors which do not really make much difference to the prospective yield; since there will be no strong roots of conviction to hold it steady. In abnormal times in particular, when the hypothesis of an indefinite continuance of the existing state of affairs is less plausible than usual even though there are no express grounds to anticipate a definite change, the market will be subject to waves of optimistic and pessimistic sentiment, which are unreasoning and yet in a sense legitimate where no solid base exists for a reasonable calculation' (Keynes 1936 [2013a], p. 154).

10.   'It might have been supposed that competition between expert professionals, possessing judgment and knowledge beyond that of the average private investor, would correct the vagaries of the ignorant individual left to himself. It happens, however, that the energies and skill of the professional investor and speculator are mainly occupied otherwise. For most of these persons are, in fact, largely concerned, not with making superior long-term forecasts of the probable yield of an investment over its whole life, but with foreseeing changes in the conventional basis of valuation a short time ahead of the general public. They are concerned, not with what an investment is really worth to a man who buys it "for keeps", but with what the market will value it at, under the influence of mass psychology, three months or a year hence. Moreover, this behaviour is not the outcome of a wrong-headed propensity. It is an inevitable result of an investment market organized along the lines described. For it is not sensible to pay 25 for an investment of which you believe the prospective yield to justify a value of 30, if you also believe that the market will value it at 20 three months hence' (Keynes 1936 [2013a], pp. 154–155).

11.   'If the reader interjects that there must surely be large profits to be gained from the other players in the long run by a skilled individual who, unperturbed by the prevailing pastime,

    continues to purchase investments on the best genuine long-term expectations he can frame, he must be answered … that there are several factors which jeopardize the predominance of such individuals in modern market investment markets. … There is no clear evidence from experience that the investment policy which is socially advantageous coincides with that which is most profitable. It needs *more* intelligence to defeat the forces of time and our ignorance of the future than to beat the gun. Moreover, life is not long enough; – human nature desires quick results, there is a peculiar zest in making money quickly' (Keynes 1936 [2013a], pp. 156–157).

12.   '[A]n investor who proposes to ignore near-term market fluctuations needs greater resources for safety and must not operate on so large a scale, if at all, with borrowed money. … it is the long-term investor, he who most promotes the public interest, who will in practice come in for most criticism, wherever investment funds are managed by committees or boards or banks. For it is in the essence of his behaviour that he should be eccentric, unconventional and rash in the eyes of average opinion' (Keynes 1936 [2013a], p. 157).

13.   'I confess I am not charmed with the ideal of life held out by those who think that the normal state of human beings is that of struggling to get on; that the trampling, crushing, elbowing, and treading on each other's heels, which form the existing type of social life, are the most desirable lot of human kind, or anything but the disagreeable symptoms of one of the phases of industrial progress. It may be a necessary stage in the progress of civilization . … But the best state for human nature is that in which, while no one is poor, no one desires to be richer, nor has any reason to fear from being thrust back, by the effects of others to push themselves forward' (Mill 1848 [2004], p. 189).

14.   Keynes's essay opens with the following words: 'We are suffering just now from a bad attack of economic pessimism. It is common to hear people say that the epoch of enormous economic progress which characterised the nineteenth century is over; that the rapid improvement in the standard of life is now going to slow down – at any rate in Great Britain; that a decline in prosperity is more likely than an improvement in the decade which lies ahead of us. I believe that this is a wildly mistaken interpretation of what is happening to us. We are suffering, not from the rheumatics of old age, but from the growing-pains of over-rapid changes, from the painfulness of readjustment between one economic period and another' (Keynes 1930 [2013b], p. 321).

15.   'The prevailing world depression, the enormous anomaly of unemployment in a world full of wants, the disastrous mistakes we have made, blind us to what is going on under the surface to the true interpretation of the trend of things. For I predict that both of the two opposed errors of pessimism which now make so much noise in the world will be proved wrong in our own time – the pessimism of the revolutionaries who think that things are so bad that nothing can save us but violent change, and the pessimism of the reactionaries who consider the balance of our economic and social life so precarious that we must risk no experiments' (Keynes 1930 [2013b], p. 322).

16.   'Now it is true that the needs of human beings may seem to be insatiable. But they fall into two classes – those needs which are absolute in the sense that we feel them whatever the situation of our fellow human beings may be, and those which are relative in the sense that we feel them only if their satisfaction lifts us above, makes us feel superior to, our fellows. Needs of the second class, those which satisfy the desire for superiority, may indeed be insatiable; for the higher the general level, the higher still are they. But this is not so true of the absolute needs – a point may soon be reached, much sooner perhaps than we all of us are aware of, when these needs are satisfied in the sense that we prefer to devote our further energies to non-economic purposes' (Keynes 1930 [2013b], p. 326).

17.   In particular, he argues that it would be convenient 'to make what work there is still to be done to be as widely shared as possible. Three-hour shifts or a fifteen-hour week may put off the problem for a great while. For three hours a day is quite enough to satisfy the old Adam in most of us!' (Keynes 1930 [2013b], p. 329).

18.   '[C]hiefly, do not let us overestimate the importance of the economic problem, or sacrifice to its supposed necessities other matters of greater and more permanent significance. It

should be a matter for specialists – like dentistry. If economists could manage to get themselves thought of as humble, competent people, on a level with dentists, that would be splendid!' (Keynes 1930 [2013b], p. 332).

19. See Skidelsky and Skidelsky (2012) and the essays collected in Pecchi and Piga (2008).

20. Joseph Stiglitz has been very impressed by what is happening in Europe with the spread of the slow food movement 'which says that the point of eating is not efficiency, providing the largest number of calories per dollar or in the shortest span of time. The movement sees eating as a pleasure in itself; it is an intellectual activity, combining sensory perceptions with an analysis of the nature of the pleasures to which the senses give rise' (Stiglitz 2008, p. 56).

21. See Skidelsky and Skidelsky (2012, pp. 34–35), Stiglitz (2008) and Zilibotti (2008).

7. Money and crisis

[T]he financial system necessary for capitalist vitality and vigor – which translates entrepreneurial animal spirits into effective demand for investment – contains the potential for runaway expansion, powered by an investment boom. This runaway expansion is brought to a halt because accumulated financial changes render the financial system fragile, so that not unusual changes can trigger serious financial difficulties. Because Keynes arrived at his views on how a capitalist economy operates by examining problems of decision-making under conditions of intractable uncertainty, in his system stability, even if it is the result of policy, is destabilizing. (Hyman Minsky 1975, pp. 11–12)

The lesson taught by the heterodox economists mentioned in the previous pages allowed us to show that the features of a monetary economy are consistent with the characteristics emerging from the explanations of the origin of the crisis elaborated by mainstream economists. Contemporary economies are structures where: 1) the supply of credit is independent of saving decisions; 2) finance creates risk; and 3) the phenomenon of speculation is relevant. Keynes uses the term 'monetary economy' to underline the fundamental role of money in understanding the concepts of investment, saving, capital, interest, profit, uncertainty, wealth and speculation. A further feature that separates a monetary economy from a corn economy is the occurrence of economic crises.

Keynes and Schumpeter have different positions on the phenomenon of economic crises. As previously discussed, Schumpeter's description of the process of change that characterizes a capitalist economy is based on the assumption that the system is always in a situation of full employment.[1] According to Keynes, instead, contemporary economies are characterized by profound fluctuations in production and employment. Starting from 1933, that is, only three years after the publication of his essay on the economic possibilities of 'his' grandchildren, Keynes no longer interprets economic crises as accidental phenomena that can be easily overcome, but rather as an essential feature of a monetary economy, which must be explained by developing a completely new theoretical approach. In the preparatory drafts of the *General Theory*, Keynes (1933a [2013c], 1933b [2013g]) referred to this theory with the expression: *monetary theory of production*.

Keynes uses this expression to emphasize that money is an essential element in explaining the phenomenon of economic crises. While Schumpeter analyses the relationship between money and the process of development of a capitalist economy, Keynes focuses on the relationship between money and crises. This chapter will show how the relationship between money and development studied by Schumpeter is a crucial element in explaining the link between money and crises that character- izes the Keynesian monetary theory of production. In other words, we will see how the very mechanisms underlying the development of a capitalist economy make this economic system fragile and prone to deep economic crises.

The monetary theory of production presented in this chapter is based on two fundamental points. The first is that a monetary economy is not ruled by Say's Law but by the principle of effective demand. The second point is that there are no measures that can truly drive a monetary economy towards a permanent state of full employment. Monetary and fiscal policies aimed at stimulating the level of aggregate demand, which are generally regarded as Keynesian policies, do not allow maintenance of a full employment balance in the long term. Michał Kalecki's and Hyman Minsky's contributions are key to understanding this point. Kalecki (1943 [1990]) emphasized the political consequences of full employment that account for entrepreneurs' reluctance to achieve this goal. Offering an alternative interpretation of Keynes's thinking in comparison with the Neoclassical Synthesis, Minsky argued that in a monetary economy 'stability, even if it is the result of policy, is destabilizing' (Minsky 1975, p. 12).

1. THE CRITIQUE OF SAY'S LAW AND THE PRINCIPLE OF EFFECTIVE DEMAND

1.1 Say's Law

Say's Law postulates that the decisions to produce goods create the conditions for a level of aggregate demand that is sufficient to absorb the entire production. In short, supply creates its own demand. Keynes argued that Say's Law cannot hold in a monetary economy: it only works in a corn economy or in what he called the economy of Robinson Crusoe.[2] By the latter expression Keynes meant an economy made of a single individual whose income consists in all the goods he is able to produce in a given period of time (a day, a month, a year), which is indicated by the letter *Y*. A portion of these goods, designated by the

letter *C*, will be consumed, while the difference between the produced
and the consumed goods, that is, $(Y - C)$, represents Robinson Crusoe's
savings (*S*). Therefore, $S = Y - C$.

Robinson Crusoe's savings thus consist in all the goods that were
produced and not consumed. Obviously, these goods do not remain
unused. They will be employed as means for producing other goods – for
example, corn used as seed, a fishing rod or a boat. Once they are used as
means of production, the saved goods become Robinson Crusoe's investments, which can be represented with the letter *I*. Since everything that
was saved is automatically invested, savings equal investments $(S = I)$.
Therefore, Robinson Crusoe is at the same time producer and consumer,
saver and investor. In the economy of Robinson Crusoe, Say's Law holds
because produced goods are either consumed or invested. In other words,
as was stated above, supply creates its own demand. Consequently,
production decisions precede consumption and saving decisions, and
saving decisions precede investment decisions.

Say's Law also applies to what Keynes defined as a real-exchange
economy, that is, an economy whose working mechanisms can be
described by the C–M–C' sequence. In this system, the goal of the
economic activity is to produce goods, and the production of goods is the
necessary condition to demand other goods. As was pointed out in
Chapter 5, in a corn economy production decisions are taken under
conditions of certainty. In fact, an additional worker will be employed in
the production of corn if his marginal productivity exceeds his real wage.
If the real wage to be paid to the available workers is lower than their
marginal productivity, the system will be characterized by a state of full
employment. Furthermore, as discussed in Chapter 6, a corn economy is
destined to reach what classical economists call a 'stationary state', a
state in which, according to Keynes's forecasts, the economic problem of
mankind will be solved.

1.2 The Principle of Effective Demand

Keynes argues that Say's Law cannot hold in a monetary economy, which
is instead governed by the principle of effective demand whereby the
level of income depends on the level of aggregate demand. The structural
instability of a monetary economy thus depends on the fluctuations in
aggregate demand.[3]

In Keynes's view, money is the key element for explaining fluctuations
in aggregate demand, which he explicitly defines as a '*monetary* phenomenon' (Keynes 1933b [2013g], p. 85).[4] The monetary nature of the
fluctuations in aggregate demand can be illustrated by referring to the

relationship between bank money, investment decisions, innovations and uncertainty, which, as was discussed in Chapter 5, is an important structural feature of a monetary economy.

This relationship allows us to emphasize that, in a monetary economy, production decisions are made under conditions of uncertainty. The M–C–M' sequence shows that the goal of economic activities is not to produce goods but to accumulate money. This applies not only to an entrepreneur-innovator who wants to build a railway, but also to a corn producer. In a monetary economy, entrepreneurs take decisions under conditions of uncertainty because their monetary proceeds do not depend on the amount of produced goods, but on the ability to sell them in exchange for money. The entrepreneurs' decisions regarding the number of workers to be employed are thus determined by their expectations on the level of aggregate demand.

The principle of effective demand that characterizes a monetary economy can be illustrated with the example used in Chapter 5 to explain the effects resulting from an investment-innovation, that is, the construction of a railway (see also the Appendix to this chapter which presents a simple linear model). The consequences of the railway construction were described by considering an economic system in which the total available workforce is equal to 1400 workers whose productivity amounts to 10 quintals of corn per unit of time, while the money wage is equal to 5 units of money. Money wages are entirely spent on buying corn at the price of a unit of money for each quintal of corn. Therefore, the real wage paid to the workers corresponds to 5 quintals of corn.

As the example in section 2.2 of Chapter 5 showed, the fact that the productivity of the 1400 workers, measured in terms of corn, is higher than the real wage is not a sufficient condition to ensure employment of all the available workers in the production of corn. In fact, farmers will decide how many workers they will employ depending on their expectations on the level of demand for corn. Since only workers consume corn, farmers decide how much corn to produce depending on their estimated number of employed workers, that is, depending on their assessment of the volume of future investments-innovations. If, for example, they estimate that all 1400 available workers will be employed, they will expect a total demand for corn of 7000 quintals. Since the productivity of a single worker is 10 quintals of corn, farmers will hire 700 workers. Thus, the farmers will hire 700 workers only if they believe that there is a sufficient number of innovative entrepreneurs driven by their animal spirits, and that banks will finance the entrepreneurs by extending a total credit equal to 3500 units of money, just enough to pay the wages of the 700 workers.

If their predictions prove to be correct, the farmers will be able to sell 7000 quintals of corn and to obtain a total revenue of 7000 units of money. Since they paid 3500 units of money for the wages of the 700 workers employed in the production of corn, their profits will amount to 3500 units of money. This example shows that the levels of income and employment depend on the flow of investments and thus on the introduction of innovations. In a monetary economy, the necessary condition for the employment of the available workforce is the existence of an adequate number of entrepreneurs willing to carry out innovations such as the construction of a railway. The existence of these entrepreneurs cannot be taken for granted; nor can it be taken for granted that banks will be willing to grant the necessary loans. In the absence of these conditions, the system will be characterized by the presence of unemployment, and farmers too will have to reduce their corn production to adjust it to the level of aggregate demand.

It should also be added that, in a monetary economy in which the level of income is a function of investment decisions, investments do not depend on savings. On the contrary, investments determine the amount of savings. The opposite of the causal relationship between saving and investment decisions that characterizes the mainstream neoclassical theory is the core of the principle of effective demand and of Keynes's criticism of Say's Law.

The example of the railway construction described above helps us to better understand this relationship. The entrepreneur-innovator will be able to build the railway because he received new money created by banks, which he will use to hire a certain number of workers. In turn, the workers will use their wages to buy corn, thereby prompting farmers to produce corn in exchange for money. In this economy, investments correspond to the monetary value of the wages paid to the workers employed in the construction of the railway. It can thus be concluded that savings, which are equivalent to the investment consisting in the construction of the railway, correspond to the quantity of corn consumed by the workers hired to build the railway.

This situation looks similar to what would have happened in a corn economy had the entrepreneurs decided to use their savings to finance the construction of the railway instead of the manufacturing of new ploughs. In fact, only the equivalence between savings and investments is unchanged, while the causal relationship between these variables is reversed. The railway is not built as a consequence of the farmers' decision to save part of the harvest. The construction of the railway rather depends on the decision taken by the entrepreneur-innovator and on the willingness of banks to finance the entrepreneur's investment project through the creation of new money.

In a monetary economy, income and employment depend not only on the flow of investments, but also on household propensity to consume, which may vary, for example, due to changes in wages. Let us assume that workers consume all of their wages and that the level of wages increases from 5 to 7 units of money, while the price of a quintal of corn remains equal to one unit of money and the overall workforce still amounts to 1400 workers. This implies that, in conditions of full employment, the aggregate demand for corn will be equal to 9800 quintals (7 quintals of corn for each of the 1400 employed workers). If we assume that the productivity of the workers employed in the production of corn is always equal to 10 quintals of corn per unit of time, and that the farmers believe that the following period will be characterized by a situation of full employment, the latter will have to hire 980 workers. However, a full employment equilibrium will be reached only if the remaining 420 workers are to be employed in the implementation of a sufficient volume of investments-innovations. This requires not only the presence of a certain number of entrepreneurs-innovators, but also the willingness of banks to fund the entrepreneurs by creating 2940 new units of money (7 units for each of the 420 employed workers).

If these conditions are fulfilled, income will correspond to 9800 quintals of corn, which, in nominal terms, amounts to 9800 units of money. The level of income equals the sum of consumption, which consists in the wages spent by the workers employed in the production of corn (6860 units of money, that is, 7 units of money for each of the 980 employed workers), and investments, which consist in the wages paid to the workers employed for the implementation of innovations. Capital expenditure thus amounts to 2940 units of money (7 units of money for each of the 420 employed workers). The propensity to consume is 70 per cent (6860/9800), while the share of investments on total income is 30 per cent (2940/9800). The volume of investments-innovations equals the quantity of savings set aside by corn producers (2940), who record overall proceeds amounting to 9800 units of money against a total production cost amounting to 6860 units of money.

This example shows that, in a monetary economy, the volume of investments required to reach a full employment equilibrium depends on the propensity to consume. The higher the propensity to consume, the smaller the amount of investments needed to achieve full employment conditions. In a monetary economy, both the production decisions taken by the farmers and those made by the entrepreneurs-innovators are influenced by their expectations to earn monetary revenues exceeding their production costs.[5]

1.3 Involuntary Unemployment in a Monetary Economy

In the years following the publication of the *General Theory*, the most critical elements of Keynes's thinking were overshadowed by an interpretation that soon became popular, known as the Neoclassical Synthesis. This interpretation led most economists to consider Keynes's theory as a special case of the neoclassical theory, as they reached the conclusion that the lack of aggregate demand ultimately depended on the rigidity of wages.

As was illustrated in Chapter 4, this is not Keynes's position. Indeed, wage flexibility can ensure the achievement of full employment in a corn economy but not in a monetary economy. If, for example, in a corn economy the productivity of labour is equal to 10 quintals of corn per unit of time and the real wage corresponds to 11 quintals of corn, not even one worker would be hired. In this case, unemployment would force a cut in real wages until they fall below the level of labour productivity and full employment is restored.

To establish whether, in a monetary economy, the flexibility of wages can ensure full employment, its effects on the two components of aggregate demand, that is, consumption and investment, must be examined. As discussed in the previous section, there is a direct relationship between the level of wages and the overall amount of consumption. In fact, an increase in the level of wages leads to an increase in consumption, thereby reducing the volume of investments required to ensure full employment. Conversely, a reduction in wages determines a drop in consumption, which implies that a higher flow of investments is required to achieve full employment. This leads to the conclusion that a reduction in wages produces a positive effect on employment only if this pushes entrepreneurs to expand their investments as far as it is necessary to reach full employment.

The supporters of the Neoclassical Synthesis claim that, thanks to the flexibility of wages and prices, the interest rate will reach a level that will lead entrepreneurs to invest as much as is necessary to achieve full employment. To support this argument, they use the relationship between the real quantity of money and the interest rate that is at the core of the liquidity preference theory described by Keynes in the *General Theory*. According to Keynes, the real quantity of money and the interest rate are inversely related. An increase in the real quantity of money can be caused either by a growth in the nominal amount of money while the general price level remains unchanged, or by a decrease in the general price level if the total amount of money is given. The supporters of the Neoclassical Synthesis conclude that the flexibility of wages and prices eliminates involuntary unemployment, as the presence of unemployment would cause a decline in money wages and, consequently, in prices. As a result, the real quantity of money will increase, thus causing a reduction in the interest rate, which in turn will trigger an increase in investments. This adjustment process will continue until investments reach a level consistent with full employment.

While he recognizes that a reduction of wages and prices may generate a positive effect on the level of employment by reducing the rate of interest, Keynes also pointed out that these effects can be entirely offset by the negative consequences that a drastic decline in wages and prices might have on the level of confidence, that is, on the expectations of entrepreneurs and bankers:

> The same reasons ... which limit the efficacy of increases in the quantity of money as a means of increasing investment to the optimum figure, apply *mutatis mutandis* to wage reductions. Just as a moderate increase in the quantity of money may exert an inadequate influence over the long-term rate of interest, whilst an immoderate increase may offset its other advantages by its disturbing effect on confidence; so a moderate reduction in money-wages may prove inadequate, whilst an immoderate reduction might shatter confidence even if it were practicable. (Keynes 1936 [2013a], pp. 266–267)

Keynes uses the concept of confidence to question the effects of the flexibility of wages and prices on the interest rate. Some economists have emphasized a logical limitation in Keynes's reasoning. In fact, they have pointed out that, in Chapter 18 of the *General Theory*, Keynes considers the economic agents' expectations as 'ultimate independent variables' (Keynes 1936 [2013a], p. 246), while in Chapter 19, the source of the above quotation, he argues that expectations may be affected by major changes in prices and wages. The specification of a relationship between changes in nominal wages and prices on the one hand and expectations on the other hand transforms the latter from an exogenous to an endogenous variable, with no previously designed theory of expectations supporting this. According to many economists this approach is not acceptable in terms of logical consistency. Messori (2012) explains this criticism very effectively:

> Keynes ... recognizes that a decline in money wages and in the general price level increases the amount of money supplied in real terms; and that, all else being equal, this increase is trending downwards the monetary interest rate

and upwards the investment demand, which in turn raises the equilibrium level of aggregate output by means of the income multiplier. However, Keynes adds that … a worsening of wealth holders' expectations can make the interest rate sticky downwards even in the presence of increments in the money supply in real terms (the 'liquidity trap'); and a worsening of entrepreneurs' long-term expectations can make investment demand sticky upwards even in the presence of a decline in interest rates. These observations of Keynes are empirically plausible because they reflect, albeit in a stylized way, what actually happened during some phases of the crisis of 1929–33 and above all during the crisis of 2007–2009, and what is now happening in the sovereign debt crisis of the European Economic and Monetary Union. From the analytical standpoint, however, Chapter 19 is one of the weakest parts of Keynes's framework. As the author explicitly underscores in Chapter 18 (246–247 pages), in the first seventeen chapters expectations are treated as 'ultimate independent variables', and Chapters 5 and 12 serve to justify this assumption. The transformation in Chapter 19 of these 'ultimate independent variables' into dependent variables, subject to changes in money wages and prices, must be written off as an *ad hoc* assumption. (Messori 2012, p. 109)

The advocates of the Neoclassical Synthesis recognize that, theoretically, the flexibility of prices and wages allows full employment to be achieved. The Keynesian theory can thus be considered as a special case of the neoclassical approach that applies when prices and wages are rigid.

This conclusion is based on the assumption that, in the monetary economy described by Keynes, there will always be a positive value of the interest rate at which enterprises will generate a flow of investments consistent with full employment. Keynes himself seems to accept this hypothesis when he argues that the liquidity preference theory explains the reasons why the interest rate 'does not automatically fall to the appropriate rate' (Keynes 1936 [2013a], p. 31). Keynes acknowledges that there is an 'appropriate' value of the rate of interest at which the amount of goods produced by employing the entire available workforce will be demanded. Starting with Dillard's interpretation (1948), this definition of the role of the liquidity preference theory characterizes a common interpretation of Keynes's principle of effective demand. For example, Rogers wrote:

> In its most general form the principle of effective demand demonstrates that the rate of interest sets a limit to the profitable expansion of output before full employment is achieved. Keynes also argued in the *General Theory* that there was no mechanism in a *laissez faire* monetary economy for automatically generating the natural rate of interest consistent with full employment. […] Keynes makes it clear that the failure of the rate of interest to automatically

fall to the level consistent with full employment is to be a key element of his analysis. (Rogers 2008, pp. 2–8; see also Dillard 1987 and Rogers 1997a, 1997b)

This hypothesis can undermine the critical content of Keynes's theoretical approach, as it leads to the conclusion that the problem of involuntary unemployment can be easily solved by eliminating the gap between the interest rate level that balances the demand and supply of money and the level that is consistent with full employment. Kurz (2013) describes Sraffa's doubts about the relevance of the liquidity preference theory as follows:

> Sraffa … was critical of [Keynes's] explanation of why liquidity preference was to prevent the money rate of interest from falling sufficiently not only in the short run, but also in the long run … Keynes's liquidity preference – which Sraffa called 'Keynes's system' – could not bear the brunt of the explanation of a downward rigidity of the interest rate. Yet if the interest rate was flexible and if investment was sufficiently elastic with respect to the rate of interest, there was no reason to presume that investment could not gravitate toward a level equal to full employment saving. According to Sraffa … Keynes's argument suffers in particular from neglecting the implications of flexible prices via the value of money for the level of the 'own rate of money interest'. (Kurz 2013, pp. 67–68)

The assumption that there exists a positive value of the interest rate at which full employment is achieved is certainly valid in a corn economy, where production decisions determine the level of income and saving decisions precede and influence investment decisions. In such an economy, the rate of interest is the price determined on the capital market by the intersection of supply and demand for loanable funds. In this case, it is appropriate to assume that entrepreneurs will be willing to pay a positive interest to savers because, thanks to the productivity of the land or to the use of spades and ploughs, they are sure that they will obtain a quantity of corn exceeding the amount that was invested initially.

However, this hypothesis does not hold in the monetary economy described in the previous pages. In a monetary economy, the existence of a flow of investments consistent with full employment of the available workforce depends on two conditions: 1) the presence of a sufficiently high number of entrepreneur-innovators who, guided by their animal spirits, are willing to make exactly that amount of investments; and 2) the willingness of banks to finance the investment projects proposed by the entrepreneurs-innovators. Fulfilling these conditions does not depend on a particular level of interest rate achieved. In other words, even a rate of interest equal to zero may not be sufficient to achieve a situation of full employment.

In a monetary economy, the rate of interest is a monetary phenomenon determined by the banking system, which can assume any value greater than or equal to zero. However, even a rate of interest equal to zero may not be sufficient to ensure full employment of the available workforce. In fact, given the level of the rate of interest set by the banking system, the flow of investments depends on the animal spirits of entrepreneurs willing to carry out innovative projects. If these entrepreneurs did not exist, unemployment would emerge even if the rate of interest were equal to zero.

Once again, let us take the example of a system in which the available workforce amounts to 1400 workers, whose productivity is equal to 10 quintals of corn per unit of time, and whose real wage amounts to 5 quintals of corn. As was discussed earlier, achieving full employment requires an amount of investments involving the employment of 700 workers. In the absence of entrepreneurs driven by their animal spirits to plan the construction of a railway or to develop similar innovations, even a rate of interest equal to zero may not be enough to ensure a flow of investments consistent with full employment.

It should be added that, given the interest rate level set by the banking system, the presence of entrepreneurs-innovators willing to create a flow of investments consistent with the employment of the available workforce is not a sufficient condition to achieve full employment. Let us suppose that, at the interest rate set by the central bank and by the banking system, for example 5 per cent, entrepreneurs-innovators wish to make a volume of investments that requires 700 workers to be employed. This is a necessary but not a sufficient condition to reach a full employment equilibrium. In fact, what is needed to achieve this goal is banks willing to finance the entrepreneurs-innovators' projects, but there is no guarantee that any bank will be willing to do so, since in a monetary economy banks are not mere intermediaries lending out resources previously collected (in kind) from savers. In fact, banks finance investments by creating new money and, similarly to the entrepreneurs-innovators, they must take their decisions under conditions of uncertainty. Thus, their evaluations of the investment projects' quality might be profoundly different from those made by the entrepreneurs. For example, they may judge an entrepreneur planning to build a railway to be an eccentric individual whose investment project has no chance of success. In this case, the innovative investments in point will not be made and the system will not reach a situation where the entire available workforce is employed.

In a monetary economy, investments and savings are determined in two separate logical steps. First, enterprises make their investments thanks to the money obtained from banks. Second, from a logical standpoint, the change in income generates an equivalent flow of savings. In fact, the construction of a railway does not depend on the corn producers' decision to lend the corn they previously saved to the entrepreneur who decided to build the railway. On the contrary, the construction of a railway depends on the funds granted by banks, which lend newly created money. The rate of interest is not determined by saving and investment decisions, as there are no ex-ante savings that, in equilibrium, match ex-ante investments. The rate of interest is a purely monetary phenomenon, that is, a phenomenon determined by the banking system.

In most cases, economists have neglected this part of Keynes's analysis. The process of removal of Keynes's thought was completed at the beginning of the 1970s, when the phenomenon of stagflation led economists to question the validity of the theoretical framework of the Neoclassical Synthesis. In those years, Milton Friedman and Robert Lucas developed a profound criticism of the version of Keynes's model of the Synthesis based on the Phillips curve. Friedman and Lucas showed that Keynesian policies aimed at stimulating the aggregate demand can produce real effects on the levels of income and employment only in the short term, if wages and prices do not react immediately to market imbalances because they are 'sticky', or if the economic agents are deceived by the monetary policy decisions taken by the central bank. Thus, the principle of effective demand can work in the short term, but in the long run, when prices and wages will finally adjust, Keynesian policies will be ineffective and Say's Law will rule the workings of the economic system. In other words, in the long run income and employment are determined only by market forces. This is why mainstream economists consider the long-term levels of income and employment as 'natural'.

These conclusions are at the core of New Classical Macroeconomics, and they are the cornerstone of the *Dynamic Stochastic General Equilibrium Models* (DSGE), which are the modern formulation of the basic features of the Neoclassical Synthesis. This version of the mainstream theory is subject to the same limitations as the Neoclassical Synthesis, for it is based on the assumption that there exists an 'appropriate' level of the interest rate that can be achieved when prices and wages are flexible.

2. THE CRISIS AND THE LIMITS OF KEYNESIAN POLICIES: KALECKI AND MINSKY

The second point that characterizes a monetary theory of production is the impossibility of achieving a permanent state of full employment through traditional Keynesian policies. This is the message of Kalecki and Minsky. Kalecki pointed out that the pursuit of full employment through expansionary fiscal policies may be hampered by the fears of entrepreneurs about the political consequences of full employment. Minsky, in turn, remarked that it is during 'tranquil' periods characterized by full employment and price stability that the conditions that can potentially cause a crisis usually develop. Minsky elaborated his thesis that stability generates instability by explicitly considering the funding mechanism of production decisions based on the creation of bank money and by recognizing the importance of the presence of speculative markets.

2.1 Kalecki and the Political Aspects of Full Employment

Kalecki argues that there may be strong resistance to the use of monetary and fiscal policies to achieve full employment. To explain the origin of this resistance, Kalecki emphasizes that capitalist economies do not consist of homogeneous individuals who, through the pursuit of their own interests, led by the action of an 'invisible hand', unconsciously realize a shared ideal of the common good. On the contrary, monetary economies are characterized by the emergence of different social groups, such as entrepreneurs, bankers and wealth owners, which express inter-ests and pursue objectives that do not necessarily match those of wage earners. According to Kalecki, the major obstacle to the employment of the entire available workforce is the resistance of entrepreneurs con-cerned about the social and political changes that might arise once full employment is achieved and maintained over time:

> the *maintenance* of full employment would cause social and political changes which would give a new impetus to the opposition of the business leaders. Indeed, under a regime of permanent full employment, the 'sack' would cease to play its role as a disciplinary measure. The social position of the boss would be undermined, and the self-assurance and class-consciousness of the working class would grow. Strikes for wage increases and improvements in conditions of work would create political tension. It is true that profits would be higher under a regime of full employment. […] But 'discipline in the factories' and 'political stability' are more appreciated than profits by business leaders. Their class instinct tells them that lasting full employment is unsound

from their point of view, and that unemployment is an integral part of the 'normal' capitalist system. (Kalecki 1943 [1990], p. 326)

Kalecki emphasizes that the combination of full employment and political democracy generates alarm among entrepreneurs and businessmen. He illustrates this thesis by stressing that the objections raised by capitalists to the maintenance of full employment can be overcome if a non-democratic government takes over, as was the case with Fascism and Nazism:

> One of the important functions of fascism, as typified by the Nazi system, was to remove capitalist objections to full employment. The dislike of government spending policy as such is overcome under fascism by the fact that the state machinery is under the direct control of a partnership of big business with fascism. The necessity for the myth of 'sound finance', which served to prevent the government from offsetting a confidence crisis by spending, is removed. In a democracy, one does not know what the next government will be like. Under fascism there is no next government [...] 'discipline in the factories' and 'political stability' under full employment are maintained by the 'new order', which ranges from the suppression of the trade unions to the concentration camp. Political pressure replaces the economic pressure of unemployment. (Kalecki 1943 [1990], pp. 326–327)

Kalecki concludes that democratic regimes will be characterized by significant fluctuations in income and employment, and governments will react to depressions but they will not be able to pursue stable full employment conditions:

> In the slump, either under the pressure of the masses, or even without it, public investment financed by borrowing will be undertaken to prevent large-scale unemployment. But if attempts are made to apply this method in order to maintain the high level of employment reached in the subsequent boom, strong opposition by business leaders is likely to be encountered. ... [T]he workers would 'get out of hand' and the 'captains of industry' would be anxious to 'teach them a lesson'. (Kalecki 1943 [1990], p. 329)

2.2   Minsky and the Neoclassical Synthesis

In the 1970s, the long phase of economic development characterized by high growth rates and low inflation, which began with the end of the Second World War, came to an end. The most remarkable phenomenon that emerged in this period was stagflation, that is, a combination of stagnant incomes and high inflation that seemed inconsistent with the theoretical framework of the Neoclassical Synthesis. Economists reacted to this new situation in two ways. The first type of reaction originated from Milton Friedman's criticism and led to the final abandonment of Keynesian principles and to the triumph of New Classical Macro-economics. The second type of reaction was that represented by Hyman Minsky's elaborations. Minsky too believed that the crisis of the 1970s had shed light on the limitations of the Neoclassical Synthesis. However, unlike Friedman, he saw the crisis as an opportunity to revive the most innovative aspects of Keynes's analysis that had been overlooked by the traditional theory.[6]

According to Minsky, the fundamental limitation of the Neoclassical Synthesis lay in its failure to recognize the relationship between money and economic crises, which can be defined by explaining the financial structure of capitalist economies.[7] Minsky argues that the crisis of the 1970s was an opportunity to replace the orthodox paradigm with a new theoretical framework in which the endogenous nature of economic crises could be fully recognized, which would hence lead to the final accomplishment of the Keynesian revolution:

> The view that instability is the result of the internal processes of a capitalist economy stands in sharp contrast to neoclassical theory, whether Keynesian or monetarist, which holds that instability is due to events that are outside the workings of the economy. (Minsky 1986a, p. 114)[8]

Two fundamental points in Minsky's work allow us to complete the description of the relationship between money and economic crises outlined in this chapter. First, Minsky emphasized the importance of what he called the stage of 'debt validation', that is, the time by which the credit and debit contracts entered into in order to finance investment decisions must be settled. Secondly, he underlined that, in a capitalist economy, the policies advocated by the supporters of the Neoclassical Synthesis would not allow the achievement or maintenance over time of a steady state characterized by high incomes and full employment because 'tranquil' periods generate the conditions that lead to an economic crisis.

2.3 Minsky and the Process of Debt Validation

As was previously discussed, in a monetary economy the presence of a developed financial system is the necessary condition in order for investments to be made, which will introduce innovations that are vital for the development of the economic system. However, the financial system is also an element of structural fragility in capitalist economies because it may trigger profound economic crises due to insufficient investments and debtors' insolvency. In fact, the credit and debit contracts entered into in order to finance investments may result in the borrowers' default. This may seem a trivial observation: entrepreneurs may be unable to repay their loans and go bankrupt. In this regard, it is worth reiterating what was anticipated in the third chapter, namely that the macroeconomic models developed since the 1970s completely neglect credit and debit relationships as they implicitly assume that borrowers will always be able to repay their loans. Thus, the debtors' default is considered as a totally irrelevant phenomenon in the mainstream theoretical framework.

The assumption that debtors are always able to fulfil their commitments may apply to a corn economy, but it is completely unjustified in a monetary economy, that is, an economy where investments with the characteristics of Schumpeter's innovations are made under conditions of uncertainty. In fact, entrepreneurs-innovators may be insolvent if their investment projects fail and they do not obtain enough monetary revenues to pay back their creditors. Minsky highlights this aspect of a monetary economy by introducing the concept of debt validation: 'A debt is validated when maturing commitments to pay are fulfilled' (Minsky1982, p. 34).

Specifying the debt validation phase allows Minsky to emphasize that, in a monetary economy, the time dimension differs from that of a corn economy. In the latter, the time dimension is the interval between the time of sowing and the time of harvest. The productive cycles are always the same and the loans obtained at the time of sowing are paid back at the time of harvest. Thus, the concepts of past, present and future do not matter in a corn economy. Minsky shows that, in a monetary economy, due to the financial relationships that must be established in order to obtain the necessary investments, the concepts of past, present and future become important. According to Minsky (1982, p. 18), '[o]ur economy has a past, which is present today in maturing payment commitments, and a future, which is present today in debts that are being created'. Therefore, the present is characterized by two distinct financial transactions: the validation of debts incurred in the past, and the provision of additional loans for new investments. Minsky points out that these financial transactions are closely interconnected.

First, he notes that the entrepreneurs' ability to repay the loans obtained in the past depends on the amount of profits earned in the present. Minsky then specifies the factors that determine the amount of current profits. Relying on an important contribution by Kalecki, he emphasizes that current profits depend on the investments made in the present based on the expectations that drive entrepreneurs-innovators to incur new debts in order to earn future profits.[9] In other words, Minsky shows that the ability of enterprises to validate debts incurred in the past depends on the amount of investments made in the present by means of new loans obtained from the banking system. Therefore, the validation of the financial structure depends on the existence of entrepreneurs willing to borrow in the present and of banks willing to extend credit by creating new money.

This conclusion can be illustrated with the same example used to describe the characteristics of a monetary economy. In this economy, there are two different categories of entrepreneurs: those producing the wage-goods demanded by workers, which we assume to be corn, and those introducing innovations such as, for example, the construction of a railway. The available workers will be employed partly for the production of corn and partly for the construction of the railway. Let us suppose that the wages are entirely spent on purchasing corn. This means that the workers employed by the farmers will have to produce a quantity of corn that can satisfy not only their own demand but also the demand of workers employed for the construction of the railway. During the construction of the railway, the entrepreneurs-innovators do not realize any profit – hence the only profits are those obtained by farmers. These profits amount to the difference between the value of corn produced and then sold and the value of wages paid to the agricultural workers. Since the total value of the farmers' sales' proceeds is the sum of the wages of the agricultural workers and those of the workers employed in the construction of the railway, the total amount of profits realized by the farmers equals the value of the wages paid to the workers employed for the construction of the railway, that is, the investment value.[10]

The numeric example used earlier may help to clarify these relationships. Let us assume that the productivity of each agricultural worker is still equal to 10 quintals of corn per unit of time, that the price of a quintal of corn amounts to one unit of money, and that the wage of a worker is equal to 5 units of money, which allows each worker to purchase 5 quintals of corn. Let us also assume that 700 workers are employed for the production of corn and that the remaining 700 workers are employed for the construction of a railway. Overall, workers will demand 7000 quintals of corn (5 quintals of corn per 1400 workers), which, in nominal terms, correspond to 7000 units of money. The farmers' profit amounts to the difference between the sales proceeds, that is, 7000 units of money, and the costs incurred, which consist in the wages paid to the 700 agricultural workers, that is, 3500 units of money. Therefore, the farmers' total profit amounts to 3500 units of money, which equals the wages paid to the workers employed for the construction of the railway, or, in other terms, the volume of investments made during the period. This example not only shows the equivalence between profits and investments, but it also clarifies the nature of their causal relationship: the investments made by the entrepreneurs-innovators thanks to the funds obtained from the financial system determine the amount of profits achieved by the farmers.

Of course, the fact that the flow of profits depends on the volume of investments does not mean that an entrepreneur who decides to make an investment will automatically obtain the profits needed to validate his debts. The aforementioned example only shows that the profits corresponding to the investments made for the construction of the railway are realized by the farmers. These profits allow the farmers to pay back the loans they obtained in the past, for example to make the investments that enabled them to increase the productivity of the agricultural workers, and thus to produce a sufficient quantity of corn to meet the demand for corn expressed by the entire workforce by employing only a fraction of it.

The entrepreneurs-innovators who build the railway will be able to repay their debts if, at the time the railway is completed, they have earned sufficient profits. Future profits are a function of the amount of investments made after the construction of the railway. These investments will allow the employment of those workers who are no longer needed to build the railway. However, this condition is not sufficient to guarantee that the entrepreneurs-innovators will earn enough profits to validate their debts. To do this, someone must purchase the train tickets sold once the railway is finished. This could be true, for example, if train tickets also became wage-goods, and thus if the workers' wages increased to a point where they would be able not only to buy corn but also to travel by train.

Minsky also remarks that the presence of the public sector makes the validation of the debts of the entrepreneurs-innovators much easier. In fact, once the construction of the railway is completed, the level of employment could be kept high if the state hired workers for the production of public services. The impact of public debt on the profits of entrepreneurs is similar to that which would occur in the case of an investment expansion. In a monetary economy, public deficits have a two-fold effect, since they affect both the level of employment and the level of corporate profits, and thus the ability of businesses to validate their debts.

2.4 Minsky and the Endogenous Nature of Economic Crises

Even though Minsky emphasizes the dual role of deficit spending, he does not believe that a capitalist economy can be steered towards a stable equilibrium characterized by the employment of the entire available workforce and by stability in the general price level. Indeed, Minsky argues that a monetary economy is structurally doomed to experience an alternation between periods of boom and periods of crisis, and that the intrinsic instability of capitalist systems is basically linked to the financial structure of monetary economies:

> [T]he primary policy message of Keynes – that slumps are unnecessary and a waste of both human and nonhuman resources – has become a fundamental political axiom guiding economic policy. […] However, this victory for Keynes's policy objectives and activist policy posture obscures the fact that implicit in his analysis is a view that a capitalist economy is fundamentally flawed. This flaw exists because the financial system necessary for capitalist vitality and vigor – which translates entrepreneurial animal spirits into effective demand for investment – contains the potential for runaway expansion, powered by an investment boom. This runaway expansion is brought to a halt because accumulated financial changes render the financial system fragile, so that not unusual changes can trigger serious financial difficulties. Because Keynes arrived at his views on how a capitalist economy operates by examining problems of decision-making under conditions of intractable uncertainty, in his system stability, even if it is the result of policy, is destabilizing. (Minsky 1975, pp. 11–12)

Minsky points out that in 'tranquil' periods businesses gain profits that enable them to validate their debts. These positive results may lead enterprises and banks to underestimate the risks of default and to take on riskier positions. Moreover, the financial system can accelerate the onset of a booming period by introducing financial innovations that drive entrepreneurs to expand their investments.[11] The transition from a state of 'tranquility' to a booming period is due to a change in the attitude of entrepreneurs and bankers. In fact, in 'tranquil' periods they tend to forget previous crises and take on a euphoric attitude, believing that the economy has entered a new era and scorning those who invite a more prudent approach.[12]

This shift from 'tranquil' to booming periods can be explained by referring to the relationship between bank money, investment decisions and uncertainty that was described in Chapters 5 and 6. In an economy where investments are made under conditions of uncertainty, it is possible to experience periods of euphoria when stories about the beginning of a new era for the economic life of humanity may appear to be credible. A key role in the transition to the booming phase is played not only by entrepreneurs and bankers, but also by the financial markets, in which shares and debt securities representing a significant part of households' wealth are continually exchanged. Euphoria, in fact, generates an increase in the stock price of companies involved in the investment projects that mark the transition to a new era. This may affect the behaviour of speculators whose goal is to make a profit by anticipating the 'psychology of the market'.

Speculative markets play an essential role in Minsky's analysis. Following Keynes's teaching on the distinction between 'enterprise' and 'speculation', Minsky remarks that, in a capitalist economy, speculation can prevail over enterprise. He uses the term 'money manager capitalism' to characterize an economic system in which the financial system's basic function is no longer to finance entrepreneurs' investment projects but to make short-term profits by means of speculative activities. Minsky underlines that in modern market economies the financial system is far from performing the function that Schumpeter identified by defining the bankers the 'ephors' of capitalism.[13]

The booming phase is bound to end up in a crisis for two fundamental reasons. First, because non-financial companies and financial companies are pushed to take increasingly risky positions by developing projects that would never have been financed in a 'tranquil' situation. Second, because the boom, being characterized by a situation of full employment, may trigger an increase in production costs due to an increase in wages. Moreover, during a boom phase, imbalances in the commodity markets may generate a further rise in production costs. These signals of growing tensions may lead enterprises to liquidate a portion of their assets in order to improve their weaker financial situation. Also speculators may be pushed to liquidate their assets in order to cash in their capital gains recorded during the boom phase. Central banks may react to these tensions by adopting restrictive monetary policies. A rush to liquidity by enterprises and speculators and a policy of high interest rates adopted by central banks can thus trigger the onset of a crisis.[14]

The experience of a crisis will drive entrepreneurs and banks to take a more prudent attitude and, as a result, the tensions on the labour market and on the financial and commodities markets will ease. Slowly, the economy will recover until a new period of 'tranquility' is reached, when the memory of the past crisis will fade away. The new period of calm will then nurture a new boom phase, which will lead to a new crisis.

3. CONCLUSIONS

This chapter has highlighted another distinctive feature that separates a monetary economy defined by the M–C–M' sequence from a real-exchange economy described by the traditional theory: a monetary economy is structurally unstable. As has been extensively discussed, the instability of a monetary economy can be explained by referring to the two relationships described in Chapters 5 and 6. The first is the relationship between bank money, investment decisions and uncertainty. The second is the relationship between wealth and saving decisions, which highlights the role of speculation.

Table 7.1 Real-exchange economy (C–M–C') and monetary economy (M–C–M')

Commodity–Money–Commodity'	Money–Commodity–Money'
Self-producers – agricultural economy	Industrial economy
Investment decisions – certainty	Investment decisions – uncertainty
Homogeneous individuals (irrelevance of the figure of the entrepreneur)	Heterogeneous individuals (entrepreneurs, workers, bankers and wealth owners)
Consumer sovereignty	Invalidity of the principle of consumer sovereignty
Satiety of needs	Insatiability of needs – scarcity of resources
Irrelevance of wealth and speculation	Wealth and speculation are relevant
Neutrality of money	Non-neutrality of money
Neutrality of finance	Non-neutrality of finance
Validity of Say's Law	Invalidity of Say's Law
Equal distribution of revenues	Unequal revenues – monetary nature of profits
Stability of the system – stationary state	Instability

These relationships allow us to conclude that in a monetary economy: 1) Say's Law does not hold; and 2) Keynesian policies aimed at stimulating aggregate demand are not sufficient to achieve a permanent condition of full employment. Table 7.1 summarizes the differences between the structure of a monetary economy and the structure of a corn economy.

NOTES

1. As is well known, Schumpeter gave a negative judgement on Keynes's *General Theory*, especially with regard to what he considers to be a static theoretical framework of the book: 'reasoning on the assumption that variations in output are uniquely related to variations in employment imposes the further assumption that all production functions remain invariant. Now the outstanding feature of capitalism is that they do not but that, on the contrary, they are being incessantly revolutionized. The capitalist process is essentially a process of change of the type which is being assumed away in this book, and all its characteristic phenomena and problems arise from the fact that it is such a process. A theory that postulates invariance of production functions ... is the theory of another world and out of all contact with modern industrial fact, unemployment included' (Schumpeter 1936, p. 794). Schumpeter's criticism seems excessive because, as was discussed in the previous pages, the investments described by Keynes are similar to Schumpeter's innovations.
2. According to Keynes, the conclusions of Say's Law 'may have been applied to the kind of economy in which we actually live by false analogy from some kind of non-exchange Robinson Crusoe economy, in which the income which individuals consume or retain as a result of their productive activity is, actually and exclusively, the output *in specie* of that activity' (Keynes 1936 [2013a], p. 20).
3. 'The explanation of how output which would be produced in a [real-exchange] economy may be "unprofitable" in [a monetary] economy, is to be found in what we may call, for short, *the fluctuations of effective demand*. ... In a [real-exchange] economy ... effective demand cannot fluctuate; and it can be neglected in considering the factors which determine the volume of employment. But in [a monetary] economy the fluctuations of effective demand may be the dominating factor in determining the volume of employment' (Keynes 1933b [2013g], p. 80).
4. Keynes holds classical economists responsible for continuing to apply Say's Law also to an economy based on the use of money, and for the '[c]onviction ... that money makes no real difference except frictionally and that the theory of production and employment can be worked out ... as being based on "real" exchanges with money introduced perfunctorily in a later chapter. ... Contemporary thought is still deeply steeped in the notion that if people do not spend their money in one way they will spend it in another' (Keynes 1936 [2013a], pp. 19–20).
5. 'It follows that in a given situation of technique, resources and factor cost per unit of employment, the amount of employment, both in each individual firm and industry and in the aggregate, depends on the amount of the proceeds which the entrepreneurs expect to receive from the corresponding output' (Keynes 1936 [2013a], p. 24).
6. '[T]he world is now performing in ways that can be interpreted as anomalous from the point of view of the current standard theory. In these circumstances a radical reformulation of economic theory, such as Keynes attempted, once again seems attractive. The synthesis of classical formulations and Keynesian constructs that Professor Joan Robinson has characterized as Bastard Keynesianism seems to be dissolving' (Minsky 1975, p. 18).
7. 'Keynes's explanation of the performance of a capitalist economy emphasized investment, the way in which investment is financed, and the effects of financial commitments. [...] Keynes's investment theory of business cycles and his financial theory of investment in the face of uncertainty were lost as the standard interpretation of Keynes's General Theory evolved into today's orthodox theory. What had started as an inspired flash of understanding into basic relations guiding our economy was reduced by the interpreting economists who followed into a banal set of prescriptions for guiding aggregate output' (Minsky 1986a, p. 133). Minsky, who was heavily indebted also to Schumpeter, as he had been one of his PhD students, stressed the opportunity to elaborate a synthesis between Keynes's and Schumpeter's analyses. On this subject see Minsky (1986b, 1993).
8. 'The conclusion to our argument is that the missing step in the standard Keynesian theory was the explicit consideration of capitalist finance within a cyclical and speculative

context. Once capitalist finance is introduced and the development of cash flows […] during the various states of the economy is explicitly examined, then the full power of the revolutionary insights and the alternative frame of analysis that Keynes developed becomes evident' (Minsky 1975, p. 129).

9. 'Profits are critical in a capitalist economy because they are a cash flow which enables business to validate debt *and* because anticipated profits are the lure that induces current and future investment. It is anticipated profits which enable business to issue debts to finance investment and positions in capital assets. Any theory that aims to explain how an investing capitalist economy works must focus upon the determination of total profits' (Minsky 1982, pp. 34–35).

10. 'Thus, profits in consumer goods equals wages in investment goods' (Minsky 1986a, p. 163).

11. 'Whenever full employment is achieved and sustained, businessmen and bankers, heartened by success, tend to accept larger doses of debt-financing. During periods of tranquil expansion, profit-seeking financial institutions invent and reinvent "new" forms of money, substitutes for money in portfolios, and financing techniques for various types of activity: financial innovation is a characteristic of our economy in good times. Each new type of money that is introduced or an old one that is used to a greater extent results in the financing of either some additional demand for capital and financial assets or of more investment. This results in a higher price of assets. Financial innovation therefore tends to induce capital gains, to increase investment, and to increase profits: the economy will try to expand beyond any tranquil full-employment state' (Minsky 1986a, p. 199).

12. '[S]uccess breeds a disregard of the possibility of failure; the absence of serious financial difficulties over a substantial period leads to the development of a euphoric economy in which increasing short-term financing of long positions becomes a normal way of life. As a previous financial crisis recedes in time, it is quite natural for central bankers, government officials, bankers, businessmen, and even economists to believe that a new era has arrived. Cassandra-like warnings that nothing basic has changed, that there is a financial breaking point that will lead to a deep depression, are naturally ignored in these circumstances' (Minsky 1986a, p. 237).

13. See Minsky (1992–93, 1993, 1996), Whalen (2001), Crotty (2011), Wray (2011, 2013, 2016) and Roncaglia (2013).

14. 'A boom once started lives a precarious life. It depends upon realization of optimistic expectations about yields, so that capital gains accrue to investors in debts and shares as well as to investors in capital assets. From a multitude of possible causes – rising wages or production costs, feedbacks from rising interest rates to the value of older long-term debt, the high cost of refunding previous debt – a large number of units can be forced to try to raise cash at the same time by taking advantage of the liquidity that some of their assets are presumed to have, that is, by attempting to sell "liquid" assets. Furthermore, for some units the burden of debt in the form of cash commitments can become so large that they are forced to sell or pledge capital assets to acquire cash to meet debt commitments. This can happen to ordinary firms and to financial organizations' (Minsky 1975, p. 115).

APPENDIX   THE PRINCIPLE OF EFFECTIVE DEMAND: A SIMPLE MODEL

The relationships underlying the principle of effective demand can be described by a simple linear model. We assume that the available workforce amounts to 1400 workers and that the workers spend all their wages on purchasing corn. The money wage (w) is equal to 5 units of money, while the price of a quintal of corn (P) equals one unit of money. We also assume that the productivity of each worker employed in the production of corn (A) is constant and equal to 10 quintals. In the previous chapters we have underlined that, in a monetary economy, investments have the characteristics of Schumpeterian innovations. Following Schumpeter, we suppose that innovations are realized by employing work as the only factor of production. Thus, the value of investments corresponds to the wages paid to the workers employed to carry out the innovations, for example the wages earned by the workers employed in the construction of a railway.[1]

Hence, there are two groups of workers: agricultural workers, who produce the wage-goods, and workers employed in the implementation of innovations. For the sake of simplicity, let us further assume that neither the farmers nor the entrepreneurs-innovators demand corn. The demand for corn will therefore match the overall amount of wages of the two groups of workers. Since only agricultural workers produce corn, the necessary condition to meet the overall corn demand is that the agricultural workers' productivity allows production of the quantity of corn demanded by the workers employed in the construction of the railway. However, although necessary, this condition is not sufficient. In fact, as the entrepreneurs-innovators do not produce corn, they cannot enter into a credit contract in which they undertake to return the corn borrowed from the farmers in real terms.

The credit agreement that enables the entrepreneurs-innovators to build the railway must therefore be defined in monetary terms. The entrepreneurs-innovators are committed to returning the amount of money to the subject, the banks, which can supply credit by creating money. The money obtained by the banks will be used by the entrepreneurs-innovators to pay the wages that the workers, employed in the construction of the railway, spend on purchasing corn. Without banks and bank money, no investment decisions can be undertaken. We identify income with Y. Since the price of a quintal of corn equals one unit of money, Y equally indicates the value of income in terms of quintals of corn or in terms of monetary units. Leaving aside the public sector and trade relationships with foreign countries, Y is the sum of consumption (C) and investments (I):

$$Y = C + I \tag{7A.1}$$

The amount of investments, which corresponds to the wages paid to the workers employed to realize the innovations, depends on two factors. The first is the presence of entrepreneurs-innovators who plan to undertake investments on the basis of their animal spirits (AS) and the interest rate level set by the banks (r^*). I_d indicates the amount of investments desired by the entrepreneurs-innovators. Hence:

$$I_d = f(AS, r^*) \tag{7A.2}$$

The second factor concerns the choices made by the banking system. As pointed out by Schumpeter, entrepreneurs can carry out their investment projects only if they borrow from banks. However, after fixing the interest rate level (r^*) bankers do not automatically accept all credit applications submitted by entrepreneurs, but only those that are deemed creditworthy. If we set the flow of credit created by the banks equal to L^*, we obtain:

$$I = L^* \leq I_d \tag{7A.3}$$

Equation 7A.3 shows that the level of investments allowed by credits granted by banks is usually lower than the level desired by businesses: in a monetary economy banks ration credit. The amount of consumption (C) corresponds to the monetary value of the corn consumed by the workers employed in the agricultural sector. Thus, consumption (C) is equal to the money wage (w) multiplied by the number of agricultural workers (N_{ag}), which, as shown in equation 7A.4, corresponds to the ratio between the corn produced (Y) and the productivity of each agricultural worker (A):

$$N_{ag} = \frac{Y}{A}. \tag{7A.4}$$

Consumption is defined by equation 7A.5:

$$C = wN_{ag} = \left(\frac{w}{A}\right)Y. \tag{7A.5}$$

The w/A ratio is less than 1, as the condition required to carry out the investments is that the agricultural workers' productivity (A) is higher than their money wage (*w*), that is, higher than the amount of corn consumed by each of them. By substituting equations 7A.3 and 7A.5 in equation 7A.1 we obtain:

$$Y = \frac{1}{\left(1 - \dfrac{w}{A}\right)} L^* . \tag{7A.6}$$

Income is a multiple of the value of the investments-innovations, which is equal to the flow of credit created by banks. Hence, the level of income depends on the value of investments and the value of the multiplier, which, in turn, depends on the value of the *w*/*A* ratio. The higher *w*/*A*, the greater the value of the multiplier. By dividing both sides of equation 7A.6 by the level of the money wage (*w*), we have:

$$\frac{Y}{w} = \frac{1}{\left(1 - \dfrac{w}{A}\right)} \frac{L^*}{w} . \tag{7A.7}$$

The *L**/*w* ratio identifies the number of workers employed by the entrepreneurs-innovators (N_i), while the *Y*/*w* ratio represents the total number of employed workers (*N*). The latter is equal to a multiple of the workers employed for the realization of innovations. If *w* is equal to 5 quintals of corn and *A* is equal to 10 quintals of corn, the value of the *w*/*A* ratio is 0.5, which means that each agricultural worker consumes half of the corn produced by his work. Thus, every worker employed in the agricultural sector realizes a surplus that is equal to his wage and to the wage of a worker employed in the construction of the railway. In this case, the value of the multiplier is 2, and the total number of employed workers (*N*) corresponds to twice the number of workers employed in the implementation of innovations. Hence, in order for the overall available workforce (1400 workers) to be employed, a number of investment projects requiring the employment of 700 workers must be implemented. If these investments are not made, there will not be full employment.

In a monetary economy, there are no mechanisms ensuring a flow of investments consistent with full employment. The flexibility of the interest rate is no guarantee that this result can actually be achieved. Indeed, not even an interest rate of zero may be sufficient to encourage employers to implement innovations. In addition, banks may not be willing to finance a flow of investments consistent with full employment.

The amount of investments needed to achieve full employment depends on the value of the w/A ratio. An increase in this ratio due, for example, to a rise in money wages implies an increase in the multiplier. For example, if w grew from 5 to 8, the value of the multiplier would be equal to 5. Thus, the employment of a new worker for the construction of the railway would cause an overall increase of 5 units of employment. In fact, the production of a quantity of corn corresponding to the wage paid to the new worker employed for the building of the railway requires employing four new agricultural workers. In the aggregate, full employment would be achieved if the implementation of new investment projects involved the employment of 280 workers.

These relationships highlight the essential role of money, which is not just a medium of exchange, but the element that shapes the structural features of an economic system. The concepts of income, investment, consumption, savings and profits can be defined only by making reference to money. Banks allow for the implementation of investments-innovations by creating new money, and investments then generate an equivalent flow of profits and savings. Suppose, for example, that the value of the multiplier is equal to 2 and that there are entrepreneurs willing to make investments requiring the employment of 700 workers. Since the money wage is equal to 5 units of money, they will need a loan of 3500 units of money. If the banks granted these loans, 700 new workers would be hired to build the railway. These workers will then use their wages to buy corn. To meet their demand for corn, farmers will have to hire another 700 workers who will produce an overall amount of 7000 quintals of corn. The sale of the 7000 quintals of corn will generate proceeds for 7000 units of money against a production cost of 3500 units of money, which corresponds to the total wages paid to the 700 agricultural workers. Thus, farmers would earn a profit equal to 3500 units of money, which equals their savings and the value of the investments made to build the railway by employing 700 workers.

The debit and credit relationships between banks and businesses determine not only the current level of income, but also the links between the past and the present and the present and the future that are characteristic of a monetary economy. The link between the past and the present is based on the debts undertaken by businesses in the past, which can be paid back with the profits made in the present. The link between the present and the future is defined by the debts undertaken in the present in order to finance innovations, which will have to be paid back in the future. Since current profits depend on the level of investments, we can note that, in the present, the ability of entrepreneurs to repay the loans obtained in the past depends on the presence of entrepreneurs-innovators and their animal spirits, and on the decisions made by the banking system.

The relationships that determine the current level of income and the link between the past, the present and the future are defined under conditions of uncertainty. The profits achieved in the present are uncertain because they depend on the entrepreneurs' investment decisions and on the choices of the banking system.[2] The future profits of the entrepreneur-innovator who builds the railway are also uncertain, as the level of the future demand for train tickets depends on a number of factors whose effects are not predictable in probabilistic terms. For example, the sale of train tickets depends on the level of wages and on the way the workers will choose to spend their wages. The construction of the railway will be a success, and will generate profits, if the level of the wages allows workers to add the purchase of train tickets to the purchase of corn.

The links between the past, the present and the future highlight two elements of fragility that characterize a monetary economy. First, it should be noted that an insufficient level of investments causes not only a low level of income and of employment, but also a low level of profits, which generates major difficulties in paying back the loans obtained in the past. The second element of fragility regards the process of wealth accumulation based on the relationship between savings and wealth decisions highlighted by Keynes, which was described in Chapter 6. The process of wealth accumulation generated by an ongoing flow of investments-innovations has determined the development of markets characterized by a continuous trade of financial instruments. These markets are a source of instability if, as Keynes pointed out, speculation overshadows enterprise.

Notes

1. This definition of investments differs from that which identifies investments with capital goods (such as spades and ploughs) used as means of production. The latter considers two productive sectors: a sector for the production of consumer goods and a sector for the production of capital goods. See, for example, Hein (2006, 2015) and Sardoni (2011).
2. As noted in Chapter 5, the farmers' production decisions are also taken under conditions of uncertainty. In fact, they take their decision on the employment of agricultural workers based on their expectations about the number of workers who will be hired to carry out the investments-innovations. Equation 7A.4, which specifies N_{ag}, should include the level of income expected by the farmers (Y^e) instead of the actual level of income (Y). For the sake of simplicity, the model was built by assuming that $Y^e = Y$.

PART III

The Endogenous Nature of the Crisis and the
Policies for a Good Life

8. The endogenous nature of the subprime crisis

> The alteration of institutions that has led to the reduction in the uncertainties of the physical environment has created the complex human environment which has produced a whole new (and in many cases still unresolved) set of uncertainties. The revolution in technology of the past several centuries has made possible a level of human well-being of unimaginable proportions as compared to the past, but it also has produced a world of interdependence and universal externalities, and in consequence a whole new set of uncertainties. The law merchant, patent laws, the institutional integration of distributed knowledge, the creation of a judicial system, have been important parts of efforts making markets more efficient in developed countries. And they are leading us into an unknown world of future uncertainties. (Douglass North 2005a, pp. 20–21)

The second part of this book presented a theoretical approach describing the underlying mechanisms of an economic system whose characteristics reflect those emerging from the explanations of the origins of the crisis elaborated by mainstream economists. The need to resort to the theories put forward by a group of heretical economists to analyse the functioning of this type of economy is justified by the limitations of the traditional theory. Our analysis shows a deep contradiction in the attitude taken by conservative economists. In fact, while they argue that the orthodox theoretical model should not undergo radical changes as a result of the current crisis, they also provide a series of explanations of the recent economic events that refer to a kind of economy that is profoundly different from that described by the orthodox theory.

This contradiction undermines the thesis whereby the current crisis is an accidental phenomenon, unrelated to the mechanisms that characterize a market economy, caused by the mistakes made by governments, the monetary authorities and the banking system. These explanations have no meaning whatsoever in the economic system described by the traditional theory where the monetary authorities control the quantity of money or the official interest rate with the aim of stabilizing the inflation rate, while banks simply gather the information they need for an optimal allocation of the saved resources. In such a context, one cannot plausibly assume that the monetary authorities are not able to determine the rate of change in the quantity of money or the value of the official interest rate that is consistent with price stability. Nor is it plausible to assume that banks do not know how to recognize good and bad borrowers.

This thesis whereby the crisis is the result of errors is not convincing even when it is applied to the monetary economy described by heretical economists. As was discussed in the second part of this book, in a monetary economy crises are endogenous phenomena. This chapter describes the elements that characterize the endogenous nature of the current crisis.

1. CHANGE AND INSTITUTIONS

The analysis presented in the second part of this book shows that a monetary economy is characterized by a process of change that does not result, either spontaneously or thanks to Keynesian policies, in an ideal state of full employment. Starting from Schumpeter's insights, Douglass North emphasized that institutions are another factor that influences the process of change in capitalist economies. North uses the term 'institutions' to indicate the set of formal and informal rules and sanctions that define the 'rules of the game' that influence the behaviour of the members of a community. This definition can be extended to include real entities such as money, central banks and enterprises.[1]

The importance of institutions depends on the characteristics of the economic system. In a corn economy, that is, the economy of a village made up of farmers and artisans, who are basically homogeneous individuals who have known each other forever, only few rules are needed to coordinate exchanges. Conversely, in a monetary economy, institutions are much more complex. As Rodrik (2011) pointed out, the functioning of such a system requires laws to define property rights, courts to ensure the execution of contracts, law enforcement officers to maintain public order, rules to protect workers and the environment, organizations that maintain financial stability, and social security systems to help those who are faced with economic difficulties.

North (2005a) points out that institutions are not born spontaneously through some sort of Darwinian process, but they are the result of decisions taken by individuals who actively play the game. In other words, institutions are the result of 'a deliberate process shaped by the perceptions of the actors about the consequences of their actions. The perceptions come from the beliefs of the players – the theories they have about the consequences of their actions – beliefs that are typically blended with their preferences'(North 2005a, p. viii). The actors or players are the organizations, that is, groups of individuals sharing common objectives.[2] The presence of organizations, that is, different social groups, is a distinctive feature of a monetary economy (or a capitalist economy), which is made up of heterogeneous subjects such as entrepreneurs, bankers, workers, wealth holders and rentiers.[3] Therefore, the process of change that characterizes a capitalist economy is affected by the institutions shaped by the 'dominant beliefs' (North 2005a, p. 2), that is, the beliefs of those organizations that manage to impose their own model of society.[4]

Conflicts of interest are an important component of a monetary economy. These include not only the conflicts dividing workers and entrepreneurs that are at the core of Marx's and Kalecki's analysis, but also those triggered by the introduction of innovations that jeopardize the interests of existing organizations. As Schumpeter (1912 [1949], pp. 86–87) observed, the entrepreneur-innovator must face the resistance of society against the introduction of elements that might disturb the existing equilibrium. A telling example of the conflicts arising from the introduction of innovations is that presented by Acemoglu and Robinson (2012). They remind us that in England, towards the end of the sixteenth century, William Lee invented a machine to process wool, but Queen Elizabeth refused to grant the patent because she was afraid of the economic and political consequences that would result from a rising unemployment due to this new technology.

North points out that the process of change driven by the introduction of Schumpeterian innovations and by institutions does not result in an ideal condition similar to the situation that Keynes imagined would be reached by his grandchildren. North develops this argument by distinguishing between ergodic systems, that is, static, and therefore timeless, systems, and non-ergodic systems subject to continuous changes and where the time dimension is relevant. North uses the concept of uncertainty to emphasize the non-ergodic nature of contemporary economies, and observes that the process of change triggered by Schumpeterian innovations and institutions generates new forms of uncertainty:

> The consequences of the evolving technology of warfare have, throughout history, produced societal changes that were not and could not have been predicted. At a more micro level, there is Schumpeter's insight about the creative destruction characteristics of innovation having continually produced unanticipated changes not only in the specific product being revolutionized but in its larger ramifications for societal change. [...] The alteration of institutions that has led to the reduction in the uncertainties of the physical environment has created the complex human environment which has produced a whole new ... set of uncertainties. The revolution in technology of the past

several centuries has made possible a level of human wellbeing of unimaginable proportions as compared to the past, but it also has produced a world of interdependence and universal externalities, and in consequence a whole new set of uncertainties. The law merchant, patent laws, the institutional integration of distributed knowledge, the creation of a judicial system, have been important parts of efforts making markets more efficient in developed countries. And they are leading us into an unknown world of future uncertainties. (North 2005a, pp. 20–21)

North's analysis allows us to point out that, over time, Keynes's monetary economy and Schumpeter's capitalist economy may take on different forms depending on the institutions that are an expression of the dominant beliefs. Recognizing that capitalism can take several forms over time allows us to single out two important aspects of economic crises. First, crises can be seen as the expression of the fragility of a particular form taken on by capitalism. Second, a crisis may mark the transition from one form of capitalism to another. Kotz defines these aspects of economic crises when he observes that:

> [c]apitalism [is] a system that evolves and changes over time. However, such change is not simply partial and gradual. While capitalism has retained certain fundamental defining features since its origin centuries ago, it has assumed a series of distinct institutional forms over time. Each form of capitalism has displayed internal coherence, with a set of economic and political institutions, as well as dominant ideas, that reinforce one another. Each form of capitalism has also persisted for a significant period of time, from a decade to several decades in duration. Transitions from one institutional form of capitalism to the next have been punctuated by crisis and restructuring. (Kotz 2015, pp. 2–3)

Under the influence of the Neoclassical Synthesis, between the late 1940s and the 1970s, a form of capitalism, which can be defined as *regulated capitalism*, developed as a result of a compromise among big business, organized workers and governments. The crisis of the 1970s favoured the emergence of a new form of capitalism, which can be defined as *neoliberal capitalism*, whose fragility, in turn, has been uncovered by the current crisis.[5]

It should be pointed out that recognizing the endogenous nature of economic crises does not mean that crises, like earthquakes, should be considered inevitable. This equivalence between economic crises and earthquakes has been frequently used by economists to defend themselves when criticized for their inability to anticipate the onset of the current crisis. This metaphor is not at all convincing because, while earthquakes are natural events, economic crises are the outcome of social dynamics. This has an important consequence. In fact, earthquakes are not only unpredictable but also inevitable, as the probability of their occurrence is completely independent of the theories developed by seismologists to explain their origin. This conclusion cannot be applied to economic crises. Economic crises are not inevitable and the probability of their occurrence is influenced by the theories elaborated by economists to explain the functioning of a market economy.[6] As remarked by Turner with regard to the Great Recession:

> This catastrophe was entirely self-inflicted and avoidable. It was not the result of war or political turmoil [...] Instead this was a crisis whose origins lay in the dealing rooms of London and New York, in a global financial system whose enormous personal rewards had been justified by the supposedly great economic benefits that financial innovation and increased financial activity were delivering. (Turner 2016, p. 2)

Since the early 1970s, economists have developed a theory whereby, in a market economy in which the price system is free to work without major obstacles, a catastrophic crisis cannot occur. The popularity of this theory has increased the probability that a crisis might actually occur, in two ways: it fostered behaviours and choices that ultimately created the conditions that caused the crisis, and led economists to neglect the signs of instability that emerged during the period of the so-called Great Moderation.[7]

2.   THE THEORETICAL ROOTS OF THE CURRENT CRISIS

2.1   The Counterrevolution of the 1970s

The crisis of the 1970s triggered two different reactions among economists. On the one hand, a small minority, represented by Hyman Minsky, considered the crisis an opportunity to revive the most innovative elements of the Keynesian theory that had been neglected by the Neoclassical Synthesis. On the other hand, the group of economists represented by Milton Friedman believed that the crisis was an opportunity to finally cut all ties with Keynes's legacy. In fact, Milton Friedman identified a theoretical gap in the model of the Neoclassical Synthesis based on the Phillips curve. He showed that, in the presence of high inflation rates and of workers who do not suffer from monetary illusion, traditional Keynesian policies cannot produce permanent effects on the levels of income and employment. If workers do not suffer from monetary illusion, employment and unemployment tend to reach their 'natural' levels, which are consistent with an equilibrium on the labour market.

Friedman first and then Lucas showed that the traditional Keynesian policies could not be used to increase employment beyond its 'natural' level at the cost of a constant inflation rate as indicated by the Phillips curve. In the long term, the level of employment inevitably tends to reach its natural value. Therefore, Friedman and Lucas presented a renewed version of the pre-Keynesian theory, which, like the older version, recognized the validity of Say's Law.

Friedman's and Lucas's criticism led economists to abandon any reference to the Keynesian theory. This reaction can be better understood by recalling that, when they accepted the Neoclassical Synthesis, economists had already forgotten the reasons why, despite the flexibility of prices and wages, a monetary economy cannot spontaneously achieve a full employment equilibrium. Economists were thus ready to accept the conclusion that the levels of income and employment depended exclusively on the workings of unfettered market forces. In fact, the specification of the conditions that made the traditional Keynesian policies ineffective did not lead economists to look for new and more effective instruments, but led them to conclude that the economy did not need any external intervention. In other words, economists assumed that if the medicine, that is, the Keynesian policies, was not effective, the disease, that is, involuntary unemployment, simply did not exist.

The monetarist counterrevolution allowed the expression of a belief system that was consistent with the interests of big businesses, which 'have perfected ways to use their profits to entrench their economic and political power. They herald the "free market" as they busily shape it to their advantage. They are the kingpins of the new economy, and average Americans are paying the price' (Reich 2015, p. 31).[8]

The collapse of Soviet communism facilitated the spreading of a story that praised the virtues of the free market and free trade. Amartya Sen's appeal that the collapse of the Soviet Union should prompt academics to look for solutions to the problems posed by the socialist criticism of capitalism, without fear of being labelled communists, went unheeded.[9] Starting from the 1980s, the institutions that reflected the dominant beliefs gave life to neoliberal capitalism, that is, a new form of capitalism based on the following pillars: 1) reduction of public spending and taxation; 2) financialization of the economic system; 3) hyper-globalization; 4) growing lack of job security; and 5) strong growth of inequality in the distribution of income and wealth.

The current crisis came as a huge surprise to economists, who had totally embraced Friedman's and Lucas's lessons. As discussed in the first part of this book, mainstream economists have tried to overcome the contradiction between theory and reality by considering the current crisis as an accidental phenomenon, alien to the normal functioning of a market economy. However, this crisis is a structural phenomenon because it is both an expression of the fragility of the form of capitalism that started to emerge in the 1980s and the result of the monetarist counterrevolution. The category of economists carries a heavy responsibility for the current crisis, since: 1) the monetarist counterrevolution provided the theoretical justification for choices and decisions that contributed to cause the crisis; and 2) the acceptance of a theoretical model that restated the fundamental principles of the pre-Keynesian theory led economists to underestimate the signs of instability that emerged during the years of the Great Moderation.

2.2 Neoliberal Capitalism: Blind Faith in Market Virtues

The triumph of the monetarist counterrevolution had two important consequences concerning the definition of the objectives of economic policy and the definition of the role of the public sector. As for economic policy, since the 1980s the only goal of economic policy has been to maintain the stability of the price level. Therefore, the objective of policy makers shifted from 'no more unemployment' to 'no more inflation'. This shift became apparent at the beginning of the 1980s, as the US monetary authorities gave absolute priority to achieving price stability. Following Wicksell's teachings, in late 1979 the newly appointed Chairman of the Federal Reserve, Paul Volcker, implemented a radical anti-inflation policy by means of a drastic rise in interest rates in the United States. The short-term real interest rate rose from the negative values of the second half of the 1970s to the highest positive level (more than 5 per cent) recorded since World War II. Between the end of the 1970s and the beginning of the 1980s, the restrictive monetary policy implemented by the Federal Reserve caused a severe recession that pushed the unemployment rate from 5 per cent in 1979 to almost 10 per cent in 1982. At the same time, the inflation rate fell from 13 per cent in 1980 to 3 per cent in 1982. The so-called 'Volcker experiment' put an end to the economic instability of the 1970s.

As regards the second consequence, the definition of the role of the public sector, we must remember that neoliberal ideas were the pillars of the economic programmes of the governments of Ronald Reagan in the United States and of Margaret Thatcher in Great Britain. The new course is well described by Ronald Reagan's famous words: 'In this present crisis, government is not the solution to our problem; government is the problem. … It is my intention to curb the size and influence of the Federal establishment' (Reagan quoted in Sachs 2011, p. 49).[10]

By accepting the monetarist counterrevolution, economists provided the theoretical justification for the deregulation of markets, especially financial markets, and the liberalization of goods and capital movements, which fed the phenomenon of speculation. The deregulation of financial markets and the liberalization of capital movements marked a clear detachment from the rules introduced after the great crash of 1929. In 1933, the United States Congress approved the Glass–Steagall Act, which introduced federal insurance on bank deposits to prevent the outbreak of financial crises due to bank runs by the depositors. Furthermore, commercial banks enjoying federal insurance on deposits were prevented from trading bonds and stocks on behalf of third parties or on their own to avoid the spread of speculative transactions. Bonds and stocks could only be traded by investment banks whose liabilities did not enjoy any form of insurance. The regulations introduced in the 1930s and 1940s ensured a long period of stability that lasted until the end of the 1960s. During this period, the bankers' job was considered to be a boring activity and was not paid handsomely (Admati and Hellwig 2013, p. 53).

However, after the marked increase in the inflation rate in the 1970s, things changed radically. When in the United States the inflation rate increased from an annual average of 2 per cent in the 1960s to an annual average of approximately 10 per cent in the 1970s, the situation of commercial banks and of savings banks became critical because they were not allowed to raise the level of the interest rates on deposits over the limits set by the regulations introduced in the 1930s. As a result, commercial banks had to face the competition of new financial institutions such as money market funds. Although their liabilities were substantially similar to bank deposits, these institutions could offer nominal interest rates that compensated for the sharp increase in the inflation rate.

The problems caused by inflation and the spread of neoliberal ideology pushed the American legislature to start a process of deregulation aimed at freeing banks from the constraints introduced by the Glass–Steagall Act. The cap on interest rates on bank deposits was removed, and in 1982, after the approval of the Garn–St Germain Act, savings banks were allowed to trade securities. From the 1980s, the differences between commercial and investment banks were progressively reduced, while the competition among financial institutions significantly increased. In 1999, the separation between the activities of commercial and investment banks was formally cancelled with the approval of the Gramm–Leach–Bliley

Act. The transformation of the banking system since the 1980s is a significant expression of the monetarist counterrevolution.

The spread of neoliberal ideology also explains the liberalization of capital movements that began after the suspension of the convertibility of the US dollar into gold and the collapse of the international monetary order established in Bretton Woods in 1944. Rodrik (2011) points out that economists in the 1970s believed that the benefits of the liberaliz- ation of capital movements exceeded the costs of a potential instability of the exchange rates. These benefits were specified with reference to the traditional concept of finance, which is based on the causal relationship between saving and investment decisions. The liberalization of capital movements would produce a more efficient use of globally saved resources, as the savings in surplus countries would be directed to the countries with the most profitable investment opportunities. In turn, the need to manage international capital flows was an important incentive for the spread of financial innovations, which culminated with the develop- ment of derivative securities.[11]

As mentioned previously, the traditional theory of finance completely ignores the phenomenon of speculation. Thus, mainstream economists believed that the deregulation of financial markets and the liberalization of capital movements would only produce positive effects, because an increase in the degree of competition would favour a more efficient functioning of the financial markets.[12] The link between market deregu- lation, greater competition and a substantial improvement in the workings of market mechanisms may be valid in non-speculative markets. In a monetary economy, however, financial innovations may generate instabil- ity and crises, because, as Keynes pointed out, speculation may prevail over enterprise.

This distinction allows the structural nature of the current crisis to be highlighted. A clear sign of the increase of the weight of speculation since the 1980s comes from the profound transformations of the banking system. As shown in the previous pages, both Schumpeter and Keynes underline the fundamental role played by the banking system in the process that generates innovations. In fact, it is the creation of new money by the banks that enables the entrepreneurs-innovators to intro- duce innovations. However, this is not the only activity carried out by the banks, as they can be faced with, or help to create, conditions that increase the attractiveness of speculative activities. The change of the rules of the game caused by the measures taken to eliminate the constraints on the working of financial markets imposed in the 1930s transformed the banking system into a homogeneous organism dominated by the presence of huge universal banks set up in the form of joint stock companies pursuing the exclusive goal of maximizing shareholders' value by means of speculation.[13]

The presence of speculation explains why the growing competition and spread of innovations have not caused a drop in profits and incomes in the financial sector as suggested by the traditional theory. An increased competition among mechanics in the second-hand car market described by Akerlof (1970) would have certainly caused a reduction of their income, but this did not happen with banks and bank managers. Mainstream economists have analysed the effects of the securitization of bank loans and the development of structured finance through the lens of a theoretical model describing a corn economy in which these factors represent a form of insurance. Think, for example, of contracts protecting lenders from the borrowers' risk of default due to poor harvests caused by bad weather. Orthodox economists have completely overlooked that, in the context of modern monetary economies, since the 1980s derivatives have been used mainly to carry out short-term speculative transactions.[14]

Several mainstream economists have recognized the link between deregulation and the current crisis. Gorton, for example, believes that the crisis that erupted in 2007 should be attributed to a lack of historical understanding among economists, as after the 1970s they failed to recognize the positive effects of the regulatory framework introduced in the 1930s, and the need to adapt those rules to the new situation created by the sharp increase in inflation rates.[15] Economists 'did not see the transformation of the financial system, the decline of traditional banking, the advent of loan sales, securitization, the rise of repo, the rise of institutional investors, and so on, all of which happened before [their] very eyes' (Gorton 2012, p. 203).

As discussed in Chapter 2, according to Rajan the current crisis was basically caused by an excessive amount of risk created by the bank managers, who sought to obtain large profits for the shareholders with the aim of obtaining high bonuses for themselves. Rajan uses the concept of speculation to clarify how bank managers have tried to increase their bonuses by creating an excessive amount of risk. Their decision to increase the supply of loans fuelled the demand for residential properties, which caused the surge of housing prices that encouraged the public to believe in the fairy tale of the beginning of a 'new era' in which real estate prices would never cease to grow. The spread of these expectations was a key element that spurred low-income households to borrow in order to purchase a house, as they hoped to meet their payment commitments thanks to an increase in the property value. Furthermore, the banking system contributed to worsening the effects of the crisis by accumulating a large amount of securitized loans. Rajan explained the behaviour of banks by referring to the concept of 'herd behaviour', a concept that is clearly derived from Keynes's analysis of speculation.

Admati and Hellwig also based their analysis on the concept of speculation. They underlined that the eruption of the crisis was favoured by bank managers' choice to increase bank profits by continuously increasing the level of leverage, that is, the ratio of total assets to shareholders' equity. A higher leverage amplifies the effects of both the positive and negative changes in the value of bank assets. In the years before the outbreak of the crisis, banks had achieved high profit margins by increasing their leverage.[16] However, they had also become very fragile and, as the mortgage market collapsed, their shareholders' equity was not sufficient to cover the losses.

3. REGULATED CAPITALISM, NEOLIBERAL CAPITALISM AND CRISES

The relationship between the theoretical counterrevolution that began in the 1970s, deregulation of the financial markets, liberalization of goods and capital movements, and the ever-increasing phenomenon of speculation shows that the current crisis is not independent of the theory developed by economists. Moreover, because of this theoretical model, economists have not understood the structural nature of the crisis of the 1970s, and have underestimated the signs of crisis that have accumulated since the 1980s.

3.1 Regulated Capitalism and the Crisis of the 1970s

As we have seen, the theoretical model that emerged from the monetarist counterrevolution states that, in a well-functioning market economy, catastrophic crises cannot occur. The adoption of this model has led mainstream economists to consider economic crises as exogenous phenomena caused by accidental factors that temporarily steered the economic system from a stable growth path. This conclusion applies not only to the current crisis, as shown in the first part of this book, but also to the stagflation of the 1970s. Bernanke (2004, 2013), for example, argues that the use of Keynesian models based on the Phillips curve led the Federal Reserve to make two major mistakes.[17] The first was to believe that monetary policy could lower the unemployment rate to 4 per cent, a value that is far below the 'natural' unemployment rate. The second was to underestimate the inflationary effects of the monetary policy. During the 1970s, these errors led the Federal Reserve to alternate expansionary policies aimed at sustaining the levels of income and employment with restrictive actions needed to reduce the inflation rate caused by the previous expansionary strategy. Thus, in Bernanke's view, the extreme volatility of the levels of income and inflation recorded in the 1970s was the result of the highly unstable conduct of monetary policy by the Federal Reserve (Bernanke 2013, p. 32).

This explanation has a significant limitation as Bernanke overlooks the fact that, during the 1950s and 1960s, the same theoretical model enabled the Federal Reserve to guarantee lower and more stable inflation rates and higher growth rates than those recorded in the years of the Great Moderation. Bernanke does not explain why the theoretical model that allowed the Federal Reserve to obtain significant results in the 1950s and 1960s had disastrous results in the 1970s. In other words, Bernanke does not explain why, during the 1970s, the Federal Reserve adopted monetary policies that put an end to a long period of price stability. It is actually unthinkable that the US monetary authorities had suddenly gone mad. The Federal Reserve's behaviour can best be understood by looking at the characteristics of a particular form of capitalism, the so-called 'regulated capitalism', that developed after the end of World War II.

This form of capitalism showed three distinctive elements. First, as Kotz pointed out, '[r]egulated capitalism had been the product of a coalition that emerged in the 1940s between two key groups in American society, big business and organized labor'(Kotz 2015, p. 46). This compromise gave rise to what Reich (2010) defines as a basic social bargain that created the conditions for the development of an industrial system that, for many years, produced goods of mass consumption, such as cars and household appliances, at relatively decreasing costs. Furthermore, because of this basic bargain, workers' wages increased as a function of the growth of labour productivity. Kotz (2015) maintains that the choices of big businesses were justified by two factors: 1) the fear of a new Great Depression; and 2) the aim of creating conditions that would limit workers' support for socialist and communist parties.

The second element was the active role played by the state. Because of the influence of Keynesian theory, public opinion recognized the positive impact of state intervention in the economy, which was not limited to the implementation of fiscal policies aimed at sustaining the level of aggregate demand. In fact, it was largely recognized that the state had also to provide public goods and to reduce income inequalities. The action of the state was an important element of the compromise between big businesses and trade unions, because, on the one hand, government spending supported private profits, and, on the other hand, it improved the workers' standards of living.

Finally, the third element was the international monetary system established with the Bretton Woods agreements of 1944. The Bretton Woods system was based on: 1) the use of the US dollar as the international means of payment; 2) the definition of a system of fixed exchange rates between the US dollar and the currencies of the other countries; and 3) the introduction of controls on international capital movements. Rodrik (2011, p. 69) considers the Bretton Woods agreements 'an amazing piece of institutional engineering'. The Bretton Woods system avoided the excesses of hyper-globalization by combining a moderate liberalization of trade with the adoption of capital controls that built a barrier, allowing national governments to pursue their own economic policy objectives.[18]

During the 1950s and 1960s, this model of economic development produced very positive results, ensuring Western industrialized countries unprecedented growth with low inflation rates. However, at the end of the 1960s worrying signs of crisis began to emerge as the system reached a state of substantially full employment. The stagflation of the 1970s marked the crisis of regulated capitalism. The origin of this crisis can be identified with the increasing conflict among the organizations within the nation states and the countries participating in the international community. Kalecki's considerations presented in the previous chapter help to explain the increasing conflict between big businesses and trade unions. In fact, at the end of the 1960s, with a situation of substantially full employment, rising conflicts were recorded on the labour markets, as evidenced by the significant increase in the number of hours of strikes in France, Italy, Germany, Great Britain and the United States (Glyn 2006).

At an international level, at the beginning of the 1970s the conflicts between oil-producing and oil-consuming countries became harsher. After the explosion of the Yom Kippur War in October 1973, oil prices increased four-fold in a few months. The abrupt rise of oil prices depended not only on political factors related to the instability of the Middle East, but also on economic factors linked to the sharp increase in the demand for oil caused by a long phase of high growth in the Western industrialized countries.

Also the crisis of the international monetary system can be interpreted as a result of a conflict between the internal policy objectives of the United States and the objectives pursued by the international community, which needed a sufficient amount of US dollars to finance international trade. The United States could fulfil this requirement by creating dollars to finance its trade deficits with foreign countries, as, unlike other countries, the US had the privilege of paying for imported goods with its national currency. This situation lasted until the countries in the rest of the world were willing to accumulate US dollars without requesting their conversion into gold. As doubts about the ability of the United States to convert dollars into gold began to spread, the US government was faced with two alternatives: 1) to change its policy in order to reduce the trade deficit, and thus the outflow of dollars towards the rest of the world; or 2) to suspend the convertibility of dollars into gold. The United States opted for the second solution and, in August 1971, President Nixon announced that the convertibility of US dollars into gold was suspended. This decision caused the collapse of the dollar–gold exchange standard, and marked the beginning of a period of great instability in exchange rates.

Bernanke's analysis completely ignores these structural changes, and assumes that the structure of the economic system in which we live is stable and does not undergo significant modifications over time. He closes his book on the relationship between the Federal Reserve and the financial crisis with a chart showing that, since 1900, the US economy has grown at a steady rate of 3 per cent in real terms. The only significant exceptions were the years of the Great Depression and the years following the financial crisis that erupted in 2007. Bernanke expressed his confidence about the fact that 'the US economy will return to a healthy annual growth rate somewhere in the 3 per cent range' (Bernanke 2013, p. 117).[19] By summarizing recent American economic history with this chart, he conveys the image of an economic system characterized by a substantially constant structure over time. Bernanke's position reflects the prevailing attitude among economists, which consists in considering the economic system as an immutable structure that can be described through models specifying a so-called 'natural' equilibrium. John Kenneth Galbraith (2004) remarked that the spread of this attitude has resulted in a modification of economists' language, as they replaced the term 'capitalism' with the more neutral expression 'market system' (see Bellamy Foster and McChesney 2012).

3.2 The Origin of the Crisis in the Years of the Great Moderation

The period that began in the mid-1980s and ended with the onset of the current crisis has been defined as the Great Moderation, as it was characterized by high stability in both the income growth rate and the inflation rate. The theoretical model developed with the monetarist counterrevolution induced economists to underestimate three signs of instability that emerged during the years of the Great Moderation:

1) financialization of the economic system; 2) hyper-globalization; and 3) a huge increase in inequality.

During the years of the Great Moderation, the most obvious signs of a process that might have ended in a devastating crisis involved the financial sector. In this regard, two significant phenomena can be identified. First, the financial system grew enormously compared with the growth of the economy as a whole. In fact, the ratio between the total value of financial instruments owned by wealth holders (stocks, public and private bonds, and bank deposits) and world GDP rose from 1.2 in 1980 to 4.4 in 2007 (Palma 2009, p. 833), while the ratio between total debt, net of shares, and world GDP increased from 1.7 in 1980 to 3.1 in 2010 (Cecchetti et al. 2011).

The second phenomenon was the increase in the share of the overall income generated by the financial sector. In the United States, the share of the value produced by the financial sector grew from 2 per cent in 1950 to 8 per cent in 2006 (Philippon 2008). In Great Britain, this share rose from 5 per cent in 1970 to 8 per cent in 2007 (Haldane et al. 2010). In a period of over 150 years, from 1856 to 2008, in Great Britain the value produced by the financial sector increased at an annual rate of 4.4 per cent versus an annual growth rate of the economy of 2.1 per cent. However, throughout this period the growth rate was not homogeneous. From 1856 to 1913, the value produced by the financial system increased very strongly, at an average annual rate of 7.6 per cent, while the average growth rate of GDP was 2 per cent. The sub-period from 1914 to 1970 featured a profound change. In fact, the annual average growth rate of the value produced by the financial sector fell to 1.5 per cent, below the annual average growth rate of GDP equal to 1.9 per cent. In the last sub-period, from 1970 to 2008, the annual average growth rate of the value produced by the financial system rose to 3.8 per cent versus an annual average growth rate of the economy of 2.1 per cent.

From the 1980s onwards, the sharp increase in the value generated by the financial system in industrialized countries caused a considerable rise in the rate of returns on capital and on labour in the financial sector. For example, in Great Britain the annual average return rate of the stocks of financial companies rose from 7 per cent in the period 1921–1961 to over 20 per cent in the period 1981–2007 (Haldane and Alessandri 2009). Since the 1980s, the average income of workers employed in the financial sector also increased significantly, well above the income earned by workers employed in other sectors (Philippon and Reshef 2007, 2009; Philippon 2008). Because of these high incomes, an increasing number of graduates from the most prestigious American universities chose to work in the financial sector. Goldin and Katz (2008) underline that, in 2008, 28 per cent of Harvard graduates went to work in the financial sector, while in the 1960s and 1970s this share was only 6 per cent. Oyer (2008) observes that, during the 1990s, the average income of Stanford graduates working in the financial sector was three times as high as the income earned by graduates working in other sectors.

There is a significant correlation between the increase in incomes earned by financial managers and the increasing inequalities in the distribution of income recorded since the 1980s.[20] Turner, for example, argues that 'the growth of a larger and highly remunerated financial sector has been – in both the United States and in the United Kingdom – a major cause of the overall increase in inequality' (Turner 2012, p. 38; see also Hein 2012).[21]

The growth in the relative size of the financial system and the increase in wages paid to the managers and employees of the financial sector should have captured the attention of mainstream economists, as they were inconsistent with the traditional theory of finance. In fact, the orthodox theory of finance states that the fundamental function of financial institutions is to facilitate the transfer of saved resources from savers to entrepreneurs because a direct relationship between creditors and borrowers is hindered by the presence of imperfect information. As was discussed in the third chapter, according to this approach banks play the same role as mechanics in the second-hand car market described by Akerlof (1970). The extraordinary growth in the income earned by financial operators since the 1980s cannot be explained by the traditional theory. If the role of bank managers were actually similar to that of the mechanics in Akerlof's example, their annual income of millions of euro earned since the 1980s could hardly be justified. If the mechanics had received salaries amounting to millions of euro, economists would have obviously been surprised and this would have captured their attention.

From the 1980s, several economists sent out alarm signals as they realized that the transformation of the financial system was making the economic system more fragile, thus creating the risk of a destructive crisis. None of them could accurately predict the timing of the crisis or the degree of its severity. However, by recognizing that a catastrophic event might actually occur, they distinguished themselves from mainstream economists who still saw the evolution of the financial system as a manifestation of its increased efficiency.

As was illustrated in the previous chapter, Hyman Minsky was the most prominent 'Cassandra', although his thinking was only appreciated ex post, after the crisis erupted. The second 'Cassandra' was James Tobin, who clearly expressed his unease vis-à-vis the continuous expansion of the financial system:

I confess an uneasy Physiocratic suspicion, perhaps unbecoming in an academic, that we are throwing more and more of our resources, including the cream of our youth, into financial activities remote from the production of goods and services, into activities that generate high private rewards disproportionate to their social productivity. I suspect that the immense power of the computer is being harnessed to this 'paper economy', not to do the same transactions more economically but to balloon the quantity and variety of financial exchanges. [...] I fear that, as Keynes saw even in his day, the advantages of the liquidity and negotiability of financial instruments come at the cost of facilitating nth-degree speculation which is short-sighted and inefficient. (Tobin 1984, p. 14)

A third author in this category is Susan Strange, who presented her analysis of the evolution of the financial system in two books significantly entitled *Casino Capitalism* (1986) and *Mad Money* (1998). In her later book, Strange identified two threats that endangered 'civilisation and the life chances of our children and grandchildren' (Strange 1998, p. 2). The first and worst threat concerned the environment, while the second, which Strange thought to be more immediate, was the potential collapse of the financial system, which might have caused a deep depression. Strange stressed that the two important financial crises of the 1980s and 1990s, namely the Wall Street crash of 1987 and the Asian financial crisis of 1997, proved that a devastating crisis such as that of 1928 might happen again.[22]

Finally, Andrew Glyn emphasized that the Asian financial crisis of 1997–1998 should have been regarded as an important warning signal of the fragility of the international financial system:

The genie of financial competition and expansion has been released by deregulation and financial innovation. Whilst the worst effects of the resulting financial fragility have been felt in the Asian countries hit by the crisis of 1997, it would be wrong to assume that the greater sophistication of financial markets in OECD countries insures them against financial problems. [...] The whole financial system can be threatened by the unrelenting search for 'value' through even more complex financial trades. (Glyn 2006, p. 152)

The inability of mainstream economists to see the warning signs concerning the evolution of the financial dimension of the economy during the years of the Great Moderation, which were instead captured by Minsky, Tobin, Strange and Glyn, is due to the limits of their theoretical model. The monetarist counterrevolution led economists to apply the analysis based on the law of supply and demand also to the financial markets.[23] The increase in the relative weight of the financial sector was justified by referring to the principle of sovereignty of the consumer-saver. Thus, it was seen as a result of the changing tastes and preferences of consumers-savers, who evidently had chosen to increase their demand for financial services. In other words, the presence of new financial instruments and new intermediaries was interpreted as the need to expand the range of financial services in order to meet savers' demand. Furthermore, the high incomes earned by financial managers and operators were considered to be the right reward for their contribution to the social product.[24]

Mainstream economists completely neglected the relationship between savings and wealth decisions that characterizes a monetary economy. While a corn economy is characterized by the causal relationship between saving and investment decisions, the crucial relationship in a monetary economy is that between saving decisions and the accumulation of wealth. In each period, in a monetary economy the increase in wealth equals the amount of savings. This is the first reason why, over time, the ratio between financial wealth and GDP has increased.[25] Neglecting the relationship between saving decisions and wealth accumulation led mainstream economists to underestimate the importance of the phenomenon of speculation.

Speculation allows us to introduce the second factor that explains the growth in the relative size of the financial sector, that is, the increased degree of intermediation and hence the higher weight of the exchanges taking place among financial intermediaries. In fact, over the last 30 years, in the United States and in advanced countries, the importance of institutional investors such as pension funds, insurance companies and investment funds has grown remarkably. At the same time, the share of households' wealth managed by these entities has also considerably increased (Davis and Steil 2001). For example, the share of American stocks owned by individual investors diminished from 93 per cent in 1945 to 56 per cent in 1986, and to 27 per cent in 2006 (Rappaport 2011, pp. 8–11). The presence of these new actors favoured the growth of the relative dimension of financial variables by increasing the degree of intermediation.[26]

Bogle (2011) measured the weight of speculation and the weight of the activities supporting the implementation of investments by businesses in Wall Street by comparing the value of the traded stocks, that is, the overall value of the purchase and sale of existing stocks, with the value of newly issued stocks. He estimated that in 2010 the value of traded stocks was equal to 40 000 billion dollars, while the value of newly issued stocks amounted to only 200 billion dollars. In 2010, the ratio between trading activities and activities aimed at supporting the implementation of investments by businesses was two hundred to one. Speculation and the presence of speculative markets explain not only the increased size of the financial system, but also the reasons for the huge difference between the incomes earned by bankers and those earned by mechanics.

The second element of instability is related to the transition from the moderate form of globalization that characterized the period of regulated capitalism to the hyper-globalization from the 1980s on. This change was the direct consequence of the policies inspired by the theoretical counter-revolution of the 1970s, according to which free trade always favours economic growth while protectionism produces underdevelopment. The Ricardian theory of comparative advantages shows that each country can benefit from importing products that incorporate a lower labour cost than that incurred if the same goods were produced at home.

The key issue in evaluating the benefits of free trade is to establish how costs are determined. This issue can be solved in a relatively easy way if countries are homogeneous, as they share similar technologies and institutions. This means, for example, that countries have similar regulations for work and environmental protection. In the absence of these conditions, the costs of a complete trade liberalization could be very high. As Rodrik (2011) pointed out, defining these costs requires a distinction between private and social costs.

Private costs are those posted in the books of any company that aims at maximizing its profits. Social costs not only measure the harmful effects of the dust and noise produced by a factory on the inhabitants of the surrounding neighbourhoods, but also reflect the importance that society attributes to the values of equality, justice and freedom. The social costs associated with trade liberalization can be very high. The free movement of goods and capital has enabled large companies to relocate their production lines to countries with less rigid labour market rules than those applied in their home countries. Many production activities were transferred to countries where the dominant working conditions would never be tolerated in their home countries. This generated heavy social costs in the industrialized countries in terms of reduced employment and increased income inequalities, which cannot be underestimated by simply stressing the benefits obtained by the emerging countries of East Asia and South America.

The third sign of instability is made up of the remarkable increase in inequalities in income distribution recorded in the Western economies during the years of neoliberal capitalism. This important change relates to the growth of the phenomenon of speculation and to the process of hyper-globalization. Between 1948 and 1979, at the time of regulated capitalism, in the United States distributional inequalities had decreased. In fact, the portion of income absorbed by the richest 5 per cent of families fell from 17.1 per cent to 15.3 per cent of GDP, while the share absorbed by the poorest 20 per cent of families grew from 4.9 per cent to 5.4 per cent. However, from 1979 to 2007, the amount of income absorbed by the top 5 per cent increased from 15.3 per cent to 20.1 per cent, while the share absorbed by the poorest 20 per cent fell from 5.4 per cent to 4.1 per cent (Kotz 2015). Picketty (2013) shows that the share of income going to the richest 1 per cent, which had reached 23.9 per cent in 1928, dropped to 10 per cent in the 1960s and 1970s. From the early 1980s, this share began to rise until it reached 23.5 per cent in 2007. Even more significant is the growth in the amount of income absorbed by the richest 0.1 per cent, which increased from 2 per cent in the 1970s to nearly 10 per cent in 2007 (Piketty 2013, p. 319). The average remuneration of the CEO of a large corporation increased from 29 times the wage of the average worker in 1978 to 351.7 times in 2007 (Mishel et al. 2012; Kotz 2015).

The dominant theoretical model has led economists to consider the increase in inequality as the natural result of the working of market forces. As pointed out by Reich (2015, pp. 3–4), according to neoliberal ideas 'whatever inequality or insecurity the market generates is assumed to be the natural and inevitable consequence of impersonal "market forces". What you're paid is simply a measure of what you're worth in the market' (see also Mankiw 2013). In fact, the increase in inequality is the consequence of the transition from the regulated form of capitalism to the neoliberal form of capitalism, which is ruled by the dominant beliefs that emerged with the monetarist counterrevolution, and is closely linked to the phenomena of financialization and of hyper-globalization that reduced the bargaining power of workers.[27]

3.3   Neoliberal Capitalism and the Crisis

Despite the major growth in inequalities in the years of neoliberal capitalism compared with the years of regulated capitalism, the current crisis was not the result of an increased level of social conflicts as in the 1970s. The Great Recession was triggered by a financial crisis caused by the burst of a speculative bubble. The prevalence of speculation over enterprise is at the root of the two great speculative bubbles that developed in the United States between the 1980s and today (2016): the dot.com bubble that burst in 2000 and the housing bubble that burst in 2007. Perez (2009) points out that the first of these two bubbles presented features that are very similar to those described by Minsky. As described in Chapter 7, according to Minsky crises are preceded by periods of boom and euphoria characterized by the spread of overly positive expectations about the returns generated by some particular innovation. The spread of the Internet phenomenon certainly featured the characteristics of a Schumpeterian innovation and was particularly suited to fuelling new euphoric profit expectations. However, the housing bubble had very different characteristics. To begin with, it was not linked to the introduction of a new technology. Furthermore, it was too close in time to the dot.com bubble to be considered a completely new phenomenon. In fact, the previous crisis was not followed by a deep recession and by a subsequent 'tranquil' period in which economic agents could forget what had happened during earlier periods of economic turmoil, and in which the conditions for a new phase of euphoria could be shaped.

To explain the rapid succession of the two speculative bubbles, Perez (2009) remarks that the burst of the dot.com bubble did not stir feelings of aversion to finance by governments and public opinion. Thus, there were no incentives to introduce new regulations that might have stopped further financial speculations, as was the case after the 1929 crash. Consequently, the burst of the dot.com bubble did not prevent bank managers from seeking high returns thanks to the development of a new speculative bubble. What had changed was simply the object of speculation. By expanding the supply of subprime mortgages, banks favoured a continuous rise in housing prices, an increase that had already started in the mid-1990s, coupled with a rise in high-tech stock prices. The fact that the housing bubble was not justified by any technological revolution makes its speculative nature even clearer.

Another element that makes the dot.com bubble radically different from the housing bubble relates to the consequences produced after their burst. While the bursting of the dot.com bubble did not generate relevant consequences on real economic activities, the bursting of the housing bubble had a catastrophic impact on levels of income and employment. The Great Recession was caused by a collapse of global demand due to two factors. First, in the case of the housing bubble, banks, which were looking for ever-growing profits, chose to stuff their books and those of their SPVs with a high share of securitized subprime mortgages, while in the case of the dot.com bubble most of the high-tech stocks were owned by private individuals. As previously discussed, the behaviour of banks was explained by referring to the concept of herd behaviour. The high level of leverage implemented by banks caused a paralysis of the financial system because, after the bursting of the bubble, the devaluation of securitized assets caused a considerable erosion of banks' equity, which brought them to the brink of bankruptcy. The banking system reacted by rationing the extension of credit to businesses and households, thereby contributing to the decline in investments and thus in aggregate demand and productive activities.

The second factor that accounts for the Great Recession is the fall in demand for goods and services by borrowers. Mian and Sufi (2014) point out that the bursting of the housing bubble caused significant capital losses for borrowers. These borrowers had purchased a house having only a small fraction of the total capital needed, that is, around 10–20 per cent of the selling price. The collapse of prices on the housing market wiped out the value of the capital of many borrowers. According to Mian and Sufi, this led to a significant reduction in their spending capacity. At the time of the bursting of the dot.com bubble, no such phenomenon occurred as the dot.com stocks were mostly owned by wealthy families, which were able to absorb the capital loss associated with the bursting of the bubble without any substantial change in their demand for goods.

4. THE LIMITS OF MAINSTREAM EXPLANATIONS OF THE CRISIS

The analysis of the endogenous nature of the crisis presented in this chapter differs considerably from the interpretations given by mainstream economists. The latter consider the crisis as an accidental event caused by the mistakes made by two main culprits, that is, the public sector and the US banking system. As mentioned in Chapter 2, the most effective analysis of the relationship between the Federal Reserve's expansionary monetary policy and the housing bubble is that developed by John Taylor based on the Taylor rule. The conclusions reached so far highlight two limitations of this analysis. First, it underestimates the reasons that led the US monetary authorities to adopt an expansionary policy. In fact, the Federal Reserve wanted to avoid the risk that the bursting of the dot.com bubble might result in a severe recession.

Until the housing bubble burst, nobody criticized the Federal Reserve's behaviour. On the contrary, Milton Friedman (2005) emphasized the positive effects of the Federal Reserve's expansionary monetary policy. He expressed this view by comparing the booming phase of the 1990s and the subsequent collapse of the stock market in 2000 with the booming phase of the 1920s that preceded the financial meltdown of 1929. Friedman stressed that the expansionary phases of the two episodes were very similar, while the periods following the peak of the booming phases were profoundly different. In fact, in 1929 the US economy was hit by a major decline in the levels of income and employment, which, however, did not occur between 2001 and 2005, after the dot.com bubble burst. According to Friedman, the fundamental reason for this difference lies in the behaviour of the monetary authorities. After the 1929 crash, the Federal Reserve adopted a restrictive monetary policy that produced a rapid contraction in money supply. However, in the aftermath of the bursting of the dot.com bubble, the US monetary authorities implemented an expansionary policy. In Friedman's view, this explains why after 2000 the recession of the US economy had been much softer than that experienced after the 'great crash' of 1929.

The second limitation of Taylor's explanation of the crisis lies in the theoretical basis of the relationship between monetary policy and the housing bubble. According to Taylor, the expansionary monetary policy allowed banks to increase the supply of credit, most notably the supply of subprime mortgages, thereby fuelling the housing bubble. But, as was described in Chapter 3, this relationship is not consistent with the mainstream theory of finance. Taylor indeed assumes that monetary policy affects the supply of credit while, according to the traditional theory of finance, the supply of credit depends on saving decisions. Moreover, Taylor's explanation is based on the concept of speculation, which is likewise alien to the orthodox theoretical model. As was explained in the second part of this book, a link between monetary policy, credit supply and asset bubbles can be defined only in the context of what Keynes called a monetary economy, that is, an economy characterized by the distinction between speculation and enterprise. This distinction clarifies that the banking system does not necessarily have to use the newly created credit money to finance the development of a speculative bubble, as the same money could be used to fund entrepreneurial initiatives.

The link between an expansionary monetary policy and the development of an asset bubble can be explained only by considering an economic system in which, as pointed out by Keynes, the presence of special conditions, such as the shift from the regulated to the neoliberal form of capitalism, makes speculation much more profitable than entrepreneurship. This aspect of modern monetary economies was completely neglected by Taylor. As illustrated in this chapter, the monetarist theoretical counterrevolution that began in the 1970s is at the root of the process that, in the years before the housing bubble burst in the United States, caused 'speculation' to prevail over enterprise.

The US government is the second public culprit of the crisis according to mainstream economists. More specifically, it is blamed for the adoption of policies that were intended to facilitate the purchase of homes by low-income families. There is no doubt that the policies aimed at promoting a growing indebtedness of low-income subjects were the result of a short-sighted decision that transformed a large number of households into insolvent borrowers. Nevertheless, as shown by the microcredits extended by Muhammad Yunus's Grameen Bank, the choice to encourage indebtedness among low-income subjects is not necessarily bound to cause their default, as long as the loans help borrowers to increase their income and thus to repay their debts.[28] In the case of the mortgages granted to low-income households in the United States, this condition certainly was not met, for the bank loans did not produce any direct effect on the borrowers' income. The only factor that gave the borrowers a chance to repay their debts was the continuous increase in the market value of the houses purchased with the newly created bank money.

The policies aimed at financially supporting low-income households inevitably ended up in heavy losses for Fannie Mae and Freddie Mac. However, these losses are not sufficient to explain the Great Recession. To do this, the role played by the banking system must be taken into consideration. As anticipated previously, Raghuram Rajan is the mainstream economist who most emphasized the responsibilities of the banking system. He maintains that the profound changes that affected the financial sector led the banking system to create an excessive amount of risk. The limit of Rajan's analysis lies in the use of concepts such as uncertainty, speculation and herd behaviour that are not consistent with the traditional theory of finance.

Rajan recognizes that the current crisis has unveiled the flaws of the mainstream theoretical model as it neglects the importance of financial factors. He justifies this choice by underlining that the models built by economists are a simplified version of reality. Thus, they neglect the elements of the real world that are deemed irrelevant. In Rajan's opinion, the lack of attention to the functioning of the financial system stems from the fact that, for a long time, the economy seemed to work smoothly. So, he compares the financial system to the plumbing of a building and emphasizes that the crisis has shown that hydraulic systems can break down. Consequently, Rajan emphasizes the need to build models taking into account the importance of the financial system and the possibility that, like a hydraulic system, it can 'break'.[29]

In addition to Rajan, many conservative economists have recognized that the crisis has exposed the limitations of the macroeconomic models used since the 1970s, as they did not explicitly take into account the dynamics of the financial system and the possibility of a crisis. Bernanke (2010b, p. 6), for example, stated that 'understanding the relationship between financial and economic stability in a macroeconomic context is a critical unfinished task for researchers'. In particular, he quotes his own works and those published with his co-authors as a significant starting point to achieve this goal.[30]

The common element in these analyses consists in the explanation of the importance of financial markets on the basis of the presence of frictions impeding the transfer of funds from savers to businesses.[31] According to the mainstream theoretical approach, the major imperfection that explains the relevance of the financial system is the presence of asymmetric information. The inclusion of asymmetric information in the analysis allows preservation of the fundamental contents of the traditional theory of finance, consisting in the description of an ideal world without frictions, in which the flexibility of prices ensures the full and efficient employment of the available resources. This ideal world, in which money and financial variables are a mere mirror image of saving and investment decisions, is not an abstract construction. Rather, it represents the condition towards which the economy converges thanks to the action of specific institutions, like the banks, born to eliminate the effects produced by the presence of asymmetric information.

The weakness of this approach is that it explains the relevance of the credit market by assuming that, although the banks were born to collect information about potential borrowers, they are not able to overcome the problems associated with the presence of asymmetric information. As Minsky remarked (1992–1993, p. 79), the theory of asymmetric information on the credit market is based on the assumption that 'non neutrality [of money] depends upon borrowers being smart and bankers being dumb'. It is impossible to explain economic crises by introducing imperfections in a model describing the working of a world without imperfections, as imperfections set off a process aimed at their elimination, and at steering the system towards the ideal state. If the function of the banks is to select the most creditworthy debtors and to avoid the saved corn being allocated to incompetent borrowers, or to swindlers, it must be concluded that they will be able to eliminate the negative consequences of the presence of asymmetric information, thereby performing the same function carried out by mechanics within the market for used cars. In other words, the function of the banks, like that of the mechanics, is to grant the realization of the results that would be obtained in an ideal world characterized by the presence of perfect information. Within such a world, the probability of the outbreak of a global economic crisis is equal to the probability of the occurrence of a general block of the automobile traffic imputable to the sudden inability of the mechanics to assess the quality of the cars in circulation.[32]

In order to explain the phenomenon of economic crises, it is necessary to abandon the mainstream model and to use a theoretical approach based on the analysis of the heretical economists cited in the second part of this book.

NOTES

1. '[W]e may define institutions as systems of established and prevalent social rules that structure social interactions. Language, money, law, systems of weight and measures, table manners, firms (and other organizations) are all institutions' (Hodgson 2006, p. 138). See also North (2005a, 2005b), Rodrik (2011) and Acemoglu and Robinson (2012).
2. 'Institutions are the rules of the game – both formal rules, informal norms and their enforcement characteristics. Organizations are the players. They are made up of a group of individuals held together by some common objectives. Economic organizations are firms, trade unions, cooperatives, etc.; political organizations are political parties, legislatures, regulatory bodies. … The immediate objective of organizations may be profit maximizing (for firms) or improving reelection prospects (for political parties); but the ultimate objective is survival' (North 2005b, p. 22).
3. According to Kotz, in contemporary economies 'the most important actors are not individuals but classes and groups, which engage in struggles and enter into alliances and coalitions as each seeks to advance its interests in the face of economic developments' (Kotz 2015, p. 4). See also Bellofiore (2011), Bellofiore and Halevi (2010–2011, 2011), Bellofiore and Vertova (2014) and Bougrine and Rochon (2015).
4. 'There is an intimate relationship between belief systems and the institutional framework. Belief systems embody the internal representation of the human landscape. Institutions are the structure that humans impose on that landscape in order to produce the desired outcome. Belief systems therefore are the internal representation and institutions the external manifestation of that representation. Thus the structure of an economic market reflects the beliefs of those in position to make the rules of the game, who enact rules that will produce the outcomes (that is, the sort of market) they desire. … When conflicting beliefs exist, the institutions will reflect the beliefs of those in the position to effect their choice' (North 2005a, pp. 49–50). See also Reich (2015).
5. The differences between these two forms of capitalism have been summarized as follows by Kotz: 'In brief, in neoliberal capitalism market relations and market forces operate relatively freely and play the predominant role in the economy. By regulated capitalism we mean a form of capitalism in which non-market institutions such as states, corporate bureaucracies, and trade unions play a major role in regulating economic activity, restricting market relations and market forces to a lesser role in the economy' (Kotz 2015, p. 2). See also Gamble (2014), Galbraith (2014) and Reich (2015).
6. Admati and Hellwig wisely observe that 'financial crises are very different from earthquakes. The analogy is convenient for many, but it is misleading. Whereas there is little we can do to prevent earthquakes, there is much we can do to reduce the likelihood of financial crises' (Admati and Hellwig 2013, p. 78).
7. See Rodrik (2011), Palley (2012), Wolf (2014) and Madrik (2014).
8. 'Few ideas have more profoundly poisoned the mind of more people than the notion of a "free market" existing somewhere in the universe, into which government "intrudes" … Government doesn't "intrude" on the "free market". It creates the market' (Reich 2015, pp. 3–5). Similarly Hodgson (2015, p. 7) states: 'While private property and markets are among the key defining institutions of capitalism and vital sources of its historically unprecedented dynamism, I argue that capitalism, property, money, markets, and corporations typically depend on, and are partly constituted by the state. This does not simply mean that the state is necessary to correct "market failures" or that empirically the role of

the state has been important. The state was vital to bring capitalism into being and is needed to sustain its existence.'

9. 'The socialist solutions may have been rather seriously undermined, but the socialist questions which build on discontent with the inadequacies of capitalism continue to be asked with much force. [...] The questions that socialists asked have grown even as the answers that socialists traditionally gave have shrunk' (Sen 1996, p. 19).

10. Jeffrey Sachs effectively summarizes this historical passage: '[The] tumult [of the 1970s] gave an extraordinary opening to the new philosophical assertion that it was "big government" itself rather than new and specific challenges (energy, the exchange rate, and so forth) that constituted the major barrier to prosperity. This was an odd assertion. The major problems that had been experienced were macroeconomic in nature: the collapse of the gold-based exchange system, the budget deficits caused by the Vietnam War, and the oil price shocks. They did not, evidently, relate to the size of government (other than the Vietnam War) as much as to shifts in the world economy. The assertion that big government had destabilized the economy was doubtful on its face, but Reagan uttered his ideas with such conviction and charm that an unhappy public was ready to vote him into office. Had the evidence been brought to bear, the flimsiness of the claim would have been exposed. Federal tax revenues as a share of GDP were nearly constant from the mid-1950s onward at 17 per cent to 18 per cent of GDP. Total federal spending as a share of GDP had increased slightly, from around 18 per cent of GDP in the late 1950s to around 20 per cent of GDP in the late 1960s and 21 per cent in the late 1970s. [...] Yet the chaos created by the oil price shocks, the new floating exchange rate regime, and lax monetary policies by the Federal Reserve reverberated into budget politics. Suddenly tax cutting, shrinking [...] and rolling back welfare policies became the vogue and the diagnostic basis for policy change. There was no turning back' (Sachs 2011, p. 55). On this point see also Judt (2010), Palley (2012, 2013), Streeck (2013) and Reich (2015).

11. Merton and Bodie have used an effective metaphor to emphasize the relationship between the globalization of the financial system and the development of the market of derivative securities: '[D]erivative-security technologies provide efficient means for creating cross-border interfaces without imposing invasive, widespread changes within each system. An analogy may prove helpful here. Imagine two countries that want to integrate their pipelines for transporting oil, gas, water, or anything else. Country A has a pipeline that is square, while country B's pipeline is triangular. Country A's plan for integrating the pipelines is to suggest to B that it replace its triangular pipeline with a square one. This, of course, will require a very large and disruptive investment by B. Decision makers in country B, not surprisingly, have an alternative – country A should tear up its square pipeline and replace it with a triangular one. But rarely would either of those two plans make sense. Almost always, the better solution is to design an efficient adapter that connects the two existing pipelines with minimum impediments to the flow across borders. This pipeline analogy captures much of what has been happening during the past twenty years in the international financial system. Financial engineers have been designing and implementing derivative contracts to function as efficient adapters that allow the flow of funds and the sharing of risks among diverse national systems with different institutional shapes and sizes' (Merton and Bodie 2005, p. 3).

12. '[T]he presumption in favor of market completion and market liquidity … was an accepted article of faith. As a result, most policymakers, far from seeking to constrain finance's remarkable growth, favored deregulation, which could unleash yet more financial innovation. Old-fashioned barriers between investment and commercial banks were dismantled, derivatives markets developments were encouraged, and financial liberalization was urged on emerging markets as a key component of successful economic development strategies' (Turner 2016, p. 29).

13. Turner points out that the current crisis has been caused by an expansion of the supply of credit by the banking system, which, rather than finance investments, has fuelled speculation: 'Credit creates purchasing power, which can fund productive investment. But it can also be used to fund wasteful investment, or the purchase of existing assets (such as

real estate and the land on which it sits), driving self-reinforcing-cycles of asset price appreciation and further credit extension' (Turner 2016, p. 140).

14. 'Derivatives and new techniques for risk management have benefited society by providing better means of sharing risks. However, the new markets and new techniques have also expanded the scope for gambling. ... Over the past twenty or thirty years, many scandals in which banks and their clients lost enormous amounts of money have involved derivatives . ... Speculation and gambling have always played a role in financial markets. In the case of derivatives, however, the gambles that individual traders take have become much larger and much more difficult to control' (Admati and Helwig 2013, pp. 70–71).

15. 'Without a historical perspective, economists are myopic. The period of the Great Moderation ... is basically a twenty-year period that began in the mid-1980s. The irony is that there was a growing credit boom in the United States, and the so-called shadow banking system was developing during this period' (Gorton 2012, p. 96). See also Acemoglu (2009) and Eichengreen (2014).

16. 'The most remarkable trend in the way banks have funded themselves since the middle of the nineteenth century has been their consistently decreased reliance on equity relative to borrowing. Early in the twentieth century, it was still typical for banks to have equity equal to 25 per cent of their total assets, but banks' equity levels declined to single digits, around 6–8 per cent of their total assets in the United States, by the early 1990s' (Admati and Hellwig 2013, p. 31).

17. '[A]fter World War II and the end of the Depression, and with the prosperity they saw, economists and policymakers became a little bit too confident about their ability to keep the economy on an even keel. They used the term *fine tuning* to refer to the notion that the Fed and fiscal policy and other government policies could keep the economy more or less perfectly on course and not worry about bumps and wiggles in the economy. That turned out to be too optimistic, too hubristic, as we collectively learned during the 1970s when the efforts of policymakers resulted, not in a lower unemployment rate, which was the original goal, but instead in a very sharp increase in inflation' (Bernanke 2013, pp. 34–35).

18. According to Rodrik, the Bretton Woods agreements 'allow enough international discipline and progress toward trade liberalization to ensure vibrant world commerce, but give plenty of space for governments to respond to social and economic needs at home. International economic policy would have to be subservient to domestic policy objectives – full employment, economic growth, equity, social insurance, and welfare state – and not the other way around. The goal would be moderate globalization, not hyperglobalization' (Rodrik 2011, pp. 69–70).

19. Bernanke justifies his confident prediction by considering the characteristics of the US economy: 'the reason that we are so productive has to do with the diverse set of industries we have; our entrepreneurial culture, which still is clearly the best in the world; the flexibility of our labor markets and our capital markets; and our technology, which remains one of our strongest points. Increasingly, technology has been driving economic growth' (Bernanke 2013, p. 116).

20. For a detailed analysis of the spread of inequalities in recent decades see, for example, Goldin and Katz (2008), Milanovic (2010), Bourguignon (2012), Galbraith (2012), Stiglitz (2012), Mankiw (2013), Piketty (2013) and Atkinson (2015).

21. Even a mainstream economist like Raghuram Rajan associates the growth of inequality with the impressive increase in the remunerations of financial managers: 'The top 1 per cent of households accounted for only 8.9 per cent of income in 1976, but this share grew to 23.5 per cent of the total income generated in the United States in 2007. Put differently, of every dollar of real income growth that was generated between 1976 and 2007, 58 cents went to the top 1 per cent of households. In 2007 the hedge fund manager John Paulson earned $ 3.7 billion, about 74 000 times the median household income in the United States' (Rajan 2010, p. 8).

22. Strange concluded her book by detailing the circumstances that could cause a new financial crisis and a subsequent severe recession: 'The question ... if a repeat of the 1929–39 scenario is to be taken seriously, is whether there are conceivable circumstances

in which another stock market fall would damage the real economy. There are. They involve an unhappy coincidence of financial and political factors. The financial scenario would have to include large disruptions in the pattern of capital flows in and out of major economies. [...] The political scenario would have to include conditions in which governments were, for one reason or another, frozen in indecision or too slow to react and therefore failed to act to restore confidence. The combination then sets off a domino effect of fear undermining confidence in the market economy and its ability to maintain credit and therefore purchasing power. Oversupply results from lack of demand' (Strange 1998, p. 183).

23. 'I think the crisis of 2008 was – in addition to being the crisis of particular institutions – a crisis of the intellectual theory that applied complete and free markets to the financial markets as well as, say, to the market for restaurants or the market for bananas or the market for automobiles. The fundamental point is that the market for finance is different, so many of the propositions in favor of free and complete markets that are powerful in other sectors of the economy are much less powerful in finance' (Turner 2015, p. 2).

24. Adair Turner describes this widespread attitude very effectively: 'The conservative narrative, asserted … that free markets were the best way to deliver prosperity, and that significant inequality was acceptable – indeed required – because it gave entrepreneurs, executives, and ordinary workers incentives that would ensure innovation, competitive success in global markets, high productivity growth, and thus increasing prosperity. Whereas in the nineteenth century conservatives defended inequality and property rights as elements of a natural order, in the late twentieth century conservative parties tended to advance an instrumental justification of both markets and inequality: that flexible markets and low taxes on the rich were good because they would make the average citizen richer' (Turner 2012, pp. 1–2). On this issue see also Stiglitz (2012).

25. Suppose, for example, that, over time, GDP assumes a constant value equal to Y. Thus, $Y_t = Y_{t+1} = Y_{t+2} = \ldots = Y_{t+n}$. Further suppose that savings are also constant and equal to S, with $S_t = S_{t+1} = S_{t+2} = \ldots = S_{t+n}$. This implies that, year after year, in correspondence with a steady level of income, wealth (W) grows by an amount that equals that of savings. Consequently, the ratio of financial wealth and GDP is continuously growing: $$\frac{W_t}{Y_t} < \frac{W_{t+1}}{Y_{t+1}} < \ldots < \frac{W_{t+n}}{Y_{t+n}}.$$

26. 'One main result is that, notwithstanding an increase in firms' indebtedness in recent years, non-financial corporations have taken advantage only partially of the huge increase in the size of the financial industry observed in the last 15 years. At least in some countries, a large part of this increase in the balance-sheet size of the overall financial sector, can be traced back to more intensive trading activity among financial intermediaries, with little impact on the ability of non-financial firms to exploit better financial conditions. This evidence may suggest a reconsideration of the positive and monotone relationship between financial development and economic growth' (Bartiloro and Di Iasio 2012, p. 158). See also Shin (2009), Turner (2016), Krippner (2011), Bellofiore and Halevi (2011), Eichengreen (2014) and Bougrine and Rochon (2015).

27. Considering the American reality, Reich (2015, pp. 131–132) states that: 'The underlying problem … is not that the average working Americans are "worth" less in the market than they had been. … The problem is that they have steadily lost the bargaining power needed to receive as large a portion of the economy's gains as they commanded in the first three decades after World War II. … To attribute this to the impersonal workings of the "free market" is to ignore how the market has been reorganized since the 1980s, and by whom. It is to disregard the power of moneyed interests who have received a steadily larger share of economic gains as a result of that power.'

28. This concept is well illustrated by the example that Muhammad Yunus (1999) makes in the book that describes his experience as 'banker to the poor'. Yunus tells the story of when he met a woman who made bamboo stools in an Indian village. The woman was so poor that she did not even have the capital of 22 cents required to buy the bamboo she needed for the work of a single day. The bamboo was supplied by the same person to whom she sold

the stools at the end of the day in exchange for an amount of 24 cents. Thus, her profit, as that of all the other women in the village involved in the building of stools, amounted to 2 cents per day. Yunus immediately realized that these women could obtain a much greater profit if only they had access to the 22 cents they needed to buy bamboo. Indeed, this way they would be free to sell the stools at a market price that was much higher than the 24 cents paid by the bamboo suppliers for the construction of the stools. Yunus's experience as 'banker to the poor' began with a loan of $27 extended to the women of this Indian village.

29.   'But as soon as the plumbing broke down, the models were an oversimplification. Indeed, the models themselves may have hastened the plumbing's breakdown: with the Fed focused on what interest rates would do to output rather than to financial risk taking (few models had a financial sector embedded in them, let alone banks), financial risk taking went unchecked. [...] In coming years, macroeconomic modeling must incorporate more of the plumbing, which has been studied elsewhere in economics' (Rajan 2010, p. 117).

30.   See Bernanke (1992–1993, 2007a), Bernanke and Blinder (1988), Bernanke and Gertler (1995), Bernanke and Lown (1991) and Bernanke et al. (1999). See also Woodford (2010), Curdia and Woodford (2010), Gertler and Karadi (2011), Brunnermeier et al. (2013) and Brunnermeier and Sannikov (2014).

31.   'In a frictionless economy, funds are liquid and can flow to the most profitable project or to the person who values the funds most. Differences in productivity, patience, risk aversion or optimism determine fund flows, but for the aggregate output only the total capital and labor matter. ... In contrast, with financial frictions liquidity considerations become important and the wealth distribution matters. External funding is typically more expensive than internal funding through retained earnings' (Brunnermeier et al. 2013, p. 3). Borio (2014, p. 11) criticizes this approach by underlining that: 'macroeconomics without the financial cycle is like *Hamlet* without the Prince ... modelling the financial cycle correctly, rather than simply mimicking some of its features superficially, requires recognizing fully the fundamental monetary nature of our economies – the financial system does not just allocate, but also generates, purchasing power, and very much has a life of its own.'

32.   For a critical analysis of the theory of finance based on the asymmetric information approach, see Bertocco (2004, 2009a).

9. Overcoming the crisis: which policies?

> There is no clear evidence from experience that the investment policy which is socially advantageous coincides with that which is most profitable. It needs more intelligence to defeat the forces of time and our ignorance of the future than to beat the gun. (John M. Keynes 1936 [2013a], p. 157)

> Politics must not be subject to the economy, nor should the economy be subject to the dictates of an efficiency-driven paradigm of technocracy. Today, in view of the common good, there is urgent need for politics and economics to enter into a frank dialogue in the service of life, especially human life. Saving banks at any cost, making the public pay the price, foregoing a firm commitment to reviewing and reforming the entire system, only reaffirms the absolute power of a financial system, a power which has no future and will only give rise to new crises after a slow, costly and only apparent recovery. (Francis, the Holy Father 2014, para. 189)

There is obviously a close relationship between the explanation of the nature of the crisis and the definition of the policies deemed necessary to overcome it. The previous chapters have emphasized the structural nature of the current crisis. In fact, economic crises are both an expression of the fragility of a specific form of capitalism and the turning point marking the transition to a new form of capitalism. The Great Depression resulted in a period of regulated capitalism, while the crisis of the 1970s evolved into the so-called 'neoliberal capitalism'. Now, one may wonder what changes will come out of the current crisis.

The answer to this question depends on the policies and the rules of the game that will be adopted, which, as North pointed out, are an expression of the dominant beliefs. Currently, the beliefs that seem to prevail are those expressed by mainstream economists, who consider the crisis as an accidental phenomenon. In fact, there is a substantial continuity between the economic policies adopted to overcome the stagflation of the 1970s and those implemented to react to the current crisis. As in the 1970s, the current economic problems are attributed to the excessive weight of the public sector in the economy. Consequently, also in the current crisis, the recommended therapy consists, first and foremost, in adopting measures aimed at cutting public spending in order to reduce the tax burden. Kotz (2015) remarks that austerity policies are consistent with the dominant beliefs of the social groups that mostly benefited from the results produced by neoliberal capitalism.[1]

The second recommended remedy consists in structural reforms aimed at removing the obstacles that prevent markets, and specifically the labour market, from functioning effectively. Finally, mainstream economists advocate the necessity to strengthen the banks' capacity to withstand the effects of a sudden collapse in their asset value by adopting more stringent capital adequacy requirements.

These policies are the manifestation of a paradox as they are inspired by the same theoretical model that led to the current crisis. As was outlined in the previous chapter, the neoliberal model provided the theoretical justification for the deregulation of financial markets and the liberalization of goods and capital movements that allowed speculation to prevail over enterprise, and it led economists to underestimate the signs of instability that emerged during the years of the Great Moderation. Thus, it is paradoxical that this very model is now being used to explain the need for austerity measures and structural reforms. This chapter has two objectives. First, to highlight the contradictions that characterize the mainstream economic policies, as it is unlikely that a wrong diagnosis may produce a successful therapy. Second, to define the characteristics of a set of policies that take into account the structural nature of the contemporary crisis.

1. THE MAINSTREAM POLICIES

Austerity policies are aimed at reducing the burden of public budgets. As explained in Chapter 1, one of the major consequences of the financial crisis has been a severe deterioration in public finances. In the Eurozone, the high level of public deficit in the peripheral countries has become the very symbol of this crisis. Thus, as in the 1970s, the public sector was identified as the main culprit of the crisis.

This attitude is testified by a letter signed by the outgoing President of the ECB, Jean-Claude Trichet, and his successor, Mario Draghi (2011), and sent to the Italian government in August 2011. In this letter, Italy was asked to achieve a balanced budget by 2013 and to reduce public spending through a reform of the pension system and a reduction in the costs of the public sector. Another important expression of the austerity policies implemented in Europe is the adoption of the Fiscal Stability Treaty (the so-called Fiscal Compact), which is part of the Treaty on

Stability, Coordination and Governance in the Economic and Monetary Union that was signed in March 2012 by all EU member states except the United Kingdom and the Czech Republic. The Treaty requires that the member states introduce a self-correcting mechanism aimed at ensuring a balance or a surplus in the public budget. The Treaty also confirms the 'debt brake' criteria outlined in the reinforced Stability and Growth Pact that define the rate at which public debt levels exceeding 60 per cent of GDP must decrease. More specifically, member states exceeding the threshold must cut the exceeding stock of debt at an average rate of at least one-twentieth (5 per cent) per year.

The second element of mainstream anti-crisis policies consists in structural reforms aimed at removing the barriers that hamper competition and market flexibility. A significant example of these reforms is provided in the letter Trichet and Draghi (2011) addressed to the Italian government. Italian authorities were asked to undertake 'pressing action … to restore the confidence of investors' through the introduction of two sets of reforms. First, reforms aimed at increasing competition in the supply of services, and especially public services. Second, a deep reform of the labour market based on the widespread use of bargaining agreements at the level of individual companies and on revised rules on hiring and dismissing workers. These proposals are inspired by the neoclassical model of the labour market in which unemployment is the result of a system of safeguards that pushes the level of wages above the workers' marginal productivity. In a report on the situation in the Euro area, the investment bank J.P.Morgan (2013) argued that the main difficulties in southern European countries (Portugal, Italy and Spain) are of a political nature, because of the characteristics of the constitutions adopted after the fall of their fascist dictatorships. According to J.P.Morgan, these constitutions are deeply influenced by socialist ideas, which inspire the provision of strong labour protections.[2] J.P.Morgan concludes that the constitutions of southern European countries represent an obstacle to the process of European integration.[3]

The third element of mainstream policies is the regulation of the financial system. Since the default of Lehman Brothers in 2008, regulating the financial system has become a top priority on the agendas of government authorities around the world.[4] According to Admati and Hellwig (2013), the main cause of the banks' fragility was their high level of leverage. Consequently, the authors conclude that the key measure of the new regulation should necessarily consist in a significant strengthening of the banks' capital adequacy requirements. The higher the banks' equity, the greater their ability to withstand the negative effects of changes in the market value of their assets without risking a default. In

Admati and Hellwig's view, the capital adequacy standards established with the new Basel III Accord, which require that by 1 January 2019 the banks' equity must be equal to at least 7 per cent of their risk-weighted assets, are far too low to stabilize the financial system. They claim that the required equity should be 20–30 per cent of the banks' total assets.

2. THE LIMITS OF THE MAINSTREAM POLICIES

The economic policy proposals described above are unquestionably acceptable. Both the idea of a mandatory considerable increase in banks' capital adequacy ratios and the suggestion to strengthen the competitiveness of the national production capacity by reducing the burden of an unnecessarily oppressive bureaucracy are certainly reasonable. Furthermore, no one would question that there are several examples of waste of resources in the public sector and that reducing such waste would lower the fiscal pressure on businesses and labour costs.

However, all these proposals have a fundamental limit, namely that they were defined with regard to the characteristics of a corn economy, in which the current crisis could not have happened. A clear proof of this statement is that, as was illustrated in the first part of this book, mainstream economists explain the origins of the crisis by referring to an economic system that is very different from that described in the traditional theory. But, making an inexplicable logical leap, as they indicate the policies needed to overcome the crisis, they refer again to a system that shows the same characteristics as a corn economy. Looking at the features of Keynes's monetary economy described in the second part of this book, three limits can be identified in the mainstream economic policies. The first concerns the proposal to increase the adequacy of the banks' capital ratios. The second regards the austerity measures. Finally, the third limit relates to the policies aimed at reforming the labour market rules.

Admati and Hellwig (2013) provide an effective description of the effects of these measures aimed at increasing the banks' capital ratios. However, they do not explain what causes fluctuations in the market value of the banks' assets. In fact, Admati and Hellwig take these fluctuations as given facts, without wondering whether or not they are connected to the banks' behaviour. This approach would be unquestionable if it were applied to a corn economy, where the activity of banks only consists in collecting the corn saved by the economic agents in order to lend it to the most skilled entrepreneurs or to the owners of the most productive plots of land. In this kind of economy, the banks' activity consists in providing an insurance against the risk that, for example, natural events might reduce the amount of corn harvested by a certain number of borrowers. Banks would be able to cope with these losses thanks to the profits made from the loans that were regularly repaid. In this case, an increase in the banks' capital provides an adequate protection, because the likelihood that bad weather conditions actually occur is completely independent of the decisions taken by the banks.

However, this hypothesis is not valid in the case of the current crisis. In fact, the decrease in the banks' asset value was caused by the bursting of the housing bubble, which the banks themselves had fuelled in order to increase their short-term profits. In other words, in a historical period characterized by the adoption of rules of the game which consisted in financial deregulation and liberalization of capital movements, the bubble allowed bank managers to expand their short-term profits by increasing the supply of subprime mortgages and the share of securitized loans held in their portfolios. Therefore, imposing higher capital requirements on banks is not a sufficient measure to reduce the likelihood of a new crisis. To quote a typical expression used by mainstream economists, what is needed is rather a limitation of the incentives that can lead banks to make speculative decisions that increase the probability of a catastrophic crisis.

In addition, the proposals aimed at ensuring the sustainability of public finances were also designed with reference to a corn economy, in which the presence of a burdensome and inefficient public sector hinders economic growth. Yet, this crisis is the endogenous outcome of a monetary economy governed by the principle of effective demand, to which Say's Law does not apply. In fact, the bursting of the housing bubble was followed by a steep fall in the levels of income and employment caused by a decline in aggregate demand. In this case, austerity policies do not free resources which could then be made available to the private sector for a more efficient use. On the contrary, austerity further compresses the level of aggregate demand, and hence the levels of income and employment.[5] Nicholas Crafts (2013) remarks that seven years after the outbreak of the crisis triggered by the collapse of the US subprime mortgage market, the situation in Europe is worse than that observed seven years after the 1929 Wall Street crash. In the same period in which the Fiscal Compact was approved, eight prestigious American economists, who can hardly be accused of representing 'heretical' positions, addressed a letter to President Obama expressing their absolute objection to the inclusion of the principle of a balanced budget in the US constitution.[6] Amartya Sen is also extremely critical of the austerity policies adopted in Europe:

There are many odd features of the experience of the world since the crisis of 2008, beginning in the United States. One of them is that what began as a clear failure of the market economy (particularly fed by misbehaving financial institutions) soon looked like a problem of the overstretched role of the state. … [S]uddenly the idea of austerity as a way out for the depressed and heavily indebted economies became the dominant priority of the financial leaders of Europe. Those with an interest in history could easily see in this a reminder of the days of the Great Depression of the 1930s when cutting public expend-iture seemed like a solution, rather than a problem. This is, of course, where Keynes made his definitive contribution in his classic book, the *General Theory*, in 1936. Keynes ushered in the basic understanding that demand is important as a determinant of economic activity, and that expanding rather than cutting public expenditure may do a better job of expanding employment and activity in an economy with unused capacity and idle labor. Austerity could do little, since a reduction of public expenditure adds to the inadequacy of private incomes and market demand, thereby tending to put even more people out of work. … How was it possible, it has to be asked, for the basic Keynesian insights and analyses to be so badly lost in the making of European economic policies that imposed austerity? (Sen 2015, pp. 5–8)

Sen does not deny that the public sector is a source of waste of money and that there is a need for serious reforms to eliminate the most blatant expressions of bad government, but he denounces the hypocrisy and lack of clarity among those who have confused two different programmes: the reform of the public administration and austerity measures. The European authorities have used reforms as an excuse to justify the adoption of austerity policies that, in the end, have exacerbated the European economic recession.

The fundamental limit of the policies aimed at reforming the labour market is that these measures are based on the assumption that the labour market works like any other market according to the law of supply and demand. Thus, as we can read in every textbook, unemployment, which corresponds to an excess in supply of labour relative to demand, depends on the rigidity of wages. Zingales (2013), for example, remarks that '[u]nemployment is nothing else than the difference between the wage that the employer is willing to pay to hire new workers and the wage at which workers are willing to work. By reducing this difference also unemployment will be reduced.' This confidence in the positive effects of 'structural' reforms of the labour market is based on the belief that there exists an ideal world in which, thanks to the unfettered action of the law of supply and demand, the labour market price ensures the achievement of a full employment equilibrium.

As pointed out in previous chapters, this analysis of the labour market may be valid in a corn economy described by the C–M–C' sequence, made of homogeneous individuals. In this context, investment decisions are undertaken under conditions of certainty and entrepreneurs are simply subjects who organize production and decide the number of employed workers based on a comparison between the workers' productivity, measured in terms of corn, and the cost of their employment, which is given by the level of wages. At each level of wages, businesses will hire all those workers whose productivity is higher than their cost. If the number of workers willing to work is greater than the number of workers whom businesses are willing to hire at a given level of wages, the excess supply of labour will cause a decline in wages that, in turn, will push businesses to expand employment. The decrease in wages will continue until they reach a level at which every labourer willing to work will be employed.

The lesson taught by heretical economists illustrated in the previous chapters leads to recognition that the economies in which we live do not work in this way. Markets are not natural phenomena, but institutions whose operation requires the introduction of rules, neither 'natural' nor eternal, reflecting the dominant beliefs. Nowadays, nobody would dare to claim that the rules banning child labour violate the principle of workers' self-determination, but in England, at the beginning of the nineteenth century, the introduction of laws aimed at prohibiting the employment of children under the age of nine and at setting a daily threshold of 12 hours of work for children aged between 10 and 16 was harshly criticized in the name of the freedom of contract (Chang 2010).

As seen in the previous chapter, the revival of the theoretical model based on the pre-Keynesian ideal figure of the 'free market' has given rise to the neoliberal form of capitalism, which is characterized by a sharp increase in economic inequalities. The fact that the current crisis is being addressed by the adoption of the same policies introduced since the beginning of the 1980s will produce a further increase of inequalities within Western economies which is likely to be inconsistent with the maintenance of a satisfactory degree of democracy:

> Over the last three decades, the rules have been shaped by large corporations, Wall Street, and very wealthy individuals in order to channel a large portion of the nation's total income and wealth to themselves. If they continue to have unbridled influence over the rules, and they gain control of the assets at the core of the new wave of innovations, they will end up with almost all the wealth, all the income, and all the political power. That result is no more in their interest than in the interests of the rest of the population, because under such conditions an economy and a society cannot endure. The coming challenge is not to technology or to economics. It is a challenge to democracy. … The central choice is not between the 'free market' and government; it is

between a market organized for broadly based prosperity and one designed to deliver almost all the gains to a few at the top. (Reich 2015, pp. 218–219)[7]

Several signs of weakness of Western economies are an expression of growing economic inequalities. The first concerns the reduction of the fertility rate for women of childbearing age to below 2.0 children. This phenomenon, which helps to explain the progressive aging of the population, is due to several factors, among which economic aspects are certainly not of secondary importance. Children have become a luxury item for young couples who are struggling to find a job, and who are paid only very low wages once they are able to find one. The second sign of weakness consists in the intense and growing hostility against migrants fleeing wars and poverty that is felt among the segments of the European population with lower incomes. This hostility is manifested through the support that this component of the European population expresses towards xenophobic parties of the extreme right.

It is therefore time to change course and address the current crisis with policies and rules of the game that are not the expression of the interests of a small social group consisting of large corporations and large speculators. The aim of these policies should be the achievement of a model of economic democracy taking into account the interests of the different social groups that characterize the heterogeneous configuration of a monetary/capitalist economy.

3.   WHICH POLICIES?

In a substantially homogeneous economic system, such as the corn economy described by the mainstream theory, the role of politics is very limited. In a corn economy, the metaphor of the invisible hand can be applied as private interests and public interests coincide. The task of politics is confined to setting few rules aimed at ensuring public order and performance of contracts, while the economic policy must remove the barriers that prevent an unfettered functioning of markets. The role of politics is totally different in a monetary economy, which is a heterogeneous system made of groups of individuals with conflicting interests. In a monetary economy, private interests and public interests do not coincide, and every social group, every organization, according to North's definition, expresses a particular vision of the common good that reflects its own specific interests. In a democratic system, the task of politics is to nurture a vision of the common good reflecting the conscious consensus of a large majority of citizens, which therefore differs from the interests of small social groups.

The two forms of capitalism that have succeeded in the post-World War II world reflect two different visions of the common good. Regulated capitalism was the expression of a compromise between the interests of big businesses and trade unions, while neoliberal capitalism, which emerged after the crisis of the 1970s, primarily reflects the interests of large multinational companies and large financial institutions. As observed by Reich (2015), the vision of the common good that, since the 1980s, has spread among the public through the rhetorical figure of the 'free market' coincides with the interests of large corporations and numerous very wealthy people. Even Pope Francis underlines the need for a shift of paradigm allowing for a definition of the common good that does not coincide with the interests of economic powers:

> Politics must not be subject to the economy, nor should the economy be subject to the dictates of an efficiency-driven paradigm of technocracy. Today, in view of the common good, there is urgent need for politics and economics to enter into a frank dialogue in the service of life, especially human life. Saving banks at any cost, making the public pay the price, foregoing a firm commitment to reviewing and reforming the entire system, only reaffirms the absolute power of a financial system, a power which has no future and will only give rise to new crises after a slow, costly and only apparent recovery. (Francis, the Holy Father 2014, para. 189)

The definition of economic policies going beyond the limits of mainstream policies must be based on the protection of human dignity. Politics and economics must strive to create the conditions that allow the citizens of a country and humanity as a whole to live what, ever since Aristotle's times, has been defined as a 'well lived' or 'good' life. Nobel laureate Michael Spence describes this concept very effectively:

> People don't really care about growth in any direct sense. After all, it is just a statistic that documents a certain aspect of change. Generally people universally care more about spiritual things: values, religion, their relations with the rest of humanity. In the material realm, humans care about opportunity, the chance to be productively employed and creative, about being valuable to society, about education and health – in short about those things that create the freedom and the opportunity to fulfill their potential. (Spence 2011, p. 31. See also Stiglitz and Greenwald 2014; Mulgan 2013)

As the next section will show, adopting Keynesian policies designed on the basis of the theoretical models developed in the 1950s and 1960s is not enough to achieve this goal.

3.1   The Limits of Keynesian Policies

In a period of worldwide economic recession such as that experienced from 2009 onwards, expansionary monetary and fiscal policies aimed at stimulating aggregate demand would undoubtedly produce positive effects on the levels of income and employment. The considerable drop in the unemployment rate recorded in the United States between 2010 and 2016 can be explained by the fact that the United States has not followed the senseless austerity measures implemented in Europe.

As discussed earlier, the limits of traditional Keynesian policies depend on the fact that they are based on the theoretical model of the Neo-classical Synthesis, which only partly captures the characteristics of a monetary economy. In fact, the presence of involuntary unemployment in this model is due only to wage and price rigidities. Thus, Keynesian policies are seen as a tool to achieve the same results that would be achieved if prices were flexible.[8] The lesson taught by heretical econo-mists analysed in the second part of this book shows that the flexibility of prices and wages does not eliminate the structural instability of a monetary economy. This conclusion was illustrated by explaining the relationship between bank money, investments-innovations and uncer-tainty. This relationship shows that the Keynesian principle of effective demand characterizes a monetary economy, in which, as Schumpeter emphasized, the introduction of innovations continuously influences the needs of households. Consequently, needs become endogenous and the principle of consumer sovereignty is not valid.

This implies that economic policies aimed at creating the conditions for a 'good life' cannot be limited to simply influencing the level of aggregate demand. Two additional objectives must be pursued. The first concerns the composition of production. Economic policies should not only focus on the level of production of goods and services, but also on the type of goods and services that are produced. Joan Robinson believed that the crisis of the 1970s was due to the limits of the particular 'Keynesian' model developed by economists in the 1950s and 1960s, in which the focus was only on the level of aggregate demand, while the issue of its composition was completely neglected:

> The first crisis arose from the breakdown of a theory which could not account for the *level* of employment. The second crisis arises from a theory that cannot account for the *content* of employment. Keynes was arguing against the dominant orthodoxy which held that government expenditure could not increase employment. He had to prove, first of all, that it could. He had to show that an increase in investment will increase consumption –that more wages will be spent on more beer and boots whether the investment is useful

or not. He had to show that the secondary increase in real income is quite independent of the object of the primary outlay. Pay men to dig holes in the ground and fill them up again if you cannot do anything else. [...] [T]he economists took over Keynes and erected the new orthodoxy. Once the point had been established, the question should have changed. Now that we all agree that government expenditure can maintain employment we should argue about what the expenditure should be for. Keynes did not want anyone to dig holes and fill them. (Robinson 1972, p. 6)

The second objective relates to the quality of work. Economic policies must deal with production methods and especially with the quality of work. In other words, economic policies must aim not only at creating jobs, but also at generating good-quality jobs. The conditions that determine the quality of work are not defined by natural laws, but must result from specific policies expressing a shared vision of the common good. The crisis of the 1970s showed that a bargain among different social groups can be broken. It is up to politics to define a set of measures governing the level of aggregate demand, its composition and the quality of work that will receive consensus from a large majority of citizens. The next sections will analyse the different elements of a policy aimed at developing the conditions for a 'good life'.

3.2 Entrepreneurship and the Socialization of Investments

Joan Robinson's position, which in the 1970s emphasized the need to complete the Keynesian revolution by adding the goal of certain composition of employment to the objective of full employment, is consistent with the argument voiced by Keynes in the last chapter of the *General Theory* in which he advocated the introduction of a certain degree of socialization of investments.[9] This expression does not merely define a policy aimed only at stimulating private investments, but it recognizes that it is important that public entities participate in the process of innovation that characterizes a monetary economy. The expression 'socialization of investments' is less heretical than it looks at first sight. As stated by Mulgan (2013) and Mazzucato (2013; Mazzucato and Wray 2015), the state has played a key role in the implementation of the most important innovations introduced in recent years.

This thesis may seem surprising as, starting with the increasing popularity of neoliberal ideology in the 1970s, the message conveyed to society identified the excessive presence of the public sector as the main obstacle to the development of the advanced economies. To explain her conclusions, Mazzucato singled out some of the elements of Keynes's and Schumpeter's thinking described in the second part of this book.

Mazzucato recalls that the investment decisions leading to the introduction of innovations are taken under conditions of uncertainty. Implementing an innovation involves the creation and the assumption of an extremely high risk of failure that a private entrepreneur is hardly willing to take by using his own resources. Therefore, institutions must be set up in order to distribute this risk across society as a whole.

Schumpeter identified these institutions with the banking system, which creates new money to finance the entrepreneurs-innovators. As was described in Chapter 5, Schumpeter emphasizes that entrepreneurs-innovators do not need to employ their own capital, and their function is independent of the availability of capital. Consequently, the entrepreneur-innovator does not take risks. The risk of the introduction of an innovation is borne by society as a whole, as it assigns the control of part of the existing productive factors (labour) to the entrepreneur-innovator through the banking system.

Schumpeter's analysis highlights the social dimension of the investments made by entrepreneurs-innovators, as it is society as a whole that, through the banking system, bears the risks of their introduction. Banks play a key role because they produce the money needed to carry out innovations under conditions of uncertainty and because they allow society to deal with the consequences of the risks arising from the introduction of innovations. Thus, on the one hand, banks generate uncertainty by creating the conditions for the implementation of innovative investment projects, but, on the other hand, they free the entrepreneurs-innovators from the risks associated with investments by transferring them to society as a whole.

Mazzucato remarks that, since the end of World War II, the Schumpeterian analytical framework based on the relationship between entrepreneurs-innovators and the banking system has undergone an evolution, as today the introduction of innovations requires a degree of scientific and technological expertise and an amount of capital that are often beyond the reach of a single 'new' man and even of large companies. In addition, the introduction of innovations requires 'patient capitals' offered by institutions willing to provide financing for longer than three to five years, the typical time horizon of venture capital funds. Since World War II, the institution that developed great visionary projects by coordinating the activities of scientists who specialize in different fields and by providing the required patient capitals has been the state.

Mazzucato illustrates her thesis by taking the United States as an example. The US is the country that symbolizes the supremacy of private entrepreneurship over the 'inefficient' public sector. Historical experience shows that the US government has played a key role in the development of computers, jets, civilian nuclear power, lasers, biotechnology and nanotechnology. The ICT revolution is a highly significant example. Public opinion tends to give credit for this revolution to the genius of individuals like Steve Jobs, who, starting with few resources, was able to create products such as the iPod, iPhone and iPad. Mazzucato stresses that Steve Jobs's genius would never have been able to produce any significant innovation without the public investments that allowed for the implementation of the technologies needed to develop Apple products (see also Mulgan 2013).

Schumpeter's analysis allows us to emphasize that the difference between public and private investments is much less marked than that described by the mainstream theory. In fact, according to the orthodox theory, private investments tend to be considered as the result of the choices of individual entrepreneurs who are risking their own resources. For this reason, they must be rewarded with profits reflecting the judgement of impersonal market forces. Nevertheless, as pointed out by Schumpeter, even in the case of private investments the risks are borne by the society as a whole, which is represented by institutions like the banks that finance the entrepreneurs by creating new money. Moreover, the analysis presented in the previous chapters highlights the purely monetary nature of profits. Profits are an expression of the rules of the game affecting the activities of big businesses and of the financial system, and they also depend on the accounting criteria used to measure private and public costs. Thus, public and private investments cannot be evaluated by simply considering the monetary values of profits (and of losses). The convenience to invest must be defined on the basis of shared criteria for the definition of private and social costs, and the degree of efficiency with which resources are employed.

Thus, the socialization of investments is an important tool in the development of a shared project for the common good. Along with enterprises, political authorities and social organizations must identify innovations and investments whose profitability is not assessed through private accounting principles, but through criteria that take into account the social costs caused by environmental damage and human degradation due to high unemployment rates. The process by which social needs are transformed into aggregate demand can be seen as a new expression of Schumpeterian innovation. In this case, the role of the entrepreneur-innovator is assumed by a political authority or by private subjects who are not guided by the objective of creating shareholder value. Environmental protection must be included among the most important social needs. In his encyclical, Pope Francis underlines the link between economic and environmental crises.[10] James K. Galbraith (2014) argues that resource costs are the source of the instability of capitalist economies, while Mazzucato (2013) calls for the creation of a green industrial revolution.

3.3 Labour and Employment

Labour and the quality of labour are key components of a good life. In a monetary economy, the concept of 'social cost of unemployment' can be defined, whereas it is completely absent in the corn economy described in the mainstream theory, in which flexibility of wages and prices ensures full employment of the labour force. In a monetary economy, there are two reasons to stress the importance of the social cost of unemployment. First, a monetary economy is typically characterized by the presence of involuntary unemployment due to fluctuations in aggregate demand. Second, labour is a key element of a person's well-being as it is a factor of social cohesion. Thanks to his job, a person performs a role that is recognized by the other members of the society. In other words, working means being a part of a system of relationships that generates well-being. Amartya Sen used the concept of 'social exclusion' to describe the costs of unemployment:

> Unemployment can be a major causal factor predisposing people to social exclusion. The exclusion applies not only to economic opportunities, such as job-related insurance, and to pension and medical entitlements, but also to social activities, such as participation in the life of the community, which may be quite problematic for jobless people. [...] The penalties of unemployment include not only income loss, but also far-reaching effects on self-confidence, work motivation, basic competence, social integration, racial harmony, gender justice, and the appreciation and use of individual freedom and responsibility. (Sen 1997, pp. 161, 168)

Similar considerations about the social importance of labour can be found in Pope Francis's encyclical.[11] This concept of labour can also be found in the Italian constitution, which, according to J.P.Morgan, represents an obstacle to the process of European integration. The first article of the Italian constitution reads: 'Italy is a democratic Republic founded on labour.' Article four also acknowledges the right to work: 'The Republic recognizes the right of all citizens to work and promotes those conditions which render this right effective.'

In the aforementioned article of 1997, Amartya Sen expressed his surprise for how little attention the European institutions devoted to the issue of unemployment, which, at the end of the twentieth century, affected approximately 10 million people. Sen was also alarmed by the fact that the European institutions appeared to be more interested in achieving the goal of reducing budget deficits than in reducing unemployment. Today, the situation is much worse than that described by Sen 20 years ago. The number of unemployed people has risen from 10 to 25 million, but the attitude of the European institutions does not seem to have changed.

Sen (1997) distinguishes between 'occupation of poor quality' and 'good jobs' to emphasize that the problem of unemployment cannot simply be solved by generating a high number of new jobs, but must create high-quality employment opportunities. Obviously, the lack of a job can push unemployed workers to accept harsh working conditions and low wages, but this is not a fair and dignified solution. In this perspective, neither Keynes's famous statement that unemployment could be eliminated by paying unemployed workers to dig holes,[12] nor his provocative assertion that, at the time of the pharaohs in Egypt, the problem of unemployment was solved by building pyramids,[13] are appropriate ways of creating 'good jobs'. The well-being that people derive from their jobs is not simply due to their wages, but also to the awareness that with their work they are contributing to achieving something that will be appreciated by the community. Thus, the examples taken from Keynes's *General Theory* could be interpreted as a provocation by the author, because government authorities must take care of creating not simply new jobs, but new 'good' jobs.

3.4   Income

A job that provides an adequate income is another important component of a 'good life'. According to the traditional theory, in a well-functioning economy markets determine a fair remuneration of labour and capital, because they are rewarded in proportion to their productivity. However, this argument does not apply to a monetary economy, as it is hard to establish a connection between profits and wages and their productivity.

As Keynes and Schumpeter underlined, in a monetary economy profits are purely a monetary phenomenon, for the entrepreneur's aim is not to produce the largest possible amount of goods, but to sell what was produced in order to gain monetary proceeds in excess of the production costs. In a monetary economy, profits have a social dimension that can be defined in relation to their monetary nature. As we have seen in Chapter 5, Schumpeter concludes that the profits from the innovations introduced by entrepreneurs are not the result of the productivity of a particular productive factor such as capital. Profits depend on two factors. First, an entrepreneur can only make profits if he first obtains credit from the

financial system, either in the form of newly created money or through
the transformation of pre-existing wealth into monetary capital. Second,
the amount of monetary profits reflects the success of an innovation. This
success does not depend on the ability to meet exogenous needs
expressed by consumers, as argued by mainstream economists. Rather, it
depends on the entrepreneurs' ability to change the habits of consumers
endowed with adequate purchasing power.

In a monetary economy, profits are not only the result of what Keynes
called enterprise. Speculation is another factor that helps to emphasize
that in a monetary economy profits and wages do not reflect the
productivity of capital and labour. It is indeed very difficult to argue that,
in the years before the onset of the crisis, the profits generated by the
banking system and the remuneration of bank managers, whose function,
according to the traditional theory, should be similar to that of mechanics
in the second-hand car market described by Akerlof (1970), reflected
some form of productivity.

As we saw in Chapter 6, Keynes, by referring to the profits generated
through speculation, observed that experience does not prove that the
activities that contribute most to the welfare of society are rewarded with
higher profits. As was pointed out in Chapter 8, the transition from the
regulated to the neoliberal form of capitalism generated a major increase
in inequalities in income distribution, which is explained not only by the
growing weight of finance and speculation, but also by the hyper-
globalization process and by the way the benefits of innovations that
allowed an increase in labour productivity have been distributed. These
innovations often result in the dismissal of thousands of workers and in a
considerable increase in the amount of profits obtained by companies, of
bonuses paid out to managers and of capital gains earned by the
companies' shareholders.

Mainstream economists tend to ignore the issue of inequalities, since
they argue that in a market economy no individual has the power to
influence the behaviour of others, and that individuals choose to co-
operate when they recognize mutual advantages.[14] For this reason,
Friedman (1970, p. 1) believed that the only goal of a company is 'to
make as much money as possible while conforming to their basic rules of
the society, both those embodied in law and those embodied in ethical
custom'. He sharply criticized the doctrine of social responsibility of
business, claiming that it 'involves the acceptance of the socialist view
that political mechanisms, not market mechanisms, are the appropriate
way to determine the allocation of scarce resources to alternative uses'
(Friedman 1970, p. 3).[15]

The growing inequalities recorded in Western economies in recent decades show that no socialist project has been realized. On the contrary, the rhetoric of free markets has been used to justify the introduction of rules of the game that have favoured the specific interests of particular social groups. In his essay of 1930, Keynes imagined that, within a few generations, technical progress would have freed the population of developed countries from the need to work. Keynes's forecast was based on two assumptions. First, he considered an economic system character-ized by a set of given needs and the principle of satiation of needs. Second, he supposed it would be relatively easy to transform the productivity gains achieved through the introduction of innovations in higher incomes and less labour time for each citizen. The experience of the last 40 years shows that this is not easy at all. The sharp increase in economic inequalities during the era of neoliberal capitalism leads to the conclusion that the benefits generated by innovations have not been distributed fairly.

It should be remembered that increasing inequality undermines the sense of belonging to the same community. The low level of income earned by an ever-growing number of workers is not consistent with the aim of ensuring a 'good life' for all members of society. Thus, measures need to be introduced with the aim of reducing inequalities and distrib-uting the benefits obtained from the implementation of innovations to the entire society.

In a society in which individuals are aware that the profits achieved through the introduction of innovations are the outcome of a shared commitment, and that working is a fundamental element of social inclusion, inequalities can be reduced also by changing the rules for labour remuneration. In this regard, Martin Weitzman (1986) and James Meade (1989) suggested a move away from a remuneration system based on fixed salaries established through bargaining between enterprises and trade unions to embrace a system based on cooperation and participation, in which wages are tied to the corporate results.

In economies with an efficient tax system, a reduction in inequalities can be achieved by easing the tax burden on low-income groups and by increasing the tax rates applied to high-income groups, as suggested, for example, by Robert Reich (2010, 2015). Considering the situation of the United States, Reich (2015) recommends the introduction of a guaranteed minimum income to all citizens, financed by taxes on higher incomes and on the possessors of large wealth. The demand for goods from citizens who do not work, but have an income, can certainly be met thanks to the productivity gains achieved through the introduction of new technologies. However, in my view, the guarantee of an income to all citizens is not enough for the achievement of a significant level of social welfare. People also need a job, as work is an essential element to transform an individual into a citizen playing a role recognized by the other members of the community.

3.5   Finance and Speculation

An economic policy aimed at creating the conditions for a 'good life' must reduce the likelihood that a financial crisis like the one that erupted in 2007 may occur again. Pursuing the goal of stabilizing the financial system should become a key component of the action plan of monetary authorities. Bernanke (2013) recognizes that during the Great Moderation monetary authorities neglected the goal of financial stability, for they behaved as if financial crises could not happen.

As discussed in the first part of this chapter, after the outbreak of the crisis a number of proposals were made to strengthen the stability of the financial system via increased capital requirements for banks. The limit of these proposals is that they do not consider the underlying causes of a sudden fall in the value of the banks' assets. If the credit market had the same characteristics as the second-hand car market described by Akerlof, such a collapse would not be possible, as it would imply that suddenly all bankers have become unable to assess the characteristics of the borrowers' projects.

As noted in Chapter 8, the current crisis shows that financial markets have different characteristics from those of the traditional markets and the market of used cars analysed by Akerlof. These features can be highlighted thanks to Keynes's and Schumpeter's lessons on the distinction between enterprise and speculation. Schumpeter stressed the essential role of money and credit in a capitalist economy. In Chapter 6 we have shown that the relationship between bank money and economic development helps to explain the process of wealth accumulation and the importance of speculative markets. Keynes stressed the danger that speculative activities might prevail over genuine entrepreneurial initiatives. The description of the crises provided in this book confirms how Keynes's concerns were real and justified.

Without citing Keynes, a mainstream economist like Zingales (2015) uses the distinction between enterprise and speculation to distinguish between 'good' and 'bad' finance. 'Good' finance promotes the introduction of innovations, while 'bad' finance allows few individuals to obtain higher incomes through activities that do not produce significant results in social terms.[16] The examples used by Zingales to describe 'bad' finance are related to the operations that enabled the banking system to achieve huge short-term profits through speculation rather than enterprise.[17]

These considerations lead to the conclusion that the primary objective of a regulation of the financial system must be to avoid speculation prevailing over entrepreneurial activities: 'we must … lean against the free market's potentially harmful bias toward the "speculative" finance of existing assets' (Turner 2015, p. 208).[18] This objective may be achieved by implementing measures that: 1) make speculative transactions less profitable; 2) redefine the objectives of the monetary authorities; and 3) prevent any financial crisis from badly affecting production activity and government budgets.

The first measure that may affect the profitability of speculative transactions is the introduction of a tax on short-term financial trans-actions, such as the tax proposed by James Tobin in 1974 (the so-called Tobin Tax) immediately after the collapse of the international monetary system outlined in Bretton Woods. More specifically, Tobin proposed the introduction of a tax on currency transactions because he believed that an excessive capital mobility would have destabilizing effects on the inter-national economy. His proposal drew inspiration from Keynes's argument outlined in the *General Theory* that a tax on financial transactions would frustrate the prevalence of speculation over entrepreneurship.[19] A second measure that would reduce the weight of speculative activities is a reform of the securitization legislation aimed at requiring banks to retain a significant share of Asset Backed Securities created to finance the acquisition of loans on their own balance sheets. This way, banks would be encouraged to grant high-quality loans (Roubini and Mihm 2010). The third measure involves the incentives system. The current crisis has shown that remuneration schemes based on the distribution of bonuses calculated in proportion to the achieved profits lead bank managers to focus on speculative transactions. Thus, redesigning the bank managers' system of remuneration is a critically important measure.

As for the redefinition of the tasks assigned to monetary authorities, it was previously underlined that, according to the traditional theory, their basic function is to maintain price stability. In a monetary economy, where speculation plays a relevant role, the central bank should also perform a macroeconomic supervisory role.[20] As discussed in Chapter 8, economic crises may be unpredictable, but they are not necessarily inevitable. Many economists have argued that monetary authorities should monitor the prices of financial assets and intervene by manipulat-ing interest rates and using administrative tools in order to avoid the development of asset bubbles. Thus, the approach taken by Alan

Greenspan in the early 2000s, whereby the Federal Reserve could not intervene to prevent the development of a speculative bubble since bubbles can only be identified once they have burst, must be abandoned.

The last set of measures should prevent the effects of a financial crisis from paralysing an entire economic system and losses generated by speculative transactions from becoming an intolerable burden on public budgets. To this end, the separation between the activities of commercial banks and investment banks, which was introduced after the outbreak of the Great Depression, should be reintroduced. In the United States, the reintroduction of this principle is established under the so-called Volcker rule, which was included in the Dodd–Frank Act, that is, the draft reform of the US banking system approved by President Obama in 2010. The adoption of this principle is also advocated in reports issued by several commissions established to submit proposals for a reform of the financial system, for example the United Kingdom's Independent Commission on Banking, chaired by John Vickers (ICB 2011), and the committee chaired by the President of the Central Bank of Finland, Erkki Liikanen (Liikanen 2012). The second measure consists in a considerable increase in the banks' share capital. As suggested by Admati and Hellwig (2013), the amount of the banks' share capital should be fixed at between 20 and 30 per cent of their assets, well above the requirements set under the new Basel agreements (Basel III).

The introduction of a regulatory framework aimed at reducing the weight of speculative activities must overcome the resistance of the financial lobby, which tends to consider the current crisis as an unforeseeable and exceptional event. Furthermore, the managers of major banks tenaciously argue that introducing measures aimed at reducing the probability that an extremely rare event occurs, such as the outbreak of a financial crisis, may severely limit the role that finance plays in supporting the production of wealth. To justify this thesis, the financial lobby claims that phenomena such as Google and Yahoo could only happen thanks to financial innovations. However, Mulgan's (2013) and Mazzucato's (2013) descriptions of the entrepreneurial role played by the state in the development of the most innovative technologies seriously question the position of the financial lobby. Admati and Hellwig (2013) compare the thesis endorsed in financial circles to the story told by Hans Christian Andersen, in which the courtiers pretend to admire the emperor's new clothes until a child cries out that the emperor is not wearing anything at all.[21]

The arguments presented by the financial lobby overlook the fact that financial innovations produce different effects as compared with innovations introduced, for example, in the second-hand car market. Most likely, in the latter case innovations allow mechanics to better assess the quality of second-hand cars. The mainstream theory's claim that financial markets work like the second-hand car market described by Akerlof (1970) led even the most skilled financial traders to believe that the complex financial instruments created since the 1980s would reduce the risks related to financial transactions. This misunderstanding spread because the importance of uncertainty and speculation as key elements of a monetary economy was underestimated.

It should finally be emphasized that past experience does not prove that the processes of deregulation and financial innovation produced a significant effect on the growth rate of advanced economies. Actually, the GDP growth rates in Europe and the United States in the years between 1945 and 1975, a period of rigid regulation of financial markets and capital movements, were higher than those recorded in the following years. In the United States, that is, the country where the most pervasive financial innovations were implemented, the GDP annual growth rate after the end of World War II averaged 3.4 per cent, whereas it decreased to 2.4 per cent from the mid-1970s to 2007.[22]

3.6 Globalization

The objective of a 'good life' cannot be pursued exclusively in a single country. The world economy is not made of homogeneous nations led by governments with similar objectives. The reality is very different. The world's population can be divided into three categories: the rich, who are about one billion and live in the West and in Japan; the poor, who are about five billion and live in hardship; and the hungry, who are about one billion and die of starvation and diseases that in the West could be treated at a minimum cost. Since the 1980s, the liberalization of goods and capital flows has strongly increased the degree of interdependence among national economies. The hyper-globalization process has been governed by the interests of large multinational companies that have transferred increasingly more production lines from industrialized to developing countries where labour costs are lower and environmental and legal constraints are softer.

The arguments used to introduce the concept of a 'good life' imply that the management of globalization and the definition of solutions to the problems of the three components of humanity cannot be entrusted to large multinational companies. It is an illusion to believe that such complex solutions can emerge spontaneously from the workings of market forces. Such solutions must rather be designed by intellectual and political forces.[23] Rodrik (2011) pointed out that hyper-globalization is incompatible with the presence of national democratic states as it enables large multinational companies to circumvent the rules that protect labour in Western countries. Thus, the task of politics is to combine the freedom of companies to choose where they want to run their business with the interests of workers in advanced as well as in emerging countries.

Creating a supranational political authority that could democratically define a set of generally applicable rules does not seem realistic. The most realistic hypothesis is that indicated by Rodrik (2011), who advocates a return to the philosophy of a regulated globalization that inspired the Bretton Woods agreements. This would require a cooperation among the United States, Europe, Japan and emerging countries such as China and India.[24] The growing awareness of the need for international coordination shows how Europe has huge responsibilities in this process. As a matter of fact, in this historical phase Europe is paralysed by the pursuit of austerity policies and does not appear to be able to play a strategic role in the global arena.

3.7   Europe

Unsustainable levels of unemployment, and especially youth unemployment, are a clear sign of the European decline. The responses to the crisis designed by the European institutions mainly consist in austerity measures justified by dominant beliefs whose content can be summarized as follows: 1) the accumulation of public debt enabled older generations to live beyond their means; 2) the excessive amount of public debt frustrates the growth prospects of the Southern European countries, as they are forced to allocate a significant share of their resources to pay interest on the accumulated debt; and 3) austerity policies are aimed at finding resources to stimulate growth by cutting public spending. The impact of these arguments on European public opinion is usually strengthened by several examples of reckless waste of public resources.

As already mentioned, the beliefs underlying austerity policies are based on the assumption that contemporary economies function as the corn economy described by classical economists. The criticism of these dominant beliefs questions the following two points: 1) the hypothesis that austerity is key to recovering the resources needed for growth; and 2) the concept of resources itself that is at the root of the 'dominant beliefs'. According to current opinion, governments know exactly what to do to generate economic growth and create new jobs, but their projects are undermined by the lack of resources. Politicians, opinion leaders and intellectuals generally claim that 'there is no money to create jobs'. The corollary to this point of view is that austerity measures are a crucial prerequisite to free the resources needed to revive the growth process and to create new jobs.

The analysis illustrated in this book shows that the currently dominant thesis is groundless, as in a monetary economy the availability of resources is not a problem. In fact, in a monetary economy the resources needed to make investments and to start production processes by using the available workforce do not correspond to the amount of unconsumed corn, but to the amount of purchasing power that the financial system can give to entrepreneurs and, more generally, to all those who need liquidity to implement their spending plans. Hence, in a monetary economy resources are virtually unlimited since the financial system can create new money or transform part of households' wealth, which in contemporary economies represents a multiple of the annual income, into readily available liquidity. Hence, what prevents contemporary economies from creating the conditions for different standards of living is not the scarcity of resources, but the spread of dominant beliefs based on the assumption that economic systems still work like corn economies, and the inability to define a shared vision of the common good aimed at creating the conditions for a 'good life'.

With regard to the notion of resources, the prevailing attitude, especially in Europe, can be considered as a manifestation of what Keynes called the 'accountant's nightmare'. With this expression, Keynes wanted to highlight the tendency to evaluate every area of life of a community in terms of income and expenditure, costs and revenues, subject to the constraint of a balanced budget. This criterion may seem to be pure common sense. At first glance, even the Fiscal Compact, which requires the countries of the Euro area to comply with the principle of a balanced budget, may seem an expression of common sense as it implies that public budgets must be managed like a family budget. Debts must be paid back and therefore they are a burden that current generations are passing on to their children.

This way of understanding a public budget does not work for the following reasons. First, a country that retains its monetary sovereignty and therefore has its own currency can repay its debt by creating new money. Of course, this option is not available to private subjects and to the countries that joined the European Monetary Union. These countries' debt is denominated in a currency that is created by a supranational central bank. The origin of the austerity policies in Europe lies in the fear of 'virtuous' countries that they may have to repay the debts of more heavily indebted countries. Second, public debts are a major component of private wealth. If public debts disappeared a significant share of private wealth would also disappear. Finally, a third reason that casts doubts on the validity of the principle of a balanced budget is the fact that the prohibition to borrow only applies to the public sector. Hence, conventional wisdom accepts the idea that private firms can borrow to carry out their investment projects. The underlying reason for this discrimination is quite clear: the public sector wastes resources while the private sector does not. Hence, only private individuals or firms should borrow to invest the resources that savers did not consume. This argument may be true in a corn economy, but it does not apply to a monetary economy where entrepreneurs do not borrow from savers but from banks, which create new money.

As was explained in the previous pages, in a monetary economy the process of innovation that influences the composition of production and the lifestyle of households cannot be managed only by banks and innovators-entrepreneurs. The quality and composition of production are key components of common good. As pointed out by Joan Robinson (1972), economic policy must be aimed not only at achieving a certain level of employment, but also at achieving a specific composition of employment. As Mazzucato (2013) and Mulgan (2013) pointed out, the innovations introduced after World War II, and the innovations that we can imagine will be developed in the near future, require quantities of resources, skills and 'patience' that are often well beyond the limits that typically characterize the relationship between banks and Schumpeterian entrepreneurs.

These considerations lead to the conclusion that the adoption of the constraint of a balanced budget by the countries of the Euro area can be regarded as an expression of Keynes's 'accountant's nightmare', which forces modern societies to build 'slums' although they possess the technology and the skills needed to erect the 'wonder city':

> The nineteenth century carried to extravagant lengths the criterion of what one can call for short the 'financial results', as a test of the advisability of any course of action sponsored by private or by collective action. The whole conduct of life was made into a sort of parody of an accountant's nightmare. Instead of using their vastly increased material and technical resources to build a wonder city, the men of the nineteenth century built slums; and they thought it right and advisable to build slums because slums, on the test of private enterprise, 'paid', whereas the wonder city would, they thought, have been an act of foolish extravagance, which would, in the imbecile idiom of the financial fashion, have 'mortgaged the future' – though how the construction to-day of great and glorious works can impoverish the future, no man can see until his mind is beset by false analogies from an irrelevant accountancy. [...] [T]he minds of this generation are still so beclouded by bogus calculations that they distrust conclusions which should be obvious, out of a reliance on a system of financial accounting which casts doubt on whether such an

operation will 'pay'. We have to remain poor because it does not 'pay' to be rich. We have to live in hovels, not because we cannot build palaces, but because we cannot 'afford' them. The same rule of self-destructive financial calculation governs every walk of life. We destroy the beauty of the countryside because the unappropriated splendors of nature have no economic value. We are capable of shutting off the sun and the stars because they do not pay a dividend. (Keynes 1933c [2013e], pp. 241–242)

A number of proposals have been made in order to overcome the 'accountant's nightmare'. One of these is to enable the countries of the Eurozone to apply the same accounting standards to both public and private investments, that is, to exclude the cost of investments from the constraint of the balanced budget. Other proposals are aimed at allowing the countries of the Euro area to take advantage of the privilege enjoyed by all governments that can issue debt securities denominated in their own currency. The countries of the Eurozone have given up this privilege, as their debt is actually denominated in a supranational currency. Therefore, many believe that a part of national debts should be transformed into a common debt to be attributed to the Union, thereby associating debts to the institution that creates the money used in the countries of the Euro area.[25]

Romano Prodi and Alberto Quadrio Curzio (2011) recommended the establishment of a European Financial Fund that can issue Euro Union Bonds (EUBs). The fund should have a capital of 1000 billion euro consisting of the gold reserves of the European System of Central Banks and of bonds and stocks owned by the European governments. As the fund is supposed to issue EUBs for a face value of 3000 billion euro, the fund's leverage would be equal to 3. The fund should allocate an amount of 2300 billion euro to buy securities issued by the governments of the EU countries in order to reduce the ratio of the public debt absorbed by the market and the GDP of these countries from 85 per cent to 60 per cent. The remaining 700 billion euro should be used to finance investments aimed at improving the European production system and at expanding public infrastructure. The payment of interest on EUBs would be financed with the revenues gained from the stocks and bonds transferred to the fund, and with a share of the VAT collected in the EU countries.

A similar proposal is that contained in the PADRE plan (Politically Acceptable Debt Restructuring in the Eurozone) developed by Pâris and Wyplosz (2014). This plan provides for the purchase of public debt securities of the Eurozone countries by the ECB, which would finance the operation through the issue of bonds placed on the financial markets.

The bonds issued by the ECB would be considered safe securities, because the ECB can repay them by creating money.

Starting from the proposal advanced by Bernanke in 2003 to address the economic crisis in Japan, several economists have stressed the need to adopt expansionary fiscal policies that do not produce an increase in public debt. In essence, these proposals are based on the idea that the ECB should purchase the bonds generated by government deficits. This would not cause an increase of the public debt held by the wealth holders, and the repayment of the bonds would not require the levy of new taxes or a cut in aggregate spending.[26] Aware of the insurmountable objections to the proposals based on the idea of financing expansionary fiscal policies by means of the creation of new money, Turner (2016) confides in the accounting and institutional creativity skills of the European authorities. In fact, European authorities should consider measures that, although they cannot be considered a form of monetary financing of public deficits from a formal point of view, nevertheless produce analogous expansionary effects on the level of aggregate demand.[27]

Proposals such as this show that contemporary economies lack neither the resources nor the ability to design accounting rules allowing the use of available resources. This aspect of a monetary economy was effectively underlined by Keynes, who, at a conference held in 1942, noted how senseless it was to stop the reconstruction of London, which had partly been destroyed by German bombing attacks, because of a shortage of money:

> Let me begin by telling you how I tried to answer an eminent architect who pushed on one side all the grandiose plans to rebuild London with the phrase: 'Where's the money to come from?' 'The money?' I said. 'But surely, Sir John, you don't build houses with money? Do you mean that there won't be enough bricks and mortar and steel and cement?' 'Oh no', he replied, 'of course there will be plenty of all that'. 'Do you mean', I went on, 'that there won't be enough labour? For what will the builders be doing if they are not building houses?' 'Oh no, that's all right', he agreed. 'Then there is only one conclusion. You must be meaning, Sir John, that there won't be enough *architects*'. But there I was trespassing on the boundaries of politeness. So I hurried to add: 'Well, if there are bricks and mortar and steel and concrete and labour and architects, why not assemble all this good material into houses?' But he was, I fear, quite unconvinced. 'What I want to know', he repeated, 'is where the money is coming from'. To answer that would have got him and me into deeper water than I cared for, so I replied rather shabbily: 'The same place it is coming from now'. (Keynes 1942 [2013f], pp. 264–265)

Keynes closed the conference stressing that what prevents a community from bridging the gap between the level of well-being that could be achieved thanks to the available technology and labour force and the current standard of living is the fact that it is not aware of its actual potentials:

> Anything we can actually *do* we can afford. Once done, it is *there*. Nothing can take it from us. We are immeasurably richer than our predecessors. Is it not evident that some sophistry, some fallacy, governs our collective action if we are forced to be so much meaner than they in the embellishments of life? (Keynes 1942 [2013f], p. 270)

What we lack is not resources, but the ability of political leaders and social forces to develop a shared project allowing every citizen to live a 'good life'. Identifying the scarcity of money as the main cause of the problems affecting contemporary economies is an alibi that hides an inability to understand the characteristics of the world in which we actually live.

NOTES

1. 'In 2008–09 the rich and powerful faced a rising tide of public anger, and where it might lead was unpredictable. Then the austerity view suddenly redirected the focus of public anger, by telling people, "It's not the banks that have done this to you, it's the government and greedy public sector workers and their powerful unions." [...] The groups that have benefited from the existing regime always mobilize to try to preserve it even when it has produced a crisis. The promotion of austerity can be seen as the second step in a two-step response by some actors; first support whatever is necessary to save the banks and stop the free-fall of the economy, then demand a shift to austerity to try to revive the neoliberal form of capitalism' (Kotz 2015, p. 174).
2. 'The political systems in the periphery were established in the aftermath of dictatorship, and were defined by that experience. Constitutions tend to show a strong socialist influence, reflecting the political strength that left wing parties gained after the defeat of fascism. Political systems around the periphery typically display several of the following features: weak executives; weak central states relative to regions; constitutional protection of labor rights; consensus building systems which foster political clientelism; and the right to protest if unwelcome changes are made to the political status quo. The shortcomings of this political legacy have been revealed by the crisis' (J.P.Morgan 2013, p. 12).
3. 'The constitutions and political settlements in the southern periphery, put in place in the aftermath of the fall of fascism, have a number of features which appear to be unsuited to further integration in the region' (J.P.Morgan 2013, p. 2).
4. For a detailed description of the various reform options see for example: Turner (2010), ICB (2011), Liikanen Group (2012), Tolley (2013), Gabbi and Sironi (2014), and Ferri and Neuberger (2014).
5. On this point see, for example, Blyth (2013), Beck (2012), Marsh (2013) and Lapavitsas (2012).
6. The letter, sent on 11 August 2011, was signed by Kenneth Arrow, Peter Diamond, William Sharpe, Charles Shultz, Alan Blinder, Eric Maskin, Robert Solow and Laura Tyson.

7. Rodrik (2011) also points out that the adoption of the neoliberal thesis in international economic relations might conflict with democracy. On the relationship between neoliberal capitalism and democracy see Judt (2010), Crouch (2011, 2013) and Gamble (2014).
8. James K. Galbraith criticizes the positions expressed by Krugman and Stiglitz, as they are based on the belief that expansionary fiscal policies would be sufficient to achieve full employment: 'even were the political and ideological barriers to stimulus swept away, even if the New Deal were reinvented at full scale and with all the same political momentum and esprit de corps, there would remain … obstacles to achieving high growth and full employment' (Galbraith 2014, p. 238).
9. '[I]t seems unlikely that the influence of banking policy on the rate of interest will be sufficient by itself to determine an optimum rate of investment. I conceive, therefore, that a somewhat comprehensive socialization of investment will prove the only means of securing an approximation to full employment' (Keynes 1936 [2013a], p. 378).
10. 'The alliance between the economy and technology ends up sidelining anything unrelated to its immediate interests.[…] [E]conomic powers continue to justify the current global system where priority tends to be given to speculation and the pursuit of financial gain, which fail to take the context into account, let alone the effects on human dignity and the natural environment. Here we see how environmental deterioration and human and ethical degradation are closely linked' (Francis, the Holy Father 2014, paras. 54–56).
11. 'Work should be the setting for [the] rich personal growth, where many aspects of life enter into play: creativity, planning for the future, developing our talents, living out our values, relating to others, giving glory to God. It follows that, in the reality of today's global society, it is essential that we continue to prioritize the goal of access to steady employment for everyone, no matter the limited interests of business and dubious economic-reasoning' (Francis, the Holy Father 2014, para. 127).
12. 'If the Treasury were to fill old bottles with bank-notes, bury them at suitable depths in disused coal-mines which are then filled up to the surface with town rubbish, and leave it to private enterprise on well-tried principles of *laissez-faire* to dig the notes up again … , there need be no more unemployment and, with the help of the repercussions, the real income of the community, and its capital wealth also, would probably become a good deal greater than it actually is' (Keynes (1936) [2013a], p. 129).
13. 'Ancient Egypt was doubly fortunate, and doubtless owed to this its fabled wealth, in that it possessed *two* activities, namely, pyramid-building as well as the search for the precious metals, the fruits of which, since they could not serve the needs of man by being consumed, did not stale with abundance. The Middle Ages built cathedrals and sang dirges. Two pyramids, two masses for the dead, are twice as good as one; but not so two railways from London to York. Thus we are so sensible, have schooled ourselves to so close a semblance of prudent financiers, taking careful thought before we add to the "financial" burdens of posterity by building them houses to live in, that we have no such easy escape from the sufferings of unemployment' (Keynes 1936 [2013a], p. 131).
14. 'The political principle that underlines the market mechanism is unanimity. In an ideal free market resting on private property, no individual can coerce any other, all cooperation is voluntary, all parties to such cooperation benefit or they need not participate' (Friedman 1970, p. 6).
15. On the shareholder value revolution, see Krippner (2011).
16. 'To separate the wheat from the chaff, we need to identify the rent-seeking component of finance, i.e. those activities that while profitable from an individual point of view are not so from a societal point of view' (Zingales 2015, p. 13).
17. Zingales also recognizes that there are no elements allowing us to define a relationship between financial innovation and economic growth: 'there is no theoretical basis for the presumption that financial innovation, by expanding financial opportunities, increases welfare. […] I am not aware of any evidence that the creation and growth of the junk bond market, the option and futures market, or the development of the over-the-counter derivatives are positively correlated with economic growth' (Zingales 2015, pp. 9–11).

18. The reform proposal advanced by Rossi (2015) is consistent with this objective. See also Lin (2013).

19. 'The introduction of a substantial government transfer tax on all transactions might prove the most serviceable reform available, with a view to mitigating the predominance of speculation over enterprise in the United States' (Keynes 1936 [2013a], p. 160). On the Tobin Tax see Tobin (1978, 1996, 1997, 1999).

20. In September 2010, the European Parliament approved the institution of the European Systemic Risk Board, that is, a macroeconomic supervisory agency, proposed by a commission chaired by de Larosière, which came into operation at the end of 2010. See also Akerlof et al. (2014).

21. 'Many of the claims made by leading bankers and banking experts actually have as much substance as the emperor's new clothes in Andersen's story. But most people do not challenge these claims, and the claims have an impact on policy. The specialists' façade of competence and confidence is too intimidating. Even people who know better fail to speak up. The emperor may be naked, but he continues his parade without being challenged about his attire' (Admati and Hellwig 2013, p. 2).

22. See, for example, Schularik and Taylor (2009), Turner (2010, 2012), Krugman (2012), Stiglitz (2012) and Ostry et al. (2016).

23. Thomas Palley (2012) emphasizes the need to move from a globalization driven by the interests and pressures of big corporations to a globalization that favours the maintenance of decent working and living conditions in developed countries while promoting the improvement of living standards in developing countries.

24. Fiorentini and Montani (2012) underline the need to design and implement a global plan for growth and employment with the involvement of the United States, Europe, United Kingdom and Japan in order to address the problem of poverty and to prevent a global ecological crisis. On this topic see also Temin and Vines (2013) and Crouch (2013).

25. For example, see De Grauwe and Moesen (2009), Delpla and von Weizsäcker (2010) and Galbraith et al. (2014).

26. See, for example, Ascari (2014), Buiter (2014), Giavazzi and Tabellini (2014), Galí (2014), Bossone et al. (2014) and Turner (2016).

27. 'The best pragmatic short-term strategy … may well involve operations that post facto turn out to be money finance, but whose essential nature can be denied for fear of legal and political challenges' (Turner 2016, p. 236).

Conclusions

> The financial crisis of 2007–08 provided an opportunity to develop a new economy, more attentive to ethical principles, and new ways of regulating speculative financial practices and virtual wealth. But the response to the crisis did not include rethinking the outdated criteria which continue to rule the world. (Francis, the Holy Father 2014, para. 189)

Economists have been accused of being unable to predict the eruption of the crisis. As a matter of fact, they carry much bigger responsibilities since, from the beginning of the 1970s, they have developed a theoretical model based on the idea that no disastrous economic crisis can occur in a market economy. Since the early 1980s, this model has provided the theoretical foundation justifying the deregulation of financial markets, the liberalization of movement of goods and capital, and the privatization of public companies. The spread of neoliberal ideology is at the root of all the behaviours that, during the years of the Great Moderation, created the conditions for the explosion of the worst economic crisis since the Great Depression of the 1930s.

The current crisis has brought out the limits of the dominant macro-economic theory. In the first part of this book, these limits were described through an analysis of the explanations of the causes of the crisis given by leading orthodox economists. These explanations share the conclusion that the current crisis should be seen as an accidental event. In other words, mainstream economists believe that the crisis was caused by a series of mistakes made by the US monetary authorities and by the US banking system. The limit of these interpretations is that they use concepts and relationships that are inconsistent with the tenets of the dominant macroeconomic theory.

The orthodox macroeconomic theory describes an economic system in which no crises can ever occur, that is, a system in which: 1) monetary authorities control the quantity of money and not the supply of credit; 2) banks, acting as financial intermediaries, do not create risk; and 3) savings finance investments and not speculative bubbles. However, when explaining the origins of the crisis, mainstream economists refer to a profoundly different system. In fact, they recognize that the crisis developed in a context in which: 1) the supply of credit depends on the choices made by the banking system and not on the agents' saving decisions; 2) the financial system can create risk; and 3) the phenomenon of speculation is relevant.

The second part of the book was devoted to outlining an alternative theoretical approach. As was demonstrated, Keynes's and Schumpeter's criticisms of the dominant theory of their time also apply to the theoretical model developed over the past 40 years. Both Keynes and Schumpeter claim that the traditional theory is unable to explain the functioning of the 'economic society in which we actually live' (Keynes 1936 [2013a], p. 3), and point out that this limitation is due to the way the classical theory defines the role of money.

Schumpeter emphasized that the key feature of capitalist economies is the process of change due to the introduction of innovations, and that money, and especially bank money, plays a crucial role in this process. Conversely, Keynes focused on the issue of fluctuations in the levels of income and employment and on the relationship between money and economic crises. The contributions made by these two great economists lead to the conclusion that money is an essential element for the explanation of the two fundamental characteristics of contemporary economies: 1) the process of economic development driven by innovations; and 2) crises. Starting from the lessons of Keynes and Schumpeter, the second part of this book puts together a theoretical model that offers an explanation of the functioning of an economic system with the characteristics specified in the mainstream economists' interpretations of the causes of the current crisis.

To explain the relationship between monetary policy and credit supply, Chapter 5 underlined that both Keynes and Schumpeter based their analyses on a kind of money that features the same characteristics as bank money, namely money created through a credit agreement. The relationship between finance and risk, which is crucial in Rajan's interpretation of the origins of the crisis (2006, 2010), was described by referring to the concepts of Keynesian uncertainty and Schumpeterian innovation. Chapter 5 also showed that bank money is a necessary element to explain the existence of a high flow of investments-innovations, and thus the importance of the dimension of uncertainty. Keynes's and Schumpeter's analyses highlight the monetary nature of uncertainty, as they define a causal relationship between the presence of bank money and the innovations implemented by entrepreneurs. This causal sequence allows us to explain the relationship between finance and risk that characterizes Rajan's analysis of the crisis.

The mainstream interpretations of the crisis also rely on concepts such as 'speculation' and 'speculative bubble' that are completely alien to a corn economy. However, these very concepts are fundamental elements of the monetary economy described by Keynes. Chapter 6 showed that the phenomenon of speculation can be explained by specifying the relationship between saving decisions and the stock of wealth. The importance of the wealth accumulation process emerges in the context of an economy in which needs are insatiable, because innovations continuously determine the production of new goods and the appearance of new needs. In a monetary economy, the fundamental function of the financial system is not only to create new money through the provision of credit, but also to 'produce liquidity', which consists in transforming wealth into capital thanks to the existence of markets in which durable goods and financial assets can be continuously exchanged. The existence of these markets explains why the phenomenon of speculation is so relevant.

The lesson taught by heretical economists such as Marx, Keynes, Schumpeter, Kalecki, Kaldor and Minsky allows development of a theoretical model that describes an economy with the characteristics specified by mainstream economists in their interpretations of the current crisis. However, following the arguments of these great economists, the nature of the crisis appears to be profoundly different from that described by mainstream economists. The analysis developed in the second part of this book emphasizes the endogenous nature of the crisis. Keynes's monetary economy and Schumpeter's capitalist economy are not stable structures converging towards a full employment equilibrium, but systems that are characterized by an evolutionary process marked by phases in which capitalism takes different forms. The economic crisis thus represents an expression of the fragility of a specific form of capitalism, and a sign of transition from one form of capitalism to another.

The third part of the book describes the endogenous nature of the subprime mortgage crisis. It also points out that, while economic crises are endogenous phenomena, they are not inevitable. In fact, they cannot be compared to natural events such as earthquakes, because they are a consequence of the economic decisions taken by the various stakeholders of a society. This implies that, while the probability that an earthquake takes place does not depend on the theories developed by seismologists to explain its origin, economic crises are not independent of the way economists theorize the functioning of the economic system. In other words, the current crisis shows that economic theories are not abstract intellectual constructions, but they do have major repercussions for the levels of income and employment.

Economists interpreted the stagflation of the 1970s as the result of a set of policies based on a wrong theoretical model. The reaction of

economists to Friedman's criticism, which showed that Keynesian policies are ineffective when workers do not suffer from monetary illusion,
was paradoxical. Instead of looking for more effective policy tools with
the aim of redesigning the development model that had worked success-
fully for almost thirty years, the majority of economists concluded that
the instability of the 1970s had been caused by the adoption of wrong
economic policies, and that there was no need for public authorities to
intervene and facilitate the definition of a new social bargain. The
counterrevolution initiated by Friedman and continued by Lucas led
economists to accept a new version of the pre-Keynesian theory, according to which the flexibility of wages and prices was sufficient to ensure
full employment conditions. The spread of the neoliberal model contributed to the current crisis in two ways. First, it favoured behaviours and
decisions that indeed caused the crisis. Second, it led to underestimation
of the signs of instability that emerged in the years before the outbreak of
the housing bubble.

In the 1930s, after the 1929 Wall Street crash, a number of important
measures were implemented to regulate the financial markets so as to
reduce the weight of speculative activities. Those years marked the
beginning of a period that ended in the late 1970s, which Reinhart and
Rogoff (2009) defined as a period of financial repression, in which no
significant financial crises occurred. However, in the early 1980s the
situation changed radically. Financial markets were heavily deregulated
and capital movements were liberalized. Neoliberal ideology led most
economists to compare the functioning of financial markets with the
workings of traditional markets and to overlook the potentially destructive effects of speculation. Chapter 8 showed that, due to the theoretical
counterrevolution that began in the 1970s, the housing bubble that
triggered the crisis was the instrument that allowed the financial system
to obtain high profits through the creation of what Rajan (2006) called an
'iceberg of risk'.

The last chapter of this book offered an analysis of the policies
adopted to overcome the crisis. These policies, and especially those
implemented in Europe, drew inspiration from the same neoliberal
ideology that created the conditions for the outbreak of the crisis. In other
words, the same doctors who contributed to causing the disease and who
could not diagnose its onset were called in to prescribe the therapy.
According to mainstream economists, the current crisis, like that of the
1970s, essentially depends on an excessive presence of the state in the
economy. Consequently, this crisis should be addressed with a combination of measures aimed, above all, at limiting the weight of the public
sector. The first measure consists in austerity policies aimed at cutting

public deficits and reducing the size of public budgets. The second measure is the introduction of structural reforms aimed at increasing the flexibility of markets, especially the labour markets. Finally, to strengthen the banks' ability to withstand the effects of a sudden fall in the value of their assets, mainstream economists recommend a reform of the financial system.

The fundamental limitation of these policies lies in the fact that they were developed with the assumption that contemporary economies work like a corn economy. In other words, these policies were designed for an economy that does not exist in reality. A monetary economy does not evolve towards the 'steady state' described by classical economists, which Keynes, in a famous essay of 1930 devoted to the analysis of the economic possibilities of 'his' grandchildren, portrayed as a situation in which humanity would finally solve the economic problem. As remarked by Schumpeter, in a monetary economy the continuous introduction of innovations nullifies the neoclassical principle of the consumer's sovereignty because needs become endogenous, thereby postponing the prospect of overcoming the economic problem to an indefinite future.

If needs are not exogenously given and are induced by the introduction of innovations resulting from the decisions taken by entrepreneurs and bankers, the focus should be shifted onto the composition of production, the way in which production is organized and the question of income distribution. For this reason, the fundamental goal of economic policies is not so much to maximize the income growth rate but to create the conditions that would allow the citizens of a country and humanity as a whole to live what, ever since Aristotle's times, has been defined as a 'good life'.

Bibliography

Quotations from works for which an English edition is not available have been translated by the author.

Acemoglu, D. (2009), 'The Crisis of 2008: structural lessons for and from economics', *CEPR Policy Insight*, No. 28, January.

Acemoglu, D. and J. Robinson (2012), *Why Nations Fail: The Origins of Power, Prosperity, and Poverty*, New York: Random House.

Admati, A. and M. Hellwig (2013), *The Bankers' New Clothes: What's Wrong With Banking and What to Do About It*, Princeton, NJ: Princeton University Press.

Akerlof, G. (1970), 'The market for "lemons": quality uncertainty and the market mechanism', *Quarterly Journal of Economics*, **84** (3), 488–500.

Akerlof, G., O. Blanchard, D. Romer and J. Stiglitz (eds) (2014), *What Have We Learned? Macroeconomic Policy After the Crisis*, Cambridge, MA: The MIT Press.

Akerlof, G. and R. Shiller (2009), *Animal Spirits: How Human Psychology Drives the Economy, and Why It Matters for Global Capitalism*, Princeton, NJ: Princeton University Press.

Aoki, M. (2001), 'To the rescue or to the abyss: notes on the Marx in Keynes', *Journal of the Economic Issues*, **XXXV** (4), 931–953.

Argitis, A. (2013), 'The illusion of the "new consensus" in macroeconomics: a Minskian analysis', *Journal of Post Keynesian Economics*, **35** (3), Spring, 483–505.

Aristotle, *Politics*, translated by Benjamin Jowett (1885), accessed 14 March 2016 at www.globalgrey.co.uk/Pages/politics-aristotle.html.

Arrow, K., A. Blinder, P. Diamond, E. Maskin, W. Sharpe, R. Solow, C. Schultze and L. Tyson (2011), Letter to President Obama and Congress, accessed 11 January 2016 at www.cbpp.org/sites/default/files/atoms/7-19-11bad-pr-sig.pdf.

Ascari, G. (2011), 'Macroeconomic models: better horses for tougher courses', *The Manchester School*, **79**, Supplement 2, 17–20.

Ascari, G. (2014), 'Deflazione, non è una fatale maledizione divina', accessed 1 February 2016 at www.lavoce.info/archives/29629/deflazione-non-fatale-maledizione-divina/.

Asensio, A. (2013–2014), 'The Achilles' heel of the mainstream explanation of the crisis and a post Keynesian alternative', *Journal of Post Keynesian Economics*, **36** (2), Winter, 355–379.

Atkinson, A. (2015), *Inequality: What Can be Done?*, Cambridge, MA: Harvard University Press.

Bagehot, W. (1873), *Lombard Street: A Description of the Money Market*, reprinted New York: Wiley & Sons (1999).

Bank of England (1999), 'The transmission mechanism of monetary policy', report by The Monetary Policy Committee, accessed 1 February 2016 at www.bankofengland.co.uk.

Barlevy, G. (2007), 'Economic theory and asset bubbles', *Economic Perspectives*, **3Q**, 44–59.

Barro, R. and X. Sala-i-Martin (2004), *Economic Growth*, Cambridge, MA: The MIT Press.

Barucci, E. and D. Magno (2009), 'Il propagarsi della crisi: svalutazioni, rischio liquidità, ricapitalizzazioni', in Emilio Barucci and Marcello Messori (eds), *Oltre lo shock. Quale stabilità per i Mercati Finanziari*, Milan: Egea.

Bartiloro, L. and G. Di Iasio (2012), 'Financial sector dynamics and firms' capital structure', in Riccardo De Bonis and Alberto Pozzolo (eds), *The Financial System of Industrial Countries*, Heidelberg: Springer, pp. 157–182.

Baskin, J.B. and P.J. Miranti Jr (1997), *A History of Corporate Finance*, Cambridge: Cambridge University Press.

Beck, U. (2012), *Das deutsche Europa: Neue Machtlandschaften im Zeichen der Krise*, Berlin: Suhrkamp Verlag. English edition, *German Europe*, Cambridge: Polity Press (2013).

Bellamy, F.J. and R. McChesney (2012), *The Endless Crisis: How Monopoly-Finance Capital Produces Stagnation and Upheaval from the U.S.A to China*, New York: Monthly Review Press.

Bellofiore, Riccardo (2005), 'The monetary aspects of the capitalist process in the Marxian system: an investigation from the point of view of the theory of the monetary circuit', in Fred Moseley (ed.), *Marx's Theory of Money: Modern Appraisals*, Basingstoke, UK: Palgrave Macmillan, pp. 124–139.

Bellofiore, R. (2011), 'Crisis theory and the Great Recession: a personal journey from Marx to Minsky', *Research in Political Economy*, **27**, 81–120.

Bellofiore, R., G. Forges Davanzati and R. Realfonzo (2000), 'Marx inside the circuit: discipline device, wage bargaining and unemployment in a sequential monetary economy', *Review of Political Economy*, **12** (1), 403–417.

Bellofiore, R. and J. Halevi (2010–2011), '"Could be raining": the European crisis after the Great Recession', *International Journal of Political Economy*, **39** (4), 5–30.

Bellofiore, R. and J. Halevi (2011), 'A Minsky moment? The subprime crisis and the "New" capitalism', in Claude Gnos and Louis-Philippe Rochon (eds), *Credit, Money and Macroeconomic Policy: A Post-Keynesian Approach*, Cheltenham, UK and Northampton, MA, USA: Edward Elgar.

Bellofiore, R. and G. Vertova (eds) (2014), *The Great Recession and the Contradictions of Contemporary Capitalism*, Cheltenham, UK and Northampton, MA, USA: Edward Elgar.

Bernanke, B.S. (1992–1993) 'Credit in the macroeconomy', *Federal Reserve Bank of New York Quarterly Review*, **18**, 50–70.

Bernanke, B.S. (2003), 'Some thoughts on monetary policy in Japan', speech at the Japan Society of Monetary Economics, Tokyo, 31 May.

Bernanke, B.S. (2004), 'The Great Moderation', speech at the Meetings of the Eastern Economic Association, Washington, DC, 20 February.

Bernanke, B.S. (2005), 'The global saving glut and the U.S. current account deficit', remarks by Governor Ben S. Bernanke at the Sandridge Lecture, Virginia Association of Economists, Richmond, Virginia, 10 March.

Bernanke, B.S. (2007a), 'The financial accelerator and the credit channel', speech at the 'Credit Channel of Monetary Policy in the Twenty-first Century' Conference, Federal Reserve Bank of Atlanta, Atlanta, Georgia, 15 June.

Bernanke, B.S. (2007b), 'Global imbalances: recent developments and prospects', speech at the Bundesbank Lecture, Berlin, Germany, 11 September.

Bernanke, B.S. (2010a), 'Monetary policy and the housing bubble', speech at the Annual Meeting of the American Economic Association, Atlanta, Georgia, 3 January.

Bernanke, B.S. (2010b), 'Implications of the financial crisis for economics', speech at the Conference Co-sponsored by the Center for Economic Policy Studies and the Bendheim Center for Finance, Princeton University, Princeton, New Jersey, 24 September.

Bernanke, B.S. (2012), 'Some reflections on the crisis and the policy response', speech at the Russell Sage Foundation and The Century Foundation Conference on 'Rethinking Finance', New York, 13 April.

Bernanke, B.S. (2013), *The Federal Reserve and the Financial Crisis*, Princeton, NJ: Princeton University Press.

Bernanke, B.S., C. Bertaut, L. Pounder DeMarco and S. Kamin (2011), 'International capital flows and the return to safe assets in the United

States, 2003–2007', Board of Governors of the Federal Reserve System, International Finance Discussion Papers, February, No. 1014.

Bernanke, B.S. and A. Blinder (1988), 'Credit, money and aggregate demand', *American Economic Review*, **78** (2), 435–439.

Bernanke, B.S. and M. Gertler (1995), 'Inside the black box: the credit channel of monetary policy transmission', *Journal of Economic Perspectives*, **9** (4), 27–48.

Bernanke, B., M. Gertler and S. Gilchrist (1999), 'The financial accelerator in a quantitative business cycle framework', in John B. Taylor and Michael Woodford (eds), *Handbook of Macroeconomics*, vol. 1C, Amsterdam: Elsevier, North-Holland, pp. 1341–1393.

Bernanke, B.S. and C. Lown (1991), 'The credit crunch', *Brookings Papers on Economic Activity*, **2**, 205–247.

Bertocco, G. (2001), 'Is Kaldor's theory of money supply endogeneity still relevant?', *Metroeconomica*, **52** (1), 95–120.

Bertocco, G. (2004), 'The new Keynesian monetary theory: a critical analysis', *Studi Economici*, **59** (2), 65–94.

Bertocco, G. (2005), 'The role of credit in a Keynesian monetary economy', *Review of Political Economy*, **17** (4), 489–511.

Bertocco, G. (2007), 'The characteristics of a monetary economy: a Keynes–Schumpeter approach', *Cambridge Journal of Economics*, **31** (1), 101–122.

Bertocco, G. (2008), 'Finance and development: is Schumpeter's analysis still relevant?', *Journal of Banking and Finance*, **32** (6), 1161–1175.

Bertocco, G. (2009a), 'The economics of financing firms: two different approaches', *History of Economic Ideas*, **17** (1), 85–123.

Bertocco, G. (2009b), 'The relationship between saving and credit from a Schumpeterian perspective', *Journal of Economic Issues*, **43** (3), 607–640.

Bertocco, G. (2010), 'The endogenous money theory and the characteristics of a monetary economy', *Rivista Italiana degli Economisti*, **15** (3), 365–401.

Bertocco, G. (2011), 'Are banks special? Some notes on Tobin's theory of financial intermediaries', *Journal of the Asia Pacific Economy*, **16** (3), 331–353.

Bertocco, G. (2013a), 'Money as an institution of capitalism: some notes on a monetary theory of uncertainty', *Economic Notes*, **42** (1), 75–101.

Bertocco, G. (2013b), 'On Keynes's criticism of the loanable funds theory', *Review of Political Economy*, **25** (2), 309–326.

Bertocco, G. (2014), 'Global saving glut and housing bubble: a critical analysis', *Economia Politica, Journal of Analytical and Institutional Economics*, **31** (2), 195–218.

Black, F. and M. Scholes (1973), 'The pricing of options and corporate liabilities', *Journal of Political Economy*, **81** (3), 637–654.

Blanchard, O. (2008), 'The state of macro', NBER Working Paper, No. 14259.

Blanchard, O., G. Dell'Ariccia and P. Mauro (2010), 'Rethinking macro-economic policy', *Journal of Money, Credit and Banking*, **42** (6), Supplement, 199–215.

Blanchard, O., D. Romer, M. Spence and J. Stiglitz (eds) (2012), *In the Wake of the Crisis*, Cambridge, MA: The MIT Press.

Blinder, A., A. Lo and R. Solow (eds) (2012), *Rethinking the Financial Crisis*, New York: Russell Sage Foundation.

Blinder, A. and R. Reis (2005), 'Understanding the Greenspan standard', paper presented at the Federal Reserve Bank of Kansas City symposium, 'The Greenspan Era: Lessons for the Future', Jackson Hole, Wyoming, 25–27 August, CEPS Working Paper, No. 114, September.

Blinder, A. and J. Stiglitz (1983), 'Money, credit constraints and economic activity', *AER Papers and Proceedings*, **73** (2), 297–302.

Blyth, M. (2013), *Austerity: The History of a Dangerous Idea*, Oxford: Oxford University Press.

Bodie, Z., A. Kane and A. Marcus (2009), *Investments*, 8th edition, Boston: McGraw-Hill.

Bogle, J. (2011), 'Preface' to A. Rappaport, *Saving Capitalism from Short-Termism: How to Build Long-Term Value and Take Back Our Financial Future*, Boston, MA: McGraw-Hill.

Böhm-Bawerk, E. (1884), 'The Problem of Interest', 'Final Conclusions' and 'Present and Future in Economic Life', in *Capital and Interest*, Volume 1, Chapter I, Chapter XV; Volume 2, Chapter I, South Holland, IL: Libertarian Press, pp. 1–7, 348–354 and 259–289, reprinted in Christopher Bliss, Avi Cohen and Geoffrey Harcourt (eds) (2005), *Capital Theory*, vol. 1, Cheltenham, UK and Northampton, MA, USA: Edward Elgar, pp. 139–193.

Borio, C. (2011), 'Rediscovering the macroeconomic roots of financial stability policy: journey, challenges and a way forward', BIS Working Papers, No. 354.

Borio, C. (2014), 'The financial cycle and macroeconomics: what have we learned and what are the policy implications?', in Edward Nowotny, Doris Ritzberger-Grünwald and Peter Backé (eds), *Financial Cycles and the Real Economy: Lessons for the CESEE Countries*, Cheltenham, UK and Northampton, MA, USA: Edward Elgar, pp. 10–35.

Bossone, B., T. Fazi and R. Wood (2014), 'Helicopter money: the best policy to address high public debt and deflation', VOX CEPR's Policy

Portal, accessed 18 March 2016 at voxeu.org/article/helicopter-money-today-s-best-policy-option/.

Bougrine, H. and L.-P. Rochon (2015), 'Transformations of entrepreneurial capitalism, crises and the need for a radical change in economic policy', *Review of Keynesian Economics*, **3** (2), 181–193.

Bourguignon, F. (2012), *La Mondialisation de l'inégalité*, Paris: Éditions du Seuil.

Bracke, T. and M. Fidora (2008), 'Global liquidity glut or global savings glut? A structural VAR approach', European Central Bank Working Paper Series, No. 911.

Braudel, F. (1977), *Afterthoughts on Material Civilization and Capitalism*, Baltimore, MD and London: The Johns Hopkins University Press.

Brunnermeier, M., T. Eisenbach and Y. Sannikov (2013), 'Macroeconomics with financial frictions: a survey', in Daron Acemoglu, Manuel Arellano and Eddie Dekel (eds), *Advances in Economics and Econometrics*, vol. 2, Cambridge: Cambridge University Press, pp. 3–94.

Brunnermeier, M. and S. Nagel (2004), 'Hedge funds and the technology bubble', *Journal of Finance*, **59** (5), 2013–2039.

Brunnermeier, M. and Y. Sannikov (2014), 'A macroeconomic model with a financial sector', *American Economic Review*, **104** (2), 379–421.

Buiter, W. (2009), 'The unfortunate uselessness of most "state of the art" academic monetary economics', *Financial Times*, 3 March.

Buiter, W. (2014), 'The simple analytics of helicopter money: why it works – analysis', Economics, The Open-Access, Open-Assessment E-Journal, Discussion Paper, No. 2014-28.

Caballero, R. (2010), 'Macroeconomics after the Crisis: time to deal with the pretense-of-knowledge syndrome', *Journal of Economic Perspectives*, **24** (4), 85–102.

Cameron, R. (1967), *Banking in the Early Stages of Industrialization*, with the collaboration of Olga Crisp, Hugh Patrick and Richard Tilly, Oxford and New York: Oxford University Press.

Cannan, E. (1921), 'The meaning of bank deposits', *Economica*, **1** (1), 28–36.

Capasso, S. (2004), 'Financial markets, development and economic growth: tales of informational asymmetries', *Journal of Economic Surveys*, **18** (3), 267–292.

Carabelli, A. and M. Cedrini (2014), 'Chapter 18 of *The General Theory* "further analysed": economics as a way of thinking', *Cambridge Journal of Economics*, **38** (1), 23–47.

Cassidy, J. (2009), *How Markets Fail: The Logic of Economic Calamities*, New York: Farrar, Straus and Giroux.

Catte, P., P. Cova, P. Pagano and I. Visco (2010), 'The role of macro-economic policies in the global crisis', Banca d'Italia, Questioni di Economia e Finanza, Occasional Papers, No. 69.

Cecchetti, S.G., M.S. Mohanty and F. Zampolli (2011), 'The real effects of debt', BIS Working Papers, No. 352.

Chancellor, E. (1999), *Devil Take the Hindmost: A History of Financial Speculation*, London: Plume.

Chang, H. (2010), *23 Things They Don't Tell You About Capitalism*, London: Penguin Books.

Chari, V. (2010), 'Testimony before the Committee on Science and Technology, Subcommittee on Investigations and Oversight', US House of Representatives, 20 July.

Chari, V. and P. Kehoe (2006), 'Modern macroeconomics in practice: how theory is shaping policy', *Journal of Economic Perspectives*, **20** (4), 3–28.

Cheng, I., S. Raina and W. Xiong (2014), 'Wall Street and the housing bubble', *American Economic Review*, **104** (9), 2797–2829.

Coase, R. (1937), 'The nature of the firm', *Economica*, **4** (16), 386–405.

Cochrane, J. (2011), 'How did Paul Krugman get it so wrong?', *IEA Economic Affairs*, June, 36–40.

Colander, D. (2011), 'How economists got it wrong: a nuanced account', *Critical Review*, **23**, (1–2), 1–27.

Colander, D., H. Föllmer, M. Goldberg, A. Hass, K. Juselius, A. Kirman, T. Lux and B. Sloth (2009), 'The financial crisis and the systemic failure of academic economics', Kiel Working Paper, No. 1489.

Coval, J., J. Jurek and E. Stafford (2009), 'The economics of structured finance', *Journal of Economic Perspectives*, **23** (1), 3–25.

Cox, J., S.A. Ross and M. Rubinstein (1979), 'Option pricing: a simplified approach', *Journal of Financial Economics*, **7**(3), 229–264.

Crafts, N. (2013), 'The Eurozone: if only it were the 1930s', Vox, 13 December, accessed 16 March 2016 at www.voxeu.org/article/eurozone-if-only-it-were-1930s.

Crotty, J. (2009), 'Structural causes of the global financial crisis: a critical assessment of the "new financial architecture"', *Cambridge Journal of Economics*, **33** (4), 563–580.

Crotty, J. (2011), 'The realism of assumptions does matter: why Keynes–Minsky theory must replace efficient market theory as the guide to financial regulation policy', PERI Working Paper Series, No. 255.

Crouch, C. (2011), *The Strange Non-Death of Neoliberalism*, Cambridge: Polity Press.

Crouch, C. (2013), *Making Capitalism Fit for Society*, Cambridge: Polity Press.

Curdia, V. and M. Woodford (2010), 'Credit spreads and monetary policy', *Journal of Money, Credit and Banking*, **46** (6), 3–35.

Cynamon, B., S. Fazzari and M. Setterfield (eds) (2013), *After the Great Recession*, Cambridge: Cambridge University Press.

Davis, P. and B. Steil (2001), *Institutional Investors*, Cambridge, MA: The MIT Press.

De Grauwe, P. (2010), 'Top-down versus bottom-up macroeconomics', *CESifo Economic Studies*, **56** (4), 465–497.

De Grauwe, P. and W. Moesen (2009), 'Gains for all: a proposal for a common Eurobond', *CEPS Commentary: Thinking Ahead for Europe*, 3 April.

de Larosière Group, High Level Group on Financial Supervision in the EU, chaired by Jacques de Larosière (2009), 'Report', Brussels, 25 February, accessed 25 January 2016 at www.ec.europa.eu/internal_market/finances/docs/de_larosiere_report_en.pdf.

Delpla, J. and J. von Weizsäcker (2010), 'The Blue Bond Proposal', *Bruegel Policy Brief*, No. 3.

Desai, M. (2010), 'Hayek: another perspective', in Robert Skidelsky and Christian Westerlind Wigström (eds), *The Economic Crisis and the State of Economics*, Houndmills, Basingstoke, UK: Palgrave Macmillan, pp. 61–66.

De Vecchi, N. (1995), *Entrepreneurs, Institutions and Economic Change: The Economic Thought of J.A. Schumpeter*, Aldershot, UK and Brookfield, VT, USA: Edward Elgar.

Diamond, D. and R. Rajan (2009), 'The credit crisis: conjectures about causes and remedies', NBER Working Paper, No. 14739.

Dillard, D. (1948), *The Economics of John Maynard Keynes: The Theory of a Monetary Economy*, Englewood Cliffs, NY: Prentice-Hall.

Dillard, D. (1984), 'Keynes and Marx: a centennial appraisal', *Journal of Post Keynesian Economics*, **6** (3), 421–432.

Dillard, D. (1987), 'Money as an institution of capitalism', *Journal of Economic Issues*, **XXI** (4), 1623–1647.

Dosi, G. (2012), 'Economic coordination and dynamics: some elements of an alternative "evolutionary" paradigm', in Giovanni Dosi (ed.), *Economic Organization, Industrial Dynamics and Development, Selected Essays,* Cheltenham, UK and Northampton, MA, USA: Edward Elgar, pp. 1–36.

Dosi, G., G. Fagiolo and A. Roventini (2010), 'Schumpeter meeting Keynes, a policy-friendly model of endogenous growth and business cycles', *Journal of Economic Dynamics and Control*, **34**, 1748–1767.

Dow, A. and S. Dow (2011), 'Animal spirits revisited', *Capitalism and Society*, **6** (2), 1–23.

ECB (2004), *The Monetary Policy of the ECB*, Frankfurt am Main: European Central Bank.

ECB (2010), 'The ECB's response to the financial crisis', *Monthly Bulletin*, October, 59–74.

ECB (2011), *The Monetary Policy of the ECB*, Frankfurt am Main: European Central Bank, 3rd edition.

Eichengreen, B. (2014), *Hall of Mirrors: The Great Depression, the Great Recession, and the Uses – and Misuses – of History*, Oxford and London: Oxford University Press.

Fama, E. (1985), 'What's different about banks?', *Journal of Monetary Economics*, **15** (1), 29–39.

Fergusson, L. (2006), 'Institutions for financial development: what are they and where do they come from?', *Journal of Economic Surveys*, **20** (1), 27–69.

Ferri, G. and D. Neuberger (2014), 'The banking regulatory bubble and how to get out of it', *Rivista di Politica Economica*, **99**, 39–69.

Fiorentini, R. and G. Montani (2012), *The New Global Political Economy: From Crisis to Supranational Integration*, Cheltenham, UK and Northampton, MA, USA: Edward Elgar.

Fitoussi, J.P. (2013), *Le Théorème du Lampadaire*, Paris: Éditions Les Liens qui Libèrent.

Francis, the Holy Father (2014), *Encyclical Letter Laudato Si'*, accessed 18 January 2016 at https://laudatosi.com/watch.

Frank, R. (2008), 'Context is more important than Keynes realized', in Lorenzo Pecchi and Giovanni Piga (eds), *Revisiting Keynes: Economic Possibilities for Our Grandchildren*, Cambridge, MA: The MIT Press, pp. 143–150.

Friedman, M. (1968), 'The role of monetary policy', *American Economic Review*, **58** (1), 1–17.

Friedman, M. (1970), 'The social responsibility of business is to increase its profits', *The New York Times Magazine*, 13 September.

Friedman, M. (1992), *Money Mischief: Episodes in Monetary History*, New York: Harvest, Harcourt Brace & Company.

Friedman, M. (2005), 'A natural experiment in monetary policy covering three episodes of growth and decline in the economy and the stock market', *Journal of Economic Perspectives*, **19** (4), 145–150.

Friedman, M. and A. Schwartz (1982), *Monetary Trends in the United States and the United Kingdom: Their Relations to Income, Prices, and Interest Rates, 1867–1975*, Chicago: The University of Chicago Press.

Gabbi, G. and A. Sironi (2014), 'Breaking up the bank: alternative proposals to separate banking activities: a critical analysis', *Rivista di Politica Economica*, **99**, 17–37.

Galbraith, John K. (1990), *A Short History of Financial Euphoria*, New York: Whittle Direct Books.

Galbraith, John K. (2004), *The Economics of Innocent Fraud*, Boston: Houghton Mifflin Company.

Galbraith, James K. (2012), *Inequality and Instability: A Study of the World Economy Just Before the Great Crisis*, Oxford: Oxford University Press.

Galbraith, James K. (2014), *The End of Normal: The Great Crisis and the Future of Growth*, New York: Simon & Schuster.

Galbraith, James K., S. Holland and Y. Varoufakis (2014), *A Modest Proposal for Resolving the Eurozone Crisis*, accessed 8 February 2016 at www.yanisvaroufakis.eu/euro-crisis/modest-proposal/.

Galí, J. (2014), 'The effects of a money-financed fiscal stimulus', CEPR Discussion Paper, No. DP 10165.

Gamble, A. (2014), *Crisis without End? The Unravelling of Western Prosperity*, Houndmills, Basingstoke, UK: Palgrave Macmillan.

Gerschenkron, A. (1962), *Economic Backwardness in Historical Perspective*, Cambridge, MA: The Belknap Press of Harvard University Press.

Gertler, M. and P. Karadi (2011), 'A model of unconventional monetary policy', *Journal of Monetary Economics*, **58** (1), 17–34.

Giavazzi, F. and G. Tabellini (2014), 'How to jumpstart the Eurozone economy', VOX CEPR's Policy Portal, accessed 11 March 2016 at voxeu.org/article/how-jumpstart-eurozone-economy.

Glyn, A. (2006), *Capitalism Unleashed: Finance, Globalization, and Welfare*, Oxford: Oxford University Press.

Goldin, C. and L. Katz (2008), 'Transitions: career and family life cycles of the educational elite', *American Economic Review*, **98** (2), 363–369.

Goldsmith, R. (1987), *Premodern Financial Systems: A Historical Comparative Study*, Cambridge: Cambridge University Press.

Goodhart, C.A.E. (1987), 'Why do banks need a Central Bank?', *Oxford Economic Papers*, **39** (1), 75–89.

Goodhart, C.A.E. (2010), 'Macro-economic failures', in Robert Skidelsky and Christian Westerlind Wigström (eds), *The Economic Crisis and the State of Economics*, Houndmills, Basingstoke, UK: Palgrave Macmillan, pp. 53–59.

Goodwin, R. (1993), 'Schumpeter and Keynes', in Salvatore Biasco, Alessandro Roncaglia and Michele Salvati (eds), *Markets and Institutions in Economic Development*, London: Macmillan Press, pp. 83–85.

Gorton, G. (2012), *Misunderstanding Financial Crises: Why We Don't See Them Coming*, Oxford: Oxford University Press.

Gorton, G. and A. Metrik (2012), 'Getting up to speed on the financial crisis: a one-weekend-reader's guide', *Journal of Economic Literature*, **50** (1), 128–150.

Gorton, G. and A. Winton (2002), 'Financial intermediation', NBER Working Paper, No. 8928, May.

Gurley, J. and E. Shaw (1956), 'Financial intermediaries and the saving–investment process', *Journal of Finance*, **11** (2), 257–276.

Hahn, F. (1982), *Money and Inflation*, Oxford: Basil Blackwell.

Haldane, A. and P. Alessandri (2009), 'Banking on the state', paper presented at the Federal Reserve Bank of Chicago Twelfth Annual International Banking Conference on 'The International Financial Crisis: Have the Rules of Finance Changed?', Chicago, Illinois, 25 September.

Haldane, A., S. Brennan and V. Madouros (2010), 'What is the contribution of the financial sector: miracle or mirage?', in LSE (ed.), *The Future of Finance: The LSE Report*, London: London School of Economics and Political Science, pp. 87–120.

Harcourt, G.C. and P. Kriesler (2011), 'The enduring importance of the General Theory', *Review of Political Economy*, **23** (4), 503–519.

Hein, E. (2006), 'Money, interest and capital accumulation in Karl Marx's economics: a monetary interpretation and some similarities to post-Keynesian approaches', *European Journal of the History of Economic Thought*, **13** (1), 113–140.

Hein, E. (2012), *The Macroeconomics of Finance-Dominated Capitalism – and its Crisis*, Cheltenham, UK and Northampton, MA, USA: Edward Elgar.

Hein, E. (2015), 'The principle of effective demand – Marx, Kalecki, Keynes and beyond', Institute for International Political Economy Berlin, Working Paper No. 60/2015.

Hicks, J. (1967), *A Theory of Economic History*, Oxford: Oxford University Press.

Hodgson, G. (2006), *Economics in the Shadows of Darwin and Marx: Essays on Institutional and Evolutionary Themes*, Cheltenham, UK and Northampton, MA, USA: Edward Elgar.

Hodgson, G. (2009), 'The great crash of 2008 and the reform of economics', *Cambridge Journal of Economics*, **33** (6), 1205–1221.

Hodgson, G. (2015), *Conceptualizing Capitalism: Institutions, Evolution, Future*, Chicago: The University of Chicago Press.

Horwitz, S. and W. Luther (2011), 'The Great Recession and its aftermath from a monetary equilibrium theory perspective', in Steven Kates (ed.), *The Global Financial Crisis: What Have We Learnt?*, Cheltenham, UK and Northampton, MA, USA: Edward Elgar, pp. 75–92.

Independent Commission on Banking, chaired by John Vickers (2011), 'Final report: recommendations', London, 12 September, accessed 7 March 2016 at www.ecgi.org/documents/icb_final_report_12sep 2011.pdf.

Jaffee, D., A. Lynch, M. Richardson and S. Van Nieuwerburgh (2009), 'Mortgage origination and securitization in the financial crisis', in Viral Acharya and Matthew Richardson (eds), *Restoring Financial Stability: How to Repair a Failed System*, Hoboken, NJ: John Wiley & Sons, pp. 61–82.

J.P.Morgan (2013), 'The Euro area adjustment: about halfway there', *Europe Economic Research*, 28 May.

Judt, T. (2010), *Ill Fares the Land*, New York: The Penguin Press.

Kaldor, N. (1982), *The Scourge of Monetarism*, Oxford: Oxford University Press.

Kaldor, N. (1985), *Economics without Equilibrium*, New York: M.E. Sharpe.

Kalecki, M. (1943), 'Political aspects of full employment', *Political Quarterly*, **14** (4), 322–331, reprinted in Jerzy Osiatyński (ed.) (1990), *Collected Works of Michał Kalecki*, vol. I, *Capitalism: Business Cycles and Full Employment*, Oxford: Clarendon Press, pp. 347–356.

Kates, S. (ed.) (2010), *Macroeconomic Theory and its Failings: Alternative Perspectives on the Global Financial Crisis*, Cheltenham, UK and Northampton, MA, USA: Edward Elgar.

Keynes, J.M. (1930), 'Economic Possibilities for our Grandchildren', in *Nation and Athenaeum*, 11 and 18 October, reprinted in J.M. Keynes (2013b), *The Collected Writings*, London: Cambridge University Press for the Royal Economic Society, vol. IX, pp. 321–332.

Keynes, J.M. (1933a), *A Monetary Theory of Production*, from *Der Stand und die nächste Zukunft der Konjunkturforschung: Festschrift für Arthur Spiethoff*, reprinted in J.M. Keynes (2013c), *The Collected Writings*, London: Cambridge University Press for the Royal Economic Society, vol. XIII, pp. 408–411.

Keynes, J.M. (1933b), 'The distinction between a co-operative economy and an entrepreneur economy', draft of the second chapter of the *General Theory* according to the last index prepared in 1933, reprinted in J.M. Keynes (2013g), *The Collected Writings*, London: Cambridge University Press for the Royal Economic Society, vol. XXIX, pp. 76–106.

Keynes, J.M. (1933c), *National Self-Sufficiency*, in *The New Statesman and Nation*, 8 and 15 July, reprinted in J.M. Keynes (2013e), *The Collected Writings*, London: Cambridge University Press for the Royal Economic Society, vol. XXI, pp. 233–246.

Keynes, J.M. (1936), *The General Theory of Employment, Interest, and Money*, reprinted in J.M. Keynes (2013a), *The Collected Writings*, London: Cambridge University Press for the Royal Economic Society, vol. VII, pp. i–xxxvii and 1–427.

Keynes, J.M. (1937a), 'The general theory of employment', *Quarterly Journal of Economics*, **51** (2), 209–223, reprinted in J.M. Keynes (2013d), *The Collected Writings*, London: Cambridge University Press for the Royal Economic Society, vol. XIV, pp. 109–123.

Keynes, J.M. (1937b), 'Alternative theories of the rate of interest', *Economic Journal*, **47** (186), 241–252, reprinted in J.M. Keynes (2013d), *The Collected Writings*, London: Cambridge University Press for the Royal Economic Society, vol. XIV, pp. 241–251.

Keynes, J.M. (1937c), 'The "ex ante" theory of the rate of interest', *Economic Journal*, **47** (188), 663–669, reprinted in J.M. Keynes (2013d), *The Collected Writings*, London: Cambridge University Press for the Royal Economic Society, vol. XIV, pp. 215–223.

Keynes, J.M. (1939), 'The process of capital formation', *Economic Journal*, **49** (195), 569–574, reprinted in J.M. Keynes (2013d), *The Collected Writings*, London: Cambridge University Press for the Royal Economic Society, vol. XIV, pp. 278–285.

Keynes, J.M. (1942), 'How much does finance matter?', from *The Listener*, 2 April, reprinted in J.M. Keynes (2013f), *The Collected Writings*, London: Cambridge University Press for the Royal Economic Society, vol. XXVII, pp. 264–270.

Kindleberger, C. (1978), *Manias, Panics, and Crashes: A History of Financial Crisis*, New York: Basic Books.

King, R. and R. Levine (1993), 'Finance and growth: Schumpeter might be right', *Quarterly Journal of Economics*, **108** (3), 717–737.

Kirman, A. (2011), 'The crisis in economic theory', *Rivista Italiana degli economisti*, **16** (1), 9–36.

Knight, F. (1921), *Risk, Uncertainty and Profit*, Boston, MA: Hart, Schaffner & Marx, reprinted New York: August M. Kelley (1964).

Kotz, D. (2015), *The Rise and Fall of Neoliberal Capitalism*, Cambridge, MA: Harvard University Press.

Krippner, G. (2011), *Capitalizing on Crisis: The Political Origins of the Rise of Finance*, Cambridge, MA: Harvard University Press.

Krugman, P. (2009), 'How did economists get it so wrong?', *New York Times*, 2 September.

Krugman, P. (2012), *End This Depression Now!*, New York: W.W. Norton & Company.

Kurz, H. (2013), 'Sraffa, Keynes, and Post-Keynesianism', in Geoffrey Harcourt and Peter Kriesler (eds), *The Oxford Handbook of Post-Keynesian Economics*, vol. 1, Oxford: Oxford University Press, pp. 51–73.

Laidler, D. (2010), 'Lucas, Keynes and the crisis', *Journal of the History of Economic Thought*, **32** (1), 39–62.

Lapavitsas, C. (2012), *Crisis in the Eurozone*, New York: Verso Books.

Lawson, T. (2009), 'The current economic crisis: its nature and the course of academic economics', *Cambridge Journal of Economics*, **33** (4), 759–777.

Leclaire, J., J. Tae-Hee and J. Knodell (eds) (2011), *Heterodox Analysis of Financial Crisis and Reform: History, Politics and Economics*, Cheltenham, UK and Northampton, MA, USA: Edward Elgar.

Leijonhufvud, A. (2009), 'Out of the corridor: Keynes and the crisis', *Cambridge Journal of Economics*, **33** (4), 741–757.

Leijonhufvud, A. (2011), 'Nature of an economy', *CEPR Policy Insight*, No. 53, February.

Levine, R. (1997), 'Financial development and economic growth: views and agenda', *Journal of Economic Literature*, **35** (2), 688–726.

Levine, R. (2002), 'Bank-based or market-based financial systems: which is better?', *Journal of Financial Intermediation*, **11** (4), 398–428.

Levine, R. (2004), 'Finance and growth: theory and evidence', NBER Working Paper, No. 10766.

Liikanen Group – High Level Expert Group on Financial Supervision in the EU, chaired by Erkki Liikanen (2012), 'Final report', Brussels, 2 October, accessed 11 January 2016 at www.ec.europa.eu/internal_market/bank/structural-reform/index_en.htm.

Lin, J.Y. (2013), *Against the Consensus: Reflections on the Great Recession*, Cambridge: Cambridge University Press.

Litner, J. (1965), 'The valuation of risk assets and the selection of risky investments in stock portfolios and capital budgets', *Review of Economics and Statistics*, **47** (1), 13–37.

Lo, A.W. (2012), 'Reading about the financial crisis: a twenty-one-book review', *Journal of Economic Literature*, **50** (1), 151–178.

Lucas, R. (1996), 'Nobel lecture: monetary neutrality', *Journal of Political Economy*, **104** (4), 661–682.

Lucas, R. (2003), 'Macroeconomic priorities', *American Economic Review*, **93** (1), 1–14.

Madrik, J. (2014), *Seven Bad Ideas: How Mainstream Economists Have Damaged America and the World*, New York: Alfred A. Knopf.

Mankiw, G. (2013), 'Defending the one percent', *Journal of Economic Perspectives*, **27** (3), 21–34.

Markowitz, H.M. (1952), 'Portfolio selection', *Journal of Finance*, **7** (1), 77–91.

Marsh, D. (2013), *Europe's Deadlock: How the Euro Crisis Could be Solved – and Why it Won't Happen*, New Haven, CT: Yale University Press.

Martin, F. (2013), *Money: The Unauthorized Biography*, London: The Bodley Head.

Marx, K. (1867–1894), *Das Kapital* (3 vols), Hamburg: Meissner. English edition, *Capital: Critique of Political Economy*, London: Penguin Classics, vol. 1 (1992), vol. 2 and vol. 3 (1993).

Mayer-Foulkes, D. (2009), 'Long-term fundamentals of the 2008 economic crisis', *Global Economic Journal*, **9** (4), 1–23.

Mazzucato, M. (2013), *The Entrepreneurial State: Debunking Public vs. Private Sector Myths*, London and New York: Anthem Press.

Mazzucato, M. and R. Wray (2015), 'Financing the capital development of the economy: a Keynes–Schumpeter–Minsky synthesis', Levy Economics Institute, Working Paper No. 837, May.

McCallum, B. (1989), *Monetary Economics: Theory and Policy*, New York: Macmillan Publishing Company.

McLeay, M., A. Radia and R. Thomas (2014), 'Money creation in the modern economy', *Quarterly Bulletin*, Q1, Bank of England.

Meade, J. (1989), *Agathotopia: The Economics of Partnership*, Aberdeen: Aberdeen University Press.

Ménard, C. and M. Shirley (eds) (2005), *Handbook of New Institutional Economics*, Heidelberg: Springer.

Merton, R. (1973), 'Theory of rational option pricing', *Bell Journal of Economics and Management Science*, **4** (1), 141–183.

Merton, R. and Z. Bodie (2005), 'Design of financial systems: towards a synthesis of function and structure', *Journal of Investment Management*, **3** (1), 1–23.

Messori, M. (2012), 'Developing a new textbook approach to macroeconomics', *Rivista di Politica Economica*, July–September, 102–117.

Mian, A. and A. Sufi (2009), 'The consequences of mortgage credit expansion: evidence from the U.S. mortgage default crisis', *Quarterly Journal of Economics*, **124** (4), 1449–1496.

Mian, A. and A. Sufi (2014), *House of Debt: How They (and You) caused the Great Recession, and How We Can Prevent It from Happening Again*, Chicago: Chicago University Press.

Milanovic, B. (2010), *The Haves and the Have-Nots: A Brief Idiosyncratic History of Global Inequality*, New York: Basic Books.

Mill, J.S. (1848), *Principles of Political Economy with some of their Applications to Social Philosophy*, abridged edition by Hackett Publishing Company, Indianapolis (2004).

Minsky, H. (1975), *John Maynard Keynes*, New York: Columbia University Press.

Minsky, H. (1980), 'Money, financial markets and the coherence of a market economy', *Journal of Post Keynesian Economics*, **3** (1), 21–31.

Minsky, H. (1982), *Can 'It' Happen Again? Essays on Instability and Finance*, New York: M.E. Sharpe.

Minsky, H. (1986a), *Stabilizing an Unstable Economy*, Yale, CT: Yale University Press.

Minsky, H. (1986b), 'Money and crisis in Schumpeter and Keynes', in Hans-Jürgen Wagener and Jan Drukker (eds), *The Economic Law of Motion of Modern Society: A Marx–Keynes–Schumpeter Centennial*, Cambridge: Cambridge University Press, pp. 112–122.

Minsky, H. (1992–1993), 'On the non-neutrality of money', *Federal Reserve Bank of New York Quarterly Review*, Spring, 77–82.

Minsky, H. (1993), 'Schumpeter and finance', in Salvatore Biasco, Alessandro Roncaglia and Michele Salvati (eds), *Markets and Institutions in Economic Development: Essays in Honour of Paolo Sylos Labini*, London: Macmillan Press, pp. 103–115.

Minsky, H. (1996), 'Uncertainty and the institutional structure of capitalist economies', *Journal of Economic Issues*, **30** (2), 357–368.

Minsky, H. (2013), *Ending Poverty: Jobs, not Welfare*, Annandale-on-Hudson, NY: Levy Economics Institute of Bard College.

Mirowski, P. (2013), *Never Let A Serious Crisis Go To Waste: How Neoliberalism Survived the Financial Meltdown*, New York: Verso Books.

Mishel, L., J. Bivens, E. Gould and H. Shierholz (2012), *The State of Working America*, 12th edition, Washington, DC: Economic Policy Institute.

Mizen, P. (2008), 'The Credit Crunch of 2007–2008: a discussion of the background, market reactions and policy responses', *Federal Reserve Bank of St. Louis Review*, **90** (5), 531–567.

Morishima, M. (1992), *Capital and Credit: A New Formulation of General Equilibrium Theory*, Cambridge: Cambridge University Press.

Mossin, J. (1966), 'Equilibrium in a capital asset market', *Econometrica*, **34** (4), 768–783.

Mulgan, G. (2013), *The Locust and the Bee: Predators and Creators in Capitalism's Future*, Princeton, NJ: Princeton University Press.

North, D. (2005a), *Understanding the Process of Economic Change*, Princeton, NJ: Princeton University Press.

North, D. (2005b), 'Institutions and the performance of economics over time', in Ménard Claude and Mary Shirley (eds), *Handbook of New Institutional Economics*, Heidelberg: Springer, pp. 21–30.

North, D. and B. Weingast (1989), 'Constitutions and commitment: the evolution of institutions governing public choice in seventeenth-century England', *Journal of Economic History*, **49** (4), 803–832.

Obstfeld, M. and K. Rogoff (2009), 'Global imbalances and the financial crisis: products of common causes', paper prepared for the Asia Economic Policy Conference, Federal Reserve Bank of San Francisco, 18–20 October.

O'Donnell, R. (2013), 'Two post-Keynesian approaches to uncertainty and irreducible uncertainty', in Geoffrey Harcourt and Peter Kriesler (eds), *The Oxford Handbook of Post-Keynesian Economics*, vol. 2, Oxford: Oxford University Press, pp. 124–142.

Offe, C. (2014), *Europe Entrapped*, Cambridge: Polity Press.

Ohanian, L. (2010), 'The economic crisis from a neoclassical perspective', *Journal of Economic Perspectives*, **24** (4), 45–66.

Orléan, A. (2009), *De l'euphorie à la panique. Penser la crise financière*, Paris: Éditions Rue d'Ulm.

Ostry, J., P. Loungani and D. Furceri (2016), 'Neoliberalism: oversold?', *Finance and Development*, June, 38–41.

Oyer, P. (2008), 'The making of an investment banker: stock market shocks, career choice, and lifetime income', *Journal of Finance*, **63** (6), 2601–2628.

Pagano, M. (1993), 'Financial markets and growth: an overview', *European Economic Review*, **37** (2–3), 613–622.

Palley, T. (2002), 'Endogenous money: what it is and why it matters', *Metroeconomica*, **53**, 152–180.

Palley, T. (2012), *From Financial Crisis To Stagnation: The Destruction of Shared Prosperity and the Role of Economics*, Cambridge: Cambridge University Press.

Palley, T. (2013), 'America's exhausted paradigm: macroeconomic causes of the financial crisis and Great Recession', in Barry Cynamon, Steven Fazzari and Mark Setterfield (eds), *After the Great Recession*, Cambridge: Cambridge University Press, pp. 31–60.

Palma, J. (2009), 'The revenge of the market on rentiers: why neo-liberal reports of the end of history turned out to be premature', *Cambridge Journal of Economics*, **33** (4), 829–869.

Pâris, P. and C. Wyplosz (2014), 'PADRE: Politically Acceptable Debt Restructuring in the Eurozone', Geneva Reports in the World Economy, Special Report 3.

Pasinetti, L. (1997), 'The principle of effective demand', in Geoffrey Harcourt and Peter Riach (eds), *A 'Second Edition' of the General Theory*, vol. 1, London: Routledge, pp. 93–104.

Pasinetti, L. (2007), *Keynes and the Cambridge Keynesians: A 'Revolution in Economics' to be Accomplished*, Cambridge: Cambridge University Press.

Pasinetti, L. (2011), 'A few counter-factual hypotheses on the current economic crisis', *Cambridge Journal of Economics*, **36** (6), 1433–1453.

Pecchi, L. and G. Piga (eds) (2008), *Revisiting Keynes: Economic Possibilities for Our Grandchildren*, Cambridge, MA: The MIT Press.

Perez, C. (2009), 'The double bubble at the turn of the century: technological roots and structural implications', *Cambridge Journal of Economics*, **33** (4), 779–805.

Phelps, E. (2009), 'Refounding capitalism', *Capitalism and Society*, **4** (3), 1–11.

Philippon, T. (2008), 'The evolution of the US financial industry from 1860 to 2007: theory and evidence', mimeo, November.

Philippon, T. and A. Reshef (2007), 'Skill biased financial development: education, wages and occupations in the U.S. financial sector', NBER Working Paper, No. 13437.

Philippon, T. and A. Reshef (2009), 'An international look at the growth of modern finance', *Journal of Economic Perspectives*, **27** (2), 73–96.

Piketty, T. (2013), *Le capital au XXIᵉ siècle*, Paris: Éditions du Seuil. English edition, *Capital in the Twenty-First Century*, Cambridge, MA: Belknap Press (2014).

Polanyi, K. (1944), *The Great Transformation: The Political and Economic Origins of Our Time*, reprinted Boston, MA: Beacon Press (2001).

Prodi, R. and A. Quadrio Curzio (2011), 'Euro Union Bond: i perché di un rilancio', *Il Sole 24 Ore*, 23 August.

Rajan, R. (2006), 'Has finance made the world riskier?', *European Financial Management*, **12** (4), 499–533.

Rajan, R. (2010), *Fault Lines: How Hidden Fractures Still Threaten the World Economy*, Princeton, NJ: Princeton University Press.

Rajan, R. and L. Zingales (1998), 'Financial dependence and growth', *American Economic Review*, **88** (3), 559–586.

Rajan, R. and L. Zingales (2003a), 'Banks and markets: the changing character of European finance', NBER Working Paper, No. 9595.

Rajan, R. and L. Zingales (2003b), 'The great reversals: the politics of financial development in the twentieth century', *Journal of Financial Economics*, **69** (1), 5–50.

Rajan, R. and L. Zingales (2003c), *Saving Capitalism from the Capitalists: Unleashing the Power of Financial Markets to Create Wealth and Spread Opportunity*, Princeton, NJ: Princeton University Press.

Rappaport, A. (2011), *Saving Capitalism from Short-Termism: How to Build Long-Term Value and Take Back Our Financial Future*, London: McGraw-Hill.

Reich, R. (2010), *Aftershock: The Next Economy and America's Future*, New York: Vintage Books.

Reich, R. (2015), *Saving Capitalism: For the Many, Not the Few*, New York: Alfred A. Knopf.

Reinhart, C. and K. Rogoff (2009), *This Time is Different: Eight Centuries of Financial Folly*, Princeton, NJ: Princeton University Press.

Robbins, L. (1932), *An Essay on the Nature and Significance of Economic Science*, London: Macmillan.

Robinson, J. (1972), 'The second crisis of economic theory', *American Economic Review*, **62** (1/2), 1–10.

Rochon, L.-P. and S. Rossi (eds) (2003), *Modern Theories of Money*, Cheltenham, UK and Northampton, MA, USA: Edward Elgar.

Rochon, L.-P. and S. Rossi (2013), 'Endogenous money: the evolutionary versus revolutionary views', *Review of Keynesian Economics*, **1** (2), 210–229.

Rodrik, D. (2011), *The Globalization Paradox: Democracy and the Future of the World Economy*, New York: Norton & Company.

Rogers, C. (1997a), 'The General Theory: existence of a monetary long-period employment equilibrium', in Geoffrey Harcourt and Peter Reich (eds), *A 'Second Edition' of the General Theory*, London: Routledge, pp. 324–342.

Rogers, C. (1997b), 'Post Keynesian monetary theory and the principle of effective demand', in Avi J. Cohen, Harald Hagemann and John Smithin (eds), *Money, Financial Institutions and Macroeconomics*, Dordrecht: Kluwer Academic Publishers, pp. 18–32.

Rogers, C. (2008), 'The principle of effective demand and the state of Post Keynesian monetary economics', The University of Adelaide School of Economics, Research Paper No. 2008-04.

Roncaglia, A. (2010), *Why the Economists Got it Wrong: The Crisis and its Cultural Roots*, London: Anthem Press.

Roncaglia, A. (2013), 'Hyman Minsky's monetary production economy', *PSL Quarterly Review*, **66** (265), 77–94.

Rossi, S. (2015), 'Structural reforms in payment systems to avoid another systemic crisis', *Review of Keynesian Economics*, **3** (2), 213–225.

Roubini, N. and S. Mihm (2010), *Crisis Economics: A Crash Course in the Future of Finance*, New York: The Penguin Press.

Ryan-Collins, J., T. Greenham, R. Wener and A. Jackson (2012), *Where Does Money Come From? A Guide to the UK Monetary and Banking System*, London: New Economics Foundations.

Sa, F., P. Towbin and T. Wieladek (2011), 'Low interest rates and housing booms: the role of capital inflows, monetary policy and financial innovation', Bank of England Working Papers, No. 411, February.

Sachs, J. (2009), 'Rethinking macroeconomics', *Capitalism and Society*, **4** (3), 1–8.

Sachs, J. (2011), *The Price of Civilization: Reawakening American Virtue and Prosperity*, New York: Random House.

Sahlins, M. (1966), 'The original affluent society', reprinted in Jacqueline Solway (ed.) (2006), *The Politics of Egalitarianism: Theory and Practice*, New York: Bergham Books, pp. 79–98.

Salin, P. (2009), *Revenir au capitalisme pour éviter les crises*, Paris: Odile Jacob.

Santos, M. and M. Woodford (1997), 'Rational asset pricing bubbles', *Econometrica*, **65** (1), 19–57.

Sardoni, C. (2011), *Unemployment, Recession and Effective Demand: The Contributions of Marx, Keynes and Kalecki*, Cheltenham, UK and Northampton, MA, USA: Edward Elgar.

Sardoni, C. (2013), 'Marx and the Post-Keynesians', in Geoffrey Harcourt and Peter Kriesler (eds), *The Oxford Handbook of Post-Keynesian Economics*, vol. 2, Oxford: Oxford University Press, pp. 231–244.

Schularik, M. and A. Taylor (2009), 'Credit boom gone bust: monetary policy, leverage cycles and financial crises, 1870–2008', CEPR Discussion Papers, No. 7570.

Schumpeter, J.A. (1912), *Theorie der wirtschaftlichen Entwicklung*, Berlin: Duncker & Humblot. English edition, *The Theory of Economic Development*, Cambridge, MA: Harvard University Press (1949).

Schumpeter, J.A. (1936), 'The General Theory of Employment, Interest and Money (review)', *Journal of the American Statistical Association*, **31** (196), 791–795.

Schumpeter, J.A. (1939), *Business Cycles: A Theoretical, Historical and Statistical Analysis of the Capitalist Process*, New York: McGraw Hill, abridged edition (1964), with an introduction by Rendigs Fels, New York: McGraw Hill.

Schumpeter, J.A. (1943), 'Capitalism in the postwar world', in S. Harris (ed.), *Postwar Economic Problems*, London: McGraw-Hill, pp. 113–126, reprinted in J.A. Schumpeter (1951) *Essays on Economic Topics of J. A. Schumpeter*, Port Washington, New York: Kennikat Press, pp. 170–183.

Schumpeter, J.A. (1954), *History of Economic Analysis*, Oxford: Oxford University Press; reprinted by Oxford University Press (1994), with a new introduction by Mark Perlman.

Sen, A. (1996), 'Social commitment and democracy: the demand of equity and financial conservatism', in Paul Barker (ed.), *Living as Equals*, Oxford: Oxford University Press, pp. 9–33.

Sen, A. (1997), 'Inequality, unemployment and contemporary Europe', *International Labour Review*, **136** (2), 155–171.

Sen, A. (2015), 'The economic consequences of austerity', *New Statesman*, 4 June.

Sharpe, W. (1964), 'Capital asset prices: a theory of market equilibrium under conditions of risk', *Journal of Finance*, **19** (3), 425–442.

Shiller, R. (2008), *The Subprime Solution: How Today's Global Financial Crisis Happened, and What to Do About It*, Princeton, NJ: Princeton University Press.

Shiller, R. (2012), *Finance and the Good Society*, Princeton, NJ: Princeton University Press.

Shin, H. (2009), 'Financial intermediation and the post-crisis financial system', paper given at the BIS Annual Conference, 25–26 June, Basel, Switzerland.

Shleifer, A. (2000), *Inefficient Markets: An Introduction to Behavioral Finance*, Oxford: Oxford University Press.

Shleifer, A. and R. Vishny (2011), 'Fire sales in finance and macroeconomics', *Journal of Economic Perspectives*, **25** (1), 29–48.

Skidelsky, R. (2009), *Keynes: The Return of the Master*, New York: Allen Lane.

Skidelsky, R. (2011), 'The relevance of Keynes', *Cambridge Journal of Economics*, **35** (1), 1–13.

Skidelsky, R. and E. Skidelsky (2012), *How Much is Enough? Money and the Good Life*, New York: Other Press.

Smith, A. (1776), *An Inquiry into the Nature and Causes of the Wealth of Nations*, reprinted by Liberty Classics, Indianapolis (1981).

Solow, R. (2010), 'Building a science of economics for the real world', prepared statement, House Committee on Science and Technology, Subcommittee on Investigations and Oversight, 20 July.

Spaventa, L. (2009), 'Economists and economics: what does the crisis tell us?', *CEPR Policy Insight*, No. 38, August.

Spence, M. (2011), *The Next Convergence: The Future of Economic Growth in a Multispeed World*, New York: Picador, Farrar, Straus and Giroux.

Stiglitz, J. (2002), 'Information and the change in the paradigm in economics', *American Economic Review*, **92** (3), 460–501.

Stiglitz, J. (2008), 'Toward a general theory of consumerism: reflections on Keynes's "Economic Possibilities for our Grandchildren"', in

Lorenzo Pecchi and Giovanni Piga (eds), *Revisiting Keynes: Economic Possibilities for Our Grandchildren*, Cambridge, MA: The MIT Press, pp. 41–85.

Stiglitz, J. (2010), *Freefall: America, Free Markets, and the Sinking of the World Economy*, New York: Norton & Company.

Stiglitz, J. (2011), 'Rethinking macroeconomics: what failed, and how to repair it', *Journal of the European American Association*, **9** (4), August, 591–645.

Stiglitz, J. (2012), *The Price of Inequality: How Today's Divided Society Endangers Our Future*, London: Penguin Books.

Stiglitz, J. and B. Greenwald (2003), *Towards a New Paradigm in Monetary Economics*, Cambridge: Cambridge University Press.

Stiglitz, J. and B. Greenwald (2014), *Creating a Learning Society: A New Approach to Growth, Development, and Social Progress*, New York: Columbia University Press.

Stiglitz, J. and A. Weiss (1990), 'Banks as special accountants and screening devices for the allocation of credit', *Greek Economic Review*, **12**, Supplement, pp. 85–118, reprinted in M. Lewis (ed.) (1995), *Financial Intermediaries*, Cheltenham, UK and Northampton, MA, USA: Edward Elgar, pp. 297–332.

Strange, S. (1986), *Casino Capitalism*, Oxford: Basil Blackwell.

Strange, S. (1998), *Mad Money*, Manchester: Manchester University Press.

Streeck, W. (2013), *Die vertagte Krise des demokratischen Kapitalismus*, Berlin: Suhrkamp Verlag. English edition, *Buying Time: The Delayed Crisis of Democratic Capitalism*, New York: Verso Books (2014).

Stulz, R. (2001), 'Does financial structure matter for economic growth? A corporate finance perspective', in Asli Demirgüç-Kunt and Ross Levine (eds), *Financial Structure and Economic Growth: A Cross-Country Comparison of Banks, Markets, and Development*, Cambridge, MA: The MIT Press, pp. 143–188.

Taleb, N. (2007), *The Black Swan: The Impact of the Highly Improbable*, New York: Random House.

Taylor, J.B. (2009), *Getting Off Track: How Government Actions Caused, Prolonged, and Worsened the Financial Crisis*, Stanford: Hoover Institution Press, Stanford University.

Taylor, J.B. (2010), 'Macroeconomic lessons from the Great Deviation', in Daron Acemoglu and Michael Woodford (eds), *NBER Macroeconomics Annual*, Chicago: University of Chicago Press, vol. 25, pp. 387–395.

Taylor, L. (2010), *Maynard's Revenge: The Collapse of Free Market Macroeconomics*, Cambridge, MA: Harvard University Press.

Taylor, L. (2013), 'Keynesianism and the crisis', in Geoffrey Harcourt and Peter Kriesler (eds), *The Oxford Handbook of Post-Keynesian Economics*, vol. 2, Oxford: Oxford University Press, pp. 458–485.

Tcherneva, P. (2012), 'Full employment through social entrepreneurship: the nonprofit model for implementing a job guarantee', Levy Economics Institute of Bard College, Policy Note, No. 2.

Temin, P. and D. Vines (2013), *The Leaderless Economy*, Princeton, NJ: Princeton University Press.

Tobin, J. (1958), 'Liquidity preference as behavior towards risk', *Review of Economic Studies*, **25** (2), 65–86.

Tobin, J. (1974), *The New Economics One Decade After*, Princeton, NJ: Princeton Legacy Library.

Tobin, J. (1978), 'A proposal for international monetary reform', *Eastern Economic Journal*, **4** (3–4), 153–159.

Tobin, J. (1982), 'Money and finance in the macro-economic process', *Journal of Money, Credit and Banking*, **16** (2), 171–204.

Tobin, J. (1984), 'On the efficiency of the financial system', *Lloyds Bank Review*, **153**, 1–15.

Tobin, J. (1996), 'A currency transactions tax: why and how', *Open Economies Review*, **7** (1), 493–499.

Tobin, J. (1997), 'Why we need sand in the market's gears', *Washington Post*, 21 December.

Tobin, J. (1999), 'Reining in the markets', interview with James Tobin, in *Information Access Company/Unesco*, 1 February.

Tolley, S. (ed.) (2013), *Banking 2020: A Vision for the Future*, London: New Economics Foundation.

Trichet, J. and M. Draghi (2011), ECB letter to the Italian Prime Minister, accessed 25 January 2016 at www.corriere.it/economia/11_settembre_29/trichet_draghi_inglese.

Turner, A. (2010), 'What do banks do? Why do credit boom and busts occur and what can public policy do about it?', in LSE (ed.), *The Future of Finance: The LSE Report*, London: London School of Economics and Political Science, pp. 3–63.

Turner, A. (2012), *Economics After the Crisis: Objectives and Means*, Cambridge, MA: The MIT Press.

Turner, A. (2015), Interview with Adair Turner, 16 April, accessed 21 March 2016 at http://moneyandbanking.com/commentary/2015/4/16/interview-with-adair-turner.

Turner, A. (2016), *Between Debt and the Devil: Money, Credit, and Fixing Global Finance*, Princeton, NJ: Princeton University Press.

Vercelli, A. (1997), 'Keynes, Schumpeter and beyond', in Geoffrey Harcourt and Peter Riach (eds), *A 'Second Edition' of the General Theory*, vol. 2, London: Routledge, pp. 284–299.

Visco, V. (2013),'Crisi finanziaria, debiti privati e debiti pubblici', in Gianni Nardozzi and Francesco Silva (eds), *La globalizzazione dopo la crisi*, Milan: Francesco Brioschi Editore, pp. 35–46.

Wachtel, P. (2003), 'How much do we really know about growth and finance?', *Federal Reserve Bank of Atlanta Economic Review*, First Quarter, 33–47.

Wang, P. and Y. Wen (2012), 'Speculative bubbles and financial crises', *American Economic Journal: Macroeconomics*, **4** (3), 184–221.

Weitzman, M. (1986), *The Share Economy: Conquering Stagflation*, Cambridge, MA: Harvard University Press.

Whalen, C. (2001), 'Integrating Schumpeter and Keynes: Hyman Minsky's theory of capitalist development', *Journal of Economic Issues*, **35** (4), 805–823.

Wicksell, K. (1898), 'The influence of the rate of interest on commodity prices', reprinted in Knut Wicksell (1958), *Selected Papers on Economic Theory*, edited by Erik Lindahl, London: George Allen & Unwin, pp. 67–89.

Wolf, M. (2014), *The Shifts and the Shocks: What We've Learned – and Have Still to Learn – from the Financial Crisis*, New York: The Penguin Press.

Woodford, M. (2003), *Interest and Prices*, Princeton, NJ: Princeton University Press.

Woodford, M. (2010), 'Financial intermediation and macroeconomic analysis', *Journal of Economic Perspectives*, **24** (2), 21–44.

Wray, R. (2011), 'Minsky's money manager capitalism and the global financial crisis', Levy Economics Institute of Bard College, Working Paper, No. 661.

Wray, R. (2013), 'Minsky's money manager capitalism: assessment and reform', in Barry Z. Cynamon, Steven Fazzari and Mark Setterfield (eds), *After the Great Recession*, Cambridge: Cambridge University Press, pp. 61–85.

Wray, R. (2016), *Why Minsky Matters: An Introduction to the Work of a Maverick Economist*, Princeton, NJ: Princeton University Press.

Wurgler, J. (2000), 'Financial markets and the allocation of capital', *Journal of Financial Economics*, **58**, 187–214.

Yunus, M. (1999), *Banker to the Poor: Micro-lending and the Battle Against World Poverty*, Washington, DC: Public Affairs Press.

Zilibotti, F. (2008), 'Economic Possibilities for Our Grandchildren 75 years after: a global perspective', in Pecchi Lorenzo and Giovanni Piga (eds), *Revisiting Keynes: Economic Possibilities for Our Grandchildren*, Cambridge, MA: The MIT Press, pp. 27–40.

Zingales, L. (2012), *A Capitalism for the People: Recapturing the Lost Genius of American Prosperity*, New York: Basic Books.

Zingales, L. (2013), 'La via americana al reddito minimo', *L'Espresso*, 16 May, accessed 14 March 2016 at http://espresso.repubblica.it/affari/ 2013/05/16/news/la-via-americana-al-reddito-minimo-1.54249.

Zingales, L. (2015), 'Does finance benefit society?', NBER Working Paper, No. 20894, January.

Index

AAA credit rating 29
absolute needs 103, 104, 107
accidental phenomena, crises perceived
    as 3, 4–5, 20, 145
'accountant's nightmare' 191, 192–3
accounting standards 193
accumulation
    of capital 89–90
    of dollar reserves 37
    of money, uncertainty and 94–5
    of securitized loans and worsening of
        the crisis 149
    of wealth 70, 91, 93, 95–6, 105, 156,
        200
Acemoglu, D. 141
acquisition, art of 92
adjustable rate mortgages 15
Admati, A. 149, 171, 172, 188
affluent society 105
aggregate demand
    austerity and 173
    credit supply and 42
    economic policies and 178, 179
    fluctuations in
        and involuntary unemployment
            182
        money as key element in 111–12
    full employment and 114
    and sales proceeds 78
    Say's Law 110
    transformation of social needs into
        181
aging population 176
agricultural economies 70; *see also* corn
    economy
AIG 17
Akerlof, G. 4, 26, 42–3, 48, 99, 148,
    154, 184
alpha index 31, 32

Alt-A mortgages 15
American Economic Association 1
Ancient Egypt 196
animal spirits 74, 76, 80, 85, 86, 105,
    109, 112, 118, 119, 127
anti-crisis policies 169–95, 201–2
anti-inflation policy 145
Aristotle 95, 96, 105–6, 177, 202
arm's length financial systems 14
Arrow–Debreu model 105
art of acquisition 92
Asian countries 5, 6, 36, 37
Asian financial crisis (1997) 37, 155
Asset Backed Securities (ABSs) 27, 28,
    34, 187
asset bubbles 161
asset liquidation 128
asymmetric information 25–6, 43–4,
    77, 99, 163
austerity policies 17, 170–71, 173–4,
    190–91, 195, 201–2
Austrian school 49

bad finance 186–7
Bagehot, W. 96
'balanced budget' principle 17, 170,
    171, 173, 191, 192, 193
bank assets
    bank loans as 26, 27
    depreciation 35–6
    devaluation of securitized 159
    fluctuations in value of 172–3
    leverage and changes in value of
        149
    strengthening bank capacity to
        withstand fall in value of 202
bank deposits 46, 81, 82, 146
Bank of England 34
bank equity 166, 171, 172

bank loans
    as bank assets 26, 27
    based on private information 31
    contracts 27
    easing of criteria, for home
        ownership 24
    incentive to grant high quality 187
    increased supply, and demand for
        residential properties 148
    liquidity of 26–7
    profit from fees on 30–31
    securitization 148, 173
    see also predatory lending
bank money 63
    and investment innovation 75–80,
        199
    investment and saving decisions 82–3
    and mainstream theory; Wicksell's
        analysis 46–50
    and post-Keynesian monetary theory
        64
    wealth and speculation 50–51
bankers
    as 'ephors of capitalism' 128
    herd behaviour 100
    remuneration 25, 31, 35, 85, 148, 187
banking system
    business model 25, 26–7
    credit rationing 159–60
    and current crisis
        contribution to worsening of 148–9
        responsibility for 4–5, 6, 24–36,
            162
    interest rate determined by 120
    Lehman Brothers bankruptcy and
        uncertainty in 16
    in mainstream theory 6
    and risk 6, 84
        see also excessive risk creation
    role in innovation 147
    rules for conduct of 85
    transformation of 24, 25–7, 147–8
bankruptcy, Lehman Brothers 16, 34
banks
    and the industrial revolution 89–91
    investment financing 119
    role in asymmetric information 43–4
    share capital 188

social function of 84–5
strengthening capacity to withstand a
    collapse 170
see also central banks; commercial
    banks; investment banks;
    savings banks
bargaining 185
bargaining agreements 171
bargaining power 158, 167
barter economy 59, 60, 63, 65, 72, 74,
    83, 95
Basel III Accord 172, 188
Bastard Keynesianism 130
BB credit rating 28
Bear Stearns 16
'beauty contest' metaphor 99–100
belief systems 164
beliefs
    and anti-crisis policies 169–70, 190
    and institutions 140
    in self-regulating markets 2
    see also dominant beliefs
belonging 185
Bernanke, B.S. 5, 6, 10, 18, 36–8, 49,
    50, 62, 149, 150, 152, 162, 166,
    186, 194
big businesses
    and profits 181
    and trade unions
        conflict between 151
        regulated capitalism as
            compromise between 142,
            177
        social bargain between 150–51
    see also large corporations;
        multinational companies
Black, F. 25
black swan event, crisis perceived as a 4
Bodie, Z. 165
Bogle, J. 156
Böhm-Bawerk, E. 44, 74, 84
bond markets 96, 97–8
bonds
    government-issued 96–7
    investment financing 96, 98
    issued by the ECB 193–4
    prices of 98–9

trading 146
bonuses (banker) 25, 31, 35, 148
boom periods 10, 127, 128, 131
Borio, C. 10, 168
borrowers
    banks' role to distinguish between
        good and bad 48
    behaviour, need to question 18
    default 124, 148, 162
    housing bubble and capital losses 160
    insolvency 28, 29, 124, 162
Braudel, F. 87
Bretton Woods system 147, 151, 166,
    190
budget deficits 17, 126, 165, 170, 183
budget surplus 171
Bush administration 24
business model (banking) 25, 26–7

C–M–C' sequence 60–61, 71, 74, 94,
    95, 111, 129
Canada 17
Cannan, E. 81
capital 87–8
    accumulation of 89–90
    in concept of primitive accumulation
        90
    monetary nature of 83–4
    rate of returns on 153
    wealth and 96–7
capital adequacy requirements 171–2,
    173
capital losses, for borrowers 160
capital movements
    controls on international 151
    liberalization 3, 25, 146, 147, 189,
        201
capitalism 68, 103, 104, 142; *see also*
        laissez-faire capitalism; neoliberal
        capitalism; regulated capitalism
capitalist economies
    central planning authority in 85
    entrepreneurial decision-making 74
    intrinsic instability 123, 127
    organizations in 141
    process of change 62–3, 76
    profits as critical in 131

role of bank money 75–6
    Schumpeter on 14, 62–3, 72, 199
cash flows, SPV securities and
        entitlement to 28–9
Casino Capitalism (Strange) 155
central banks 20–21, 49, 128, 187; *see
        also* Bank of England; European
        Central Bank; Federal Reserve
certainty
    in credit agreements 80
    and investment 71–2
    production decisions 111
    see also uncertainty
change, *see* process of change
child labour 175
childbearing women, fertility rate 176
children 176
China 5, 37, 38, 190
chrematistics 95
'circulation of money as capital', *see*
        M–C–M' sequence
classical economists 44, 105; *see also*
        Mill; Ricardo; Smith
classical theory
    economic systems 67
    Keynes and limits of 57–8, 59, 60
    stationary state 101, 102
    see also neoclassical theory
Clinton administration 24
Coase, R. 65, 66
collateralized debt obligations (CDOs)
        34, 39
commercial banks 146, 165, 188
Committee of Statistical Experts of the
        League of Nations 105
common debt 193
common good 121, 169, 176–7, 179,
        181, 191, 192
comparative advantages 157
compensation schemes (bank manager)
        25, 31
competition 62, 146, 147, 148, 155, 171
complex financial instruments 25
confidence 116
conflict 151–2
conflicting beliefs 164
conflicts of interest 141
conglomerates (banking) 31

conservative economists 3, 7, 20, 51,
        139, 162
constitutions, European periphery
        countries 171, 195
consumer needs
    absolute 103, 104, 107
    and innovation, *see* innovation(s)
    and productive processes 72
    relative 103, 104
    see also insatiability; satiety
consumer sovereignty 84, 86, 155, 178,
        202
consumption
    increased credit supply due to
        reduced 42
    wage level and 115
    see also propensity to consume
consumption decisions 70, 93
contemporary economies 57, 61, 82,
        109, 141, 164, 199
conventional evaluation 99, 100, 106
cooperation
    regulated globalization 190
    remuneration systems based on 185
corn economy
    absence of social cost of
        unemployment 182
    asymmetric information and role of
        banks 43–4
    bank money and innovation 76–7
    capital in 90
    classical economics 44, 45
    debtors in 124
    full employment 114, 115, 182
    institutions in 140
    investment 70–71
    investment decisions 74
        and degree of certainty 71–2
        dissociation between saving
            decisions and 77
    limits of mainstream policies 172,
        173, 174–5
    natural rate of interest 47, 64
    principle of effective demand
        112–13, 114
    production decisions 79–80, 111
    profits 79
        and ability to repay loans 125–6

role of politics in 176
savings
    and investment 92–3
    and wealth 50–51, 93, 94
Say's Law 110
structured finance 148
time dimension 124
corporate bonds 97
counterrevolution, *see* monetarist
        counterrevolution
Cox, J. 25
Crafts, N. 173
'creating risk' 24
creative destruction 19, 141
credit
    based on creation of bank money 76
    investment decisions and demand for
        42
    in mainstream theory 41–2
    and money, in monetary economies
        81–3
    purchasing power 165–6
credit agreements 77–8, 79, 80
credit creation 41, 46, 81, 87
credit instruments 82
credit market
    information economics 43, 163
    money market confused with 41
    rate of interest on money 47
credit rating 28, 29
credit rationing 159–60
credit supply
    monetary policy and 6, 40, 41, 50,
        161, 199
    in orthodox economics 7
    and saving decisions 6, 42, 161
credit–debit contracts 25–6, 123, 124
critical economists 4; *see also* Akerlof;
        Krugman; Shiller; Stiglitz
Crouch, C. 197
Czech Republic 171

debt, *see* common debt; indebtedness;
        public debt; sovereign debt crisis
'debt brake' criteria 171
debt financing 131
debt securities 128, 193

debt to GDP ratios 17, 171
debt validation 123–6, 127
debtors 76; *see also* borrowers
decision-making
  entrepreneurial 119
  institutions as result of deliberate 140
  see also investment decisions; saving
    decisions
default
  borrowers 124, 148, 162
  risk of, borne by society 84–5
default probability, senior securities 29
default rate, mortgages 15, 16
deficit to GDP ratios 17
deflation 48
deleverage 36
demand
  for goods and services, fall in 160
  Great Recession due to collapse in
    159
  Keynesian understanding of 174
  see also aggregate demand; effective
    demand; supply and demand
democracy(ies)
  fluctuations in income and
    employment 122
  hyper-globalization as incompatible
    in presence of 190
  inequalities and challenge to 175–6
  neoliberal capitalism and 196
  politics in 176–7
depreciation, bank assets 35–6
deregulation 3, 25, 31, 146, 147, 148,
    155, 165, 189, 201
derivatives 28, 29, 34, 35, 147, 148, 165,
    166
devaluation, securitized assets 159
development
  classical economics 102
  concept of primitive accumulation 90
  current path 103
  global plan for 197
  government role in 180–81
  public sector as main obstacle to 179
  Schumpeter's theory of 63, 76, 82, 83
  social bargain and 150
  see also underdevelopment
Dillard, D. 117

discipline in the factories 121, 122
distorted incentives, excessive risk
    creation 5
distributional inequalities, *see* income
    distribution
division of labour
  criticism of enterprises based on 65–6
  financial intermediaries 27–8
  in pure exchange economies 62
Dodd–Frank Act (2010) 188
dollar reserves, accumulation of 37
dollar–gold exchange standard 152
dominant beliefs 140, 141, 144, 158,
    169, 170, 175, 190, 191
dot.com bubble 6, 18, 21, 37, 39, 158,
    159, 160, 161
Draghi, M. 170, 171
*Dynamic Stochastic General
    Equilibrium Models* 120

earthquake metaphor 142–3
economic activities
  in contemporary economies 61
  in pre-industrial economies 89
  as stemming from propensity to truck
    61
economic actors
  in contemporary economies 164
  in a monetary economy 81
  see also banks; monetary authorities
economic crises
  of the 1970s
    as an opportunity to recognise
      endogenous nature of crises
      123
    questioning of Keynesian policies
      3
    regulated capitalism 149–52
    Robinson on causes of 178–9
  current
    as a crisis of intellectual theory 167
    as crisis of intellectual theory 167
    due to lack of historical
      understanding 148
    economists' passive attitude
      towards 1
    lessons to be learned from 1–2

limitations of mainstream
    explanations 1, 4–7, 40–52,
    160–64, 198–9
mainstream theory and causes of
    4–5, 20–38
need for a new theoretical model
    2–4, 7–9
outbreak in the US 13–15
policies for overcoming 169–95
questions concerning 18–19
split in economics profession 4
subprime mortgage market 15–16
theoretical roots 143–9
three phases of 16–17
denial of possibility of, in a market
    economy 1, 4
endogenous nature 60, 102, 123,
    127–8, 139–64, 200
Keynes and Schumpeter on 109
and the limits of Keynesian policies
    121–8
link between environmental crises
    and 181
as a monetary phenomenon 59
and non-neutrality of money 60
see also Asian financial crisis; Great
    Depression; Great Recession
economic growth 63, 157, 166, 167,
    173, 177, 189, 191, 197
economic growth theory 45
economic historians 89
economic models 10
economic pessimism 107
economic policy
    international 166
    since 1980s 145
    see also anti-crisis policies; fiscal
        policies; monetary policies
economic systems
    based on chrematistics 95
    belief in stability of 152
    classical theory 67
    financial system transformation and
        fragility of 154
    mainstream theory 5–6
    politics in 176
economic theory(ies)

crises, and the need for a new 3–4,
    7–9
Kaldor on fundamental task of 82
and societal welfare 2
see also classical theory; mainstream
    theory; neoclassical theory
economics
    Aristotle's use of term 95
    as the study of human behaviour 101
economists
    Keynes's prediction on future of
        103–4
    neglect of the signs of instability 1,
        170
    passive attitude towards current
        crisis 1
    reaction to stagflation 122–3
    see also classical economists;
        conservative economists; critical
        economists; heretical
        economists; mainstream
        economists
economy(ies)
    alliance between technology and 196
    fine tuning 166
    frictionless 168
    see also barter economy; capitalist
        economies; contemporary
        economies; fishing economy;
        market economies; monetary
        economies; real exchange
        economies
effective demand
    fluctuations of 130
    principle of 111–15, 117–18, 120,
        178
    simple linear model 132–6
efficient markets theory, speculative
    bubbles 34–5
employment
    and conditions for a good life 182–3
    economic policy and 192
    fluctuations in 3, 58, 59, 63, 122, 199
    impact of crisis on 18–19
    impact of housing bubble on 159
    Keynesian policies 120
    market forces and 120, 144
    in monetary economies 114

natural level of 144
see also full employment; job
    creation; job scarcity;
    unemployment
endogenous nature, economic crises 60,
    102, 123, 127–8, 139–64, 200
England 90, 96, 102, 141, 175; *see also*
    London
enterprise(s)
    criticism of those based on division of
        labour 65–6
    prevalence of speculation over 100,
        147, 158
    remuneration based on bargaining
        between trade unions and 185
    and socialization of investments
        179–82
    speculation contrasted with 98, 128
entrepreneur-coordinators 65, 66, 68
entrepreneur-innovators
    bank money
        and ability to control production 84
        and investment decisions 77–8, 80
    decision-making 73, 112, 119
    development dependent on presence
        of 76
    financial systems and ability to
        borrow 14
    Keynes's introduction of 105
    lack of risk on part of 180
    production decisions 114–15
    societal resistance to 14, 141
    transfer of risk 85
entrepreneurs 66
    consumption decisions as funds for
        93
    decision-making in barter economies
        74
    investment decisions 106
    in monetary economies 61, 74, 125
    profit and the ability to repay loans
        124–6
    resistance to full employment 121–2
entrepreneurship, *see* enterprise(s)
environmental crises 181
'ephors' of capitalism 128
ergodic systems 141

ethnic minorities, promotion of home
    ownership 24
euphoria 127, 128, 131, 159
Euro Union Bonds (EUBs) 193
European authorities 194
European Central Bank (ECB) 193, 194
European countries
    banks and industrialization 91
    financial systems 14–15
    GDP growth rate 189
    policies for a good life 190–95
    signing of Treaty on Stability 17
    situation seven years after the crisis
        173
    see also individual countries
European Financial Fund 193
European institutions 182–3
European integration 171
European Monetary Union (EMU) 191
European Systemic Risk Board 197
Eurozone countries
    accounting standards 193
    austerity policies 17
    public deficits 170
    sovereign debt 17
excessive risk creation, banking system
    and 5, 25, 30–33, 148, 162
exogenous phenomenon, crisis
    perceived as an 4–5, 20–38
expansionary fiscal policies 121, 178,
    194, 196
expansionary monetary policies 4–6,
    21, 22, 23, 37, 50, 160, 161, 178
expectations
    and borrowing by low-income
        households 148
    long-term 99, 100, 107, 117
    and shareholder accountability 100
    and speculative bubbles 33–4
    as ultimate independent variables
        116–17
explorers 85
external debt contracts 26, 27

fair value accounting principle 35
Fannie Mae 16, 24, 162
Fascism 122

federal funds rate 16, 21, 22, 38, 49
Federal Housing Enterprises Safety and
        Soundness Act (1992) 24
federal insurance, bank deposits 146
Federal Reserve
    control of interest rates 49–50
    crisis blamed on mistakes by 4–6,
        20–23, 149–50
    non-intervention in speculative
        bubbles 35
fertility rate, childbearing women 176
fiat money 63
finance
    'bad' and 'good' 186–7
    mainstream theory of 42–50, 154
    portfolio allocation theory 25
    and risk 69–86
    standard theory of 6
    and uncertainty 70
    see also structured finance
financial accounting 192–3
financial assets
    prices 99, 100
    see also bank assets
financial innovations 13–14, 29–30,
        127, 147, 155, 188–9
financial instability
    capitalist economies and intrinsic
        123, 127
    emergence during Great Moderation
        152–8
    innovations and 147
    in a macroeconomic context 10,
        162–3
    neglect of the signs of 1, 170
    resource costs and 182
financial institutions
    competition from new 146
    fundamental function of 154
    impact of crisis on 16
    uncertainty in, and rise in interest
        rates 16
    see also banks
financial intermediaries
    existence of 42
    fundamental role of 26
    growth of financial sector 156

increasing share of wealth managed
        by 156
    specialization 27
    see also banks
financial lobby 188
financial markets
    compared to traditional markets 201
    deregulation 25, 31, 146, 155, 165,
        189, 201
    efficient markets theory 35
    increase in workers' income 153–5
    second-hand car market analogy 189
    transitions to booming periods 128
financial performance, bonuses based
        on 31, 35
financial repression 201
financial results 192
financial stability 146, 152, 186
financial system(s)
    active role 89–90
    advantage of well-developed,
        England 96
    criteria for measuring development of
        13–14
    European 14–15
    fragility, *see* fragility
    fundamental function in monetary
        economies 200
    government interventions to support
        17
    growth, *see* financialization
    impact of mortgage market collapse
        18
    and industrial revolution 89–90
    Minsky on 109
    passive role 89
    pipeline analogy 165
    regulation 171–2, 187, 201
    textbook definition 13
    transformation 154
    underdeveloped 14, 15
    United States
        as benchmark for other countries 5,
            13
        difficulties and global
            repercussions 17
        and innovation 13, 14
        questions concerning 18

value produced by 153
well-developed 14, 96
see also banking system
financial transactions
  and asymmetric information 25–6
  belief in innovation and reduced risk
    in 189
  tax on short-term 187, 197
financialization 153, 155–6, 158; *see
  also* financial innovations
fine tuning 166
Fiorentini, R. 197
firms
  in a real-exchange economy 65–6
  see also enterprises
Fiscal Compact 17, 170, 173, 191
fiscal policies, *see* anti-inflation policy;
  expansionary fiscal policies
fishing economy 44, 45, 52, 74, 84, 90
fixed exchange rates 151
fixed-income compensation scheme 25
flow of investments 6, 37, 76, 113, 114,
  115, 117, 118, 119, 134, 136, 199
flow of profits 126, 135
flow of savings 6, 37, 50, 80, 96, 120,
  126, 135
fluctuations
  in aggregate demand 111–12, 182
  of effective demand 130
  in income and employment 58, 59,
    63, 122, 199
  of output and employment 3, 57
  in propensity to save 48
forecast error, Keynes's 104
foreign capital, stock market boom, US
  37
fragility 42, 123–4, 142, 145, 154, 155,
  169, 171, 200
France 17, 90, 96, 151
Francis, the Holy Father 169, 177, 181,
  182
Freddie Mac 16, 24, 162
free market(s) 2, 144, 164, 167, 175,
  177, 185, 187, 196
free trade 144, 157
freedom of contract 175
freedom from work 185
frictionless economy 168

Friedman, M. 21, 41, 48, 58, 120, 123,
  143, 144, 160, 161, 184, 201
  criticism of Keynesian policies 3
full employment
  classical theory and 57
  in a corn economy 114, 115, 182
  and debt financing 131
  expansionary fiscal policies 196
  innovations introduced under 75
  insufficiency of Keynesian policies to
    achieve 129
  interest rate and 117–19
  Kalecki and political aspects of
    121–2
  price adjustment mechanism and 59
  wage and price flexibility 117, 201

Galbraith, James K. 181–2, 196
Galbraith, John K. 105, 152
Garn–St Germain Act (1982) 146
GDP
  federal funds rate and control of 21
  growth rate 153, 189
  see also debt to GDP ratios; deficit to
    GDP ratios; per capita GDP
*General Theory of Employment,
  Interest and Money* (Keynes) 3, 57,
  58, 63, 64, 72, 97, 98, 105, 109,
  115, 116, 130, 174, 179, 183, 187
Germany 17, 90, 96, 151
Gershenkron, A. 89–91
Glass–Steagall Act (1933) 146
global demand, recession due to
  collapse in 159
global plan, for growth and
  development 197
global savings glut 36–8
globalization 189–90, 197; *see also*
  hyper-globalization
Glorious Revolution 96
Glyn, A. 155
gold deposits 82
Goldin, C. 153–4
good finance 186
good jobs 183
good life 177
  amount of property required for 95

limits of Keynesian policies 178–9
policies for developing conditions for
    179–95, 202
goods and services 45, 160, 178
Google 188
Gorton, G. 148
government bonds 96–7
government interventions, to support
    international financial system 17
government (US)
    as culprit of crisis 161–2, 165
    role in development 180–81
Government-Sponsored Enterprises
    (GSEs) 49
graduate workers, financial sector
    153–4
Grameen Bank 162
Gramm–Leach–Bliley Act (1999)
    146–7
Great Britain, *see* United Kingdom
Great Depression 1, 2, 25, 102, 150,
    152, 169, 174, 198
Great Moderation 1, 143, 150, 152–8,
    166, 186, 198
Great Recession 4, 7, 8, 9, 13, 18, 143,
    158, 159, 160, 162
greed 104
green industrial revolution 182
Greenspan, A. 2, 5, 21, 30, 35, 187–8
gregarious attitude, professional
    speculators 35
growth, *see* economic growth; personal
    growth
guaranteed minimum income 185–6

Hahn, F. 94–5
Harrod, R.F. 104
Harvard graduates 154
Hellwig, M. 149, 171, 172, 188
herd behaviour 34–6, 39, 100, 149, 159,
    162
heretical economists 57, 164, 175, 178,
    200; *see also* Kaldor; Kalecki;
    Keynes; Marx; Minsky;
    Schumpeter
heterogeneous subjects, in capitalist and
    monetary economies 80, 141

Hicks, J. 82
high interest rates 26, 47, 128
high quality loans 187
high-risk securities 28
historical understanding, crisis due to
    lack of 148
History of Economic Analysis
    (Schumpeter) 81
Hodgson, G. 164
Home Equity Line of Credit (HELOC)
    mortgages 15
home ownership, American promotion
    of 24–5
homogenous path, of development 90
homogenous subjects, corn economies
    80, 87, 140, 175
hostility, against migrants 176
housing bubble 4–5, 6, 19, 29, 34, 36,
    37, 38, 158, 159, 160, 161, 173,
    201
housing prices 33–4, 37, 38, 100, 148,
    159, 160
human dignity 177, 196
human well-being 139, 142, 182, 183,
    195
humanity
    best state for 107
    inborn desire to improve living
        conditions 104
    Keynes's prediction on future of
        103–4
Hume, D. 41
hungry population 189
hyper-globalization 151, 157, 158, 184,
    189–90

iceberg of risk 6, 31, 48, 201
ICT revolution 25, 26, 31, 37, 159, 181,
    188
ignorant speculators 98, 99, 106
illiquid financial assets 26, 27
imperfect information 39, 154
improvement, human inborn desire for
    104
incentive systems 5, 187
income
    as a component of the good life 183–6
    fluctuations in 58, 59, 63, 122, 199

impact of crisis on 18–19
impact of housing bubble on 159
increase in 153–4
Keynesian policies 120
market forces and 120, 144
in monetary economies 114
volatility, 1970s 150
income allocation decisions 97
income determination 67
income distribution, inequalities in
    24–5, 154, 157–8, 166, 184
indebtedness, low-income subjects 24,
    161–2
Independent Commission on Banking
    (UK) 188
India 190
industrial revolution 102
    banks and the 89–91
industrialized countries, social costs
    157
inequalities
    and the challenge to democracy
        175–6
    conservatives' defence of 167
    ignored by mainstream economists
        184
    income distribution 24–5, 154,
        157–8, 166, 184
    neoliberal capitalism and 175
    reducing 185
    wealth distribution 95
    Western economies 175, 176, 185
inflation
    federal funds rate and control 21,
        38
    increase in, 1970s 146, 150
    money supply and 41
    Western economies, 1950s and 1960s
        151
    Wicksell's view on 48
    see also anti-inflation policy;
        deflation; stagflation
information availability, change in
    business model of banking 26–7
information and communications
    technology, *see* ICT revolution
information economics 42–4; *see also*
    asymmetric information

innovation(s)
    bank money and 75–80, 199
    investment decisions and uncertainty
        72–5, 180
    in monetary economies 192
    and needs 72–3, 200, 202
        influence on 178
        satisfaction of relative 104
        social function of banks 84–5
        transformation into aggregate
            demand 181
    profits as reflection of success of 184
    resistance to 14, 141
    risks borne by society 180, 181
    role of banking system 147
    state role in 179, 188
    wealth accumulation 96
    see also entrepreneur-innovators;
        financial innovations; new
        combinations; process of change
insatiability 94, 95, 101, 103, 104, 200
insolvency 16, 28, 29, 46, 124, 162
instability, *see* financial instability;
    political instability
institutional engineering 151
institutional investors 156
institutions
    change and 140–43
    see also European institutions;
        financial institutions
insurance companies 17, 24, 32, 156
insurance policies 32
intellectual theory, current crisis as
    crisis of 167
interbank rate 16–17
interdependence 139, 189
interest payments on EUBs 193
interest rate(s)
    anti-inflation policy and rise in 145
    assumption of appropriate level 117,
        120
    central bank influence/control 21,
        49–50
    determined by the banking system
        120
    'fishing economy' analogy 44
    and full employment 117–19
    monetary nature of 84

neoclassical theory 84
  as price of credit 41, 48
  price and wage flexibility 116
  propensity to save and fall in 37
  and real quantity of money 115, 116
  reduced consumption and fall in 42
  uncertainty in and rise in 16
  see also federal funds rate; high
       interest rates; interbank rate;
       monetary interest rate; natural
       rate of interest
internal debt contracts 26
international community, conflict
       between US and 151–2
International Monetary Fund (IMF) 34
international monetary system 151
Internet phenomenon 159
investment(s)
  entrepreneurship and socialization of
       179–82
  in a monetary economy 120, 191
  revaluations 106
  see also flow of investments
investment banks 16, 146, 165, 171,
       182, 188
investment decisions
  bank money and innovation 75–80
  credit demand 42
  entrepreneurial 106
  and saving decisions
    bank money 82
    causal relationship between 92–3
    dissociation between 42, 77
    mainstream models 45
    and natural rate of interest 49
  and uncertainty 70–75, 112, 180
investment financing 63–4, 96, 98, 119,
       180
investment funds 156
invisible hand 61, 67, 121, 176
involuntary unemployment 115–20,
       178, 182
IS–LM tradition 105
Italy 17, 90, 151, 170, 171, 182

Jackson Hole Conference 30, 35
Japan 17, 189, 190, 194

job creation 191
job scarcity 183
Jobs, S. 181
joint stock companies 147–8
J.P.Morgan 171, 182
junior security 28–9

Kaldor, N. 7, 82–3, 97
Kalecki, M. 7, 110, 141, 151
  political aspects of full employment
       121–2
Katz, L. 153–4
Keynes, J.M. 7, 169
  on 'accountant's nightmare' 191,
       192–3
  on characteristics of money 62–5
  on concept of monetary economy
       59–62
  on consumption decisions 93
  on economic possibilities of his
       grandchildren 101, 102–4, 202
  on entrepreneur-innovators 85
  explanation for forecast error 102,
       104–5
  on fluctuations of income and
       employment 63, 199
  on fluctuations in output and
       employment 3
  on investment decisions under
       uncertainty 73–4
  on investment financing 98
  on phenomenon of economic crises
       109–10
  on professional speculators 99–100
  on profits 83, 183, 184
  on real quantity of money 115–16
  on reconstruction of London 194–5
  on role of banking system in
       innovation 147
  on saving 92
  on speculation 97, 98
  on technical progress and freedom
       from labour 185
  on unsolved problem of crises 57
  on wastefulness of slumps 127
  on wealth accumulation 96
  on wealth and saving decisions 94

see also General Theory of Employment, Interest and Money
Keynesian policies
  crisis as an opportunity to review 143
  criticisms of 3, 58–9
  effect on income and employment 120
  as insufficient to ensure full employment 129
  limits of 121–8, 178–9, 201
Keynesian revolution 41, 123, 179
Knight, F. 66
Kotz, D. 142, 150, 164, 170
Krugman, P. 4, 196
Kurz, H. 118

labour
  and conditions for a good life 182–3
  demand for, and increase in wage levels 76
  rate of returns on 153
  technical progress and freedom from 185
labour market flexibility 202
labour market reform 170, 171, 174–5, 202
labour productivity 84, 112, 114, 115, 150, 184, 185
labour protections 171, 190
laissez-faire capitalism 101, 117
large corporations 65, 66, 98, 158, 175; *see also* big businesses; multinational companies
Lee, W. 141
legal tender 20, 46, 82
legislation, securitization 187
Lehman Brothers 16, 34, 171
leverage 36, 149, 159, 171
liberalization
  capital movements 3, 25, 146, 147, 189, 201
  of trade 151, 157, 166, 189
Liikanen, E. 188
liquidity
  of bank loans 26–7
  crises due to a rush to 128

  excessive
    on causes of 5
    and need to question origins of 18
  financial systems and 200
  relationship between wealth and capital 97
  see also 'whole liquidity position'
liquidity preference theory 115, 117, 118
liquidity trap 117
Litner, J. 25
living conditions, human inborn desire to improve 104
living standards 104, 191, 195
loanable funds theory 63
Lombard Street (Bagehot) 96
London 194
long-term bonds and shares 97, 98
long-term expectations 99, 100, 107, 117
long-term financing 98, 180
long-term interest rates 49
long-term investors 107
long-term levels of income and employment 120
love, for money, Keynes's emphasis on 104
low income families
  belief in 'new era' and increased borrowing 148
  belief in 'this time is different' message 34
  loans designed to appeal to 32–3
  promotion of home ownership and indebtedness 24, 161–2
low inflation rates 151
low rate of interest on money 47
Lucas, R. 1, 41, 58, 120, 144, 201

M–C–M' sequence 60, 61–2, 65, 66, 69, 74, 95, 112, 129
McCallum, B. 40, 45
macroeconomic models 97, 124, 162, 168
macroeconomic supervisory role 187
macroeconomics 1, 168, 198; *see also* new classical macroeconomics

Mad Money (Strange) 155
mainstream economists
    inability to see warning signs 155
    issue of inequalities ignored by 184
    neglect of relationship between
        savings and wealth decisions
        156
    recognition of link between
        deregulation and crisis 148
mainstream policies
    to overcome crisis 170–72
        limits to 172–6
mainstream theory
    assumption of an appropriate rate of
        interest 120
    continued acceptance of 4
    contradictions of 101–5
    current crisis
        explanations for 4–5, 20–38
        limitations of 1, 4–7, 40–52,
            160–64, 198–9
    economic systems in 5–6
    of finance 42–50, 154
    on fundamental function of financial
        institutions 154
    money and credit in 41–2
    questioning of validity of 2
market(s)
    belief in self-regulating ability 2
    blind faith in 145–9
    equilibrium 43
    flexibility 167, 171, 202
    imbalances 128
    liquidity 165
    relationships and financial systems
        14
    see also financial markets; free
        market(s)
market completion 165
market economies
    belief in impossibility of crises
        occurring 1, 4, 143
    fluctuations, *see* fluctuations
    homogenous subjects 87
market forces 59, 164, 181, 189
    and income and employment 120,
        144
    and inequality 158

market mechanism 196
market system 152
Markowitz, H.M. 25
Marx, K. 7, 60, 61, 89, 95, 96, 141
mass psychology 106
maximization, shareholder value 31,
    148
Mazzucato, M. 179–80, 182, 188,
    192
Meade, J. 185
mechanics, *see* 'second hand car
    market' analogy
Merton, R. 25, 165
Messori, M. 116–17
Mian, A. 160
microcredits 162
Middle Ages 196
Middle East 151
migrants, hostility against 176
Mill, J.S. 102
Minsky, H. 7, 154
    on asymmetric information on credit
        market 163
    certainty in credit agreements 80
    crises
        on endogenous nature of 121,
            127–8
        as an opportunity to revive
            Keynesianism 143
    debt validation 123–6
    on financial system 109
    on monetary economy stability 110
    and the Neoclassical Synthesis
        122–3
modern economies, *see* contemporary
    economies
monetarism 3
monetarist counterrevolution 3, 21, 41,
    143–5, 146, 149, 155, 161, 201
monetary authorities
    in first phase of crisis 16
    mainstream theory 5–6
    neglect of goal of financial stability
        186
    neoclassical theory 5–6, 7
    setting of annual growth rate of
        money supply 21
    see also central banks

monetary base 20–21
monetary economies
    characteristics of 80–85, 121
    compared to real exchange
        economies 129
    conflicts of interest in 141
    consumption in 93
    debtors in 124
    financial system in 200
    income and employment 114
    innovation in 84, 192
    institutions in 140
    interest rates in 84
    investment financing 96
    investment and uncertainty 71, 73,
        112
    involuntary unemployment in
        115–20
    Keynes on concept of 59–62
    main actors in 81
    organizations in 141
    production decisions 112, 114–15
    production and uncertainty in 69
    profits in 75, 183–4
    public deficits 126
    resources for investment 191
    role of politics in 176
    savings and investment in 120
    social cost of employment 182
    structural instability 129
    time dimension 124
    types of entrepreneur 125
    wealth accumulation 96
monetary illusion 3, 58, 143, 201
monetary interest rates 47–8, 49
monetary policies
    and credit supply 6, 40, 41, 50, 161,
        199
    price stability 49
    see also expansionary monetary
        policies; restrictive monetary
        policies
monetary sovereignty 191
monetary theory of production 7,
    57–68, 102, 109, 110, 121
money
    and credit, in monetary economies
        81–3

and fluctuations
    in aggregate demand 111–12
    in income and employment 59, 63
Keynes's emphasis on love and greed
    for 104
Keynes, Schumpeter and the
    characteristics of 62–5
in mainstream theory 41–2
neutrality of 60, 67
non-neutrality of 60, 163
relationship between economic crises
    and 123
and savings 92–5
see also bank money; C–M–C'
    sequence; fiat money; M–C–M'
    sequence
money creation 41, 46, 62, 64, 76,
    80–81, 87
money manager capitalism 128
money market, credit market confused
    with 41
money market funds 146
money supply, monetary authorities and
    rate of 21
Montani, G. 197
moral hazard issue 30
Mortgage Backed Securities (MBSs)
    27, 28
mortgage market
    agencies, see Fannie Mae; Freddie
        Mac
    collapse of 16, 18, 34
    see also subprime mortgage crisis;
        subprime mortgages
Mossin, J. 25
Mulgan, G. 179, 188, 192
multinational companies 177, 189, 190

national debt, see public debt
natural equilibrium 152
natural rate of interest 47–8, 49, 50, 53,
    64, 68, 84, 117
Nazism 122
needs, see consumer needs
Neoclassical Synthesis 3, 21, 58, 59,
    105, 178

identification of theoretical gap in
    143–4
Minsky and 122–3
prices, wages and involuntary
    unemployment 115, 116, 117
regulated capitalism 142
stagflation and questioning of 120
neoclassical theory
  Great Depression and the
      undermining of confidence in 3
  interest rates 84
  labour market 171
  monetary authorities 6, 7
  of money 6
  re-acceptance of pre-Keynesian 3
  see also mainstream theory
neoliberal capitalism 164, 177
  austerity and 195
  blind faith in market virtues 145–9
  and the crisis 158–60
  and democracy 196
  emergence of 142, 144, 175
  inequality due to transition to 158
neoliberal ideology 3, 198, 201
neutrality of money 60, 67
new classical macroeconomics 3, 120,
    123
new combinations 86, 88, 97
new entrepreneurs 14
new era 34, 35, 127, 128, 131, 148
ninja loans 15
Nixon, President 152
non-democratic regimes 122
non-ergodic systems 141
non-financial corporations 167
non-neutrality of money 60, 163
non-prime mortgages 15
non-professional speculators 35
North, D. 139, 140, 141–2, 169
Northern Rock 16

Obama, President 173, 188
'occupation of poor quality' 183
official interest rate 21
oil prices 37, 38, 151, 165
oil-producing countries

conflict between oil consuming and
    151
'savings glut' hypothesis 5, 36
oligarchic goods 104
organizations 141
organized labour, *see* trade unions
'originate to distribute' model 25, 27
'originate to hold' model 25, 26, 27
orthodox theory, *see* mainstream theory

PADRE plan 193–4
Palley, T. 197
Pâris, P. 193
participation, remuneration systems
    based on 185
patient capitals 180
Pecchi, L. 104
pension funds 156
per capita GDP 17
Perez, C. 158, 159
perfect information 43, 163
peripheral European countries 170, 171,
    195
personal growth 196
Phelps, E. 4
Phillips curve 58, 120, 143, 144, 149
Piga, G. 104
Piketty, T. 158
pin factory 66
pipeline analogy 165
planned economies 85
Polanyi, K. 89, 105
political aspects, of full employment
    121–2
political change, and resistance to full
    employment 121
political instability 151
political stability 121, 122
political systems, European periphery
    countries 195
politics, role of 176–7
poor population 189
Pope Francis 169, 177, 181, 182
population categories 189
portfolio allocation theory 25
portfolio diversification 25, 27–9
Portugal 171

positional goods 104
post-Keynesian theory 64
pre-industrial economies
    economic activities 89
    individuals in 87
    wealth in 95–6
pre-Keynesian theory 3, 144, 145, 201
predatory lending 32–3
prehistoric subsistence economies
        105
premiums, for money creation, interest
        rate as 84, 88
price(s)
    of credit 41, 48
    of financial assets 99, 100
    flexibility 58, 115, 116, 117, 120,
        144, 163, 178, 182, 201
    level 41, 42, 46–7, 115–16
    of money 41
    reduction in 116
    rigidity 58, 117, 178
    stability 48, 49, 121, 127, 140, 145,
        150, 187
    stickiness 120
price adjustment mechanism 58, 59
price system 61, 65, 66
prime mortgages 15
primitive accumulation 89–90
private business, investment in 106
private costs 157, 181
private firms 192
private information, bank loans based
        on 31
private investments 181, 193
private property 62, 87, 164, 196
private wealth, public debt and 191
privatization 4
probability distribution, portfolio
        diversification 28, 29
process of change
    capitalist economies 14, 62–3,
        76
    contemporary economies 82
    and institutions 140–43
    Keynes's forecast error due to
        overlooking 102
    see also innovation
Prodi, R. 193

production
    and the common good 192
    consumer needs 72
    economic policies and 178
    in a monetary economy 112
    specialization in 61
    transfer of 157, 189
    uncertainty in 69
    see also M–C–M' sequence
production costs 63, 82, 128
production decisions 79–80, 111, 112,
        114–15, 136
professional speculators 35, 98,
        99–100, 106
profit(s) 87
    and ability to repay loans 124–6
    in a corn economy 79
    as critical in capitalist economies
        131
    as an expression of the 'rules of the
        game' 181
    from fees on bank loans 30–31
    in a monetary economy 75, 183–4
    monetary nature of 83
    in a real-exchange economy 74
    wealth accumulation and 96
propensity to consume 114–15
propensity to save 6, 36–7, 48, 63
propensity to truck 61
property rights 140, 167
protectionism 157
prudence 128
'psychology of the market' 98, 99, 100,
        128
public budgets 191; *see also* balanced
        budget principle; budget deficits
public debt 191
    bond markets 96, 97
    and entrepreneurial profit 126
    Eurozone countries 17
    securities 193
    United Kingdom 96, 97
public finances, government
        intervention and deterioration in
        17
public investments 181, 193
public sector(s)
    as culprit of the crisis 170

and debt validation 126
as main obstacle to development 179
as source of waste of money 174
purchasing power 47, 73, 76, 78, 81, 87, 90, 91, 94, 96, 165, 191
pure-exchange economy 62

Quadrio Curzio, A. 193
quality of loans 15
quality of production 192
quality of work/labour 179, 182, 183
quantitative easing 49
quantity theory of money 5–6, 41, 46, 97

Radcliffe Report 97
railroad construction 73, 77–8, 98, 112, 113–14, 119, 120, 125, 126
railway cloakrooms 81–2
Rajan, R. 5, 6, 13, 14, 15, 18, 23, 24, 30, 31, 34, 35, 48, 62, 69, 70, 100, 148, 162, 166, 199, 201
rate of returns on capital and labour 153
Reagan, R. 3, 25, 145–6, 165
real estate bubble, *see* housing bubble
real quantity of money 115–16
real-exchange economies 80
compared to monetary economies 129
entrepreneurial profit 74
money in 59, 60, 61, 64
the nature of the firm in 65–6
purpose of 84
Say's Law as applicable to 111
see also agricultural economies; C–M–C' sequence
receipts (bankers) 82
receipts (cloakroom) 82
reference interest rate 21
regulated capitalism 142, 164
and the common good 177
and crisis of the 1970s 149–52
inequality as consequence of transition to neoliberal capitalism 158
regulated globalization 190

regulation, financial system 171–2, 187, 201
Reich, R. 150, 158, 167, 177, 185
Reinhart, C. 34, 201
relation-based financial systems 14
relative needs 103, 104
remuneration
bankers 25, 31, 35, 85, 148, 187
based on bargaining 185
need for redesigning of 187
CEOs, large corporations 158
rent-seeking 196
reputation 100
residential mortgages
default rate 15, 16
as an external debt contract 27
questions concerning expansion in supply of 18
supply of loans and increased demand for 148
transfer to SPVs 27
types 15
resource allocation 6, 65, 184; *see also* transfer of funds
resource costs, and financial instability 182
resources, for investment in monetary economies 191
restrictive monetary policies 128, 145, 161
revaluations 106
Ricardo, D. 44, 74, 157
rich population 189
risk(s)
banking system and creation of 6, 84
see also excessive risk creation
borne by society 84–5, 180, 181
credit–debit contracts 25
finance and 69–96
financial innovation and belief in reduced 189
mortgages and transfer of 34, 84
see also iceberg of risk
risk management 166
Robbins, L. 101
Robinson Crusoe economy 110–11
Robinson, J. 130, 141, 178–9, 192

Rodrik, D. 140, 147, 151, 157, 166, 189–90, 196
Rogers, C. 117
Rogoff, K. 34, 201
rules, for the conduct of banking 85
'rules of the game' 140, 147, 164, 169, 173, 176, 181, 185
runaway expansion 109, 127

Sachs, J. 165
satiety 95, 101, 103, 185
saved resources 6, 7, 48, 64, 69, 93, 139, 147, 154
savings
   in a monetary economy 120
   money and 92–5
   see also flow of savings
savings banks 146, 169
saving decisions
   and credit supply 6, 42, 161
   and investment decisions
      bank money and 82
      causal relationship between 92–3
      dissociation between 42, 77
      mainstream model 45
      and natural rate of interest 49
   and speculation/speculative bubbles 6
   and wealth 50, 93, 156, 200
   see also propensity to save
'savings glut' hypothesis 5, 6, 36–8, 49
Say's Law 61, 110–11, 120, 129, 130, 144, 173
scarce resources, allocation of 65, 184
scarcity, and insatiability 101
Scholes, M. 25
Schumpeter, J.A. 7
   on bank money
      creation 87
      role in capitalist economies 75–6
   banks/banking
      role in innovation 147
      on rules for conduct of 85
      on social function of 85
   on capitalist economies 14, 62–3, 72, 199
   on characteristics of money 62–5
   on concept of capital 96
   on entrepreneur-innovators 141, 180
   on innovation 199
      and needs 72–3, 178, 181
      role of banking system 147
      societal resistance 141
   on investment financing 98
   on monetary nature
      of credit 81
      of profit, capital and interest rates 83–4
   negative judgement on *General Theory* 130
   on phenomenon of economic crises 109, 110
   on profits in a monetary economy 183–4
   on risk of default 84–5
   on risks of private investments 181
   on wealth accumulation 96
Schwartz, A. 41, 48
'second hand car market' analogy 43, 99, 148, 154, 184, 188–9
securities, loan purchasing 28–9
securitization
   of bank loans 148, 173
   and expansion in supply of mortgages 30–31
   legislation 187
   misuse of 31
   moral hazard issue 30
   process 27–30
securitized assets, devaluation 159
self-destructive financial calculation 192–3
self-fulfilling prophecy 33
self-regulating market, belief in 2
selfishness 61
Sen, A. 144, 173–4, 182–3
senior security 28, 29
sequence economies 105
shadow banking system 166
shareholder accountability 100
shareholder equity 35–6, 149
shareholder value, maximization 31, 148
shares
   investment financing 88, 96
   prices of 98–9

trading 97, 146
Sharpe, W. 25
Shiller, R. 4, 33–4
short-term financial transactions, tax on
    187
short-term interest rates 49, 145
'simple circulation of commodities',
    see C–M–C' sequence
Skidelsky, E. 103
Skidelsky, R. 102, 103
slow food movement 108
slumps 122, 127
small producers 61, 65, 66, 71, 73, 80,
    98
Smith, A. 44, 61, 66, 74, 99, 102
social bargain 150–51
social change, and resistance to full
    employment 121
social cohesion 182
social costs 157, 181, 182
social exclusion 182
social function of banks 84–5
social inclusion 185
social needs 181
social responsibility 184
social welfare 186
socialism 165, 171, 184
socialization of investments 179–82
societal welfare 2, 184, 196
society, risks borne by 84–5, 180, 181
Solow, R. 4
southern European countries 170, 171,
    195
sovereign debt crisis 117
Soviet communism 103, 144
Spain 171
Special Purpose Vehicle (SPV) 27, 28
specialization
    financial intermediaries 27
    in production 61
speculation 6, 33, 50
    and economic crises 199–200
    euphoria and 128
    growth of the financial sector
        156–7
    ignored in traditional theory of
        finance 147

maximization of shareholder value
    through 148
measures affecting profitability of
    187
prevalence over entrepreneurship
    100, 147, 158
profits generated by 184
wealth and 97–101
see also ignorant speculators;
    non-professional speculators;
    professional speculators
speculative bubbles
    and economic crises 199–200
    efficient market theory 34–5
    expectations and 33–4
    mainstream analysis 51
    professional speculators and
        generation of 100
    saving decisions and 6
    see also dot.com bubble; housing
        bubble
Spence, M. 177
Sraffa, P. 118
stability, *see* financial stability; political
    stability; price(s), stability
Stability and Growth Pact 171
stagflation 3, 58, 120, 122–3, 149, 151,
    200–201
standards of living 104, 191, 195
Stanford graduates 154
state role
    in innovation 179, 188
    in regulated capitalism 150–51
stationary state 101, 102, 111
steady state 202
Stiglitz, J. 4, 39, 43, 77, 78, 108, 196
stock, value of traded (2010) 156
Stock Exchange 106
stock market boom, foreign capital
    inflow and 37
stock market crash (2000) 4, 16, 21, 37
Strange, S. 155, 166–7
strikes 151
structural nature, of the crisis 147
structural reforms 170, 171, 174–5, 202
structurally limited goods 104
structured finance 27, 29, 148

subprime mortgage crisis 15–16, 18–19, 22, 33–4, 200
subprime mortgages 15, 18, 32–3, 173
subsistence economies 52, 105
Sufi, A. 160
supply and demand 33, 41, 64, 110, 155, 174
supranational political authority 190

tail risk 31–2
'taking on risk' 24
TARP (Troubled Assets Relief Program) 17
tax
  on financial transactions 187, 197
  and reduction of inequalities 185
Taylor, J. 21, 22, 37, 42, 62, 160, 161
Taylor rule 21–2, 37–8, 160
teaser loans 15
technical progress, and freedom from work 185
technology
  alliance between economy and 196
  and uncertainty 139, 141–2
  see also ICT revolution
Temin, P. 197
Thatcher, M. 3, 25, 145
'this time is different' message 34
time dimension 124, 141
Tobin, J. 25, 105, 154–5, 187
Tobin tax 187
trade, and wealth accumulation 95–6
trade deficit (US) 36
trade liberalization 151, 157, 166, 189
trade unions
  and big businesses
    conflict between 151
    regulated capitalism as compromise between 142, 177
    social bargain between 150–51
  remuneration based on bargaining between enterprise and 185
traded stock, value of (2010) 156
traditional markets 33
tranching 28–9
tranquil periods 121, 123, 127, 128, 159

transaction costs 65, 66
transfer of funds
  from saver to business 6, 154, 163
  see also resource allocation
transfer of mortgages 27
transfer of production 157, 189
transfer of risk 34, 85
Treasuries 49
Treatise on Money (Keynes) 64, 68
Treaty on Stability, Coordination and Governance in the Economic and Monetary Union 17, 170–71
Trichet, J.-C. 170, 171
Turner, A. 143, 154, 165, 167, 194
Twin Towers terrorist attack 4, 16, 21

ultimate independent variables, expectations as 116–17
unanimity 196
uncertain knowledge 71
uncertainty 66
  and accumulation of money 94–5
  concept of 70–72
  entrepreneurial decision-making 119
  finance and 70
  of future expectations 99
  innovations
    institutions and new forms of 141–2
    investment decisions and 72–5, 180
  Lehman Brothers' bankruptcy and 16
  in a monetary economy 69
  monetary nature of 75–80, 199
  and non-ergodic nature of contemporary economies 141
  production decisions 112
  technology and 139, 141–2
  see also certainty
underdeveloped countries 90
underdeveloped financial systems 14, 15
underdevelopment 157
unemployment 57, 174
  costs of 182
  drop in, due to absence of austerity 178

Europe 190
European institutions' lack of
	attention to 182, 183
resistance to innovation due to fear of
	141
see also involuntary unemployment
United Kingdom
	bond market 96
	conflict between big business and
		trade unions 151
	deficit to GDP ratio 17
	financial sector
		growth 154
		share of value produced by 153
	Independent Commission on
		Banking 188
	non signatory to Treaty on Stability
		171
	per capita GDP 17
	public debt 96, 97
	see also England
United States 190
	banking system, transformation 24,
		25–7
	bond market 97
	capital inflows and stock market
		boom 37
	distributional inequalities 157–8
	federal tax revenue and spending 165
	financial crisis
		blamed on mistakes of banking
			system 4–5, 6, 24–36
		government as culprit of the 161–2
		outbreak in 13–15
		in subprime mortgage market
			15–16
	financial system
		as a benchmark for other countries
			5, 13
		difficulties and global
			repercussions 17
		growth 154
		and innovation 13, 14
		questions concerning 18
	GDP growth rate 189
	government role in development
		180–81
	inflation rates (1970s) 146

strikes 151
trade deficit 36
unemployment (1932) 57
unemployment rate (2010–16) 178
universal banks 31, 147
unpredictable shock, crisis perceived as
	a result of an 4, 5
use values 95

Veblen goods 104
'veil' analogy 50, 60, 69, 74, 83, 86, 93
venture capital funds 180
Vickers, J. 188
Vines, D. 197
Volcker, P. 145
Volcker rule 145, 188

wage(s)
	and consumption 115
	flexibility 58, 115, 116, 117, 120,
		144, 178, 182, 201
	increases in 76, 115, 128, 150
	reduction in 115, 116
	rigidity 58, 117, 174, 178
	stickiness 120
Wall Street 101, 175
Wall Street crash (1929) 102, 201
Wall Street crash (1987) 155
warfare technology, and uncertainties
	141–2
wealth 50
	accumulation of 70, 91, 93, 95–6,
		105, 156, 200
	and capital 96–7
	contribution to industrialization
		90–91
	increasing share managed by
		intermediaries 156
	lower propensity to save and
		increased 37
	in pre-industrial economies 95–6
	public debt and private 191
	savings and 50, 93–4, 200
	and speculation 97–101
	subprime mortgage crisis and
		destruction of 18–19
Weiss, A. 43–4, 77, 78

Weitzman, M. 185
well-developed financial systems 14, 96
Western economies
  inequalities 175, 176, 185
  low inflation rates, 1950s and 1960s
    151
  role of financial system in
    transformation of 89–90
  stagflation, 1970s 3
'whole liquidity position' 97, 106
Wicksell, K. 145
  bank money and mainstream theory
    46–50, 64

working conditions, job scarcity and
  harsh 183
world economy 17, 165, 189
Wray, R. 179
Wyplosz, C. 193

Yahoo 188
youth unemployment 190
Yunus, M. 162, 167–8

zero interest rate 119
Zingales, L. 13, 14, 15, 18, 20, 23, 30,
  174, 186–7, 196